embodiment

AN APPROACH TO SEXUALITY AND CHRISTIAN THEOLOGY

JAMES B. NELSON

Augsburg Publishing House • Minneapolis, Minnesota

Contents

For Wilys Claire

Foreword

LTHOUGH MANY church people, as well as leaders in Christian communions, do not always recognize it, we are today in the midst of a sexual revolution. The older and generally accepted conventions regarding human sexuality and its expression are being questioned—not only by many outside the religious traditions but also by many within them; not only by young people but also by older ones; not only by revolutionaries but by relatively conservative men and women who find those conventions meaningless under the very different conditions in which we are all obliged to live today.

For the most part, the response of theologians and thinkers about ethics has been defensive. They have frequently failed to see that what is needed is a radical investigation of human sexuality, an investigation which (as the very word 'radical' indicates) will get at the *root* of the matter and not rest content with treating the symptoms while forgetting the basic cause of contemporary concern and dissatisfaction.

Dr. Nelson's splendid study of the subject, which I have the honour here to introduce, is a notable exception in this respect. He has had the insight and the courage to grasp the nettle boldly, as

Shakespeare said in another (and very different) connexion. He
sees that human sexuality is not only part of God's creation; it is
also one of the clues, indeed the central clue, to what God is up to
in the world. Our sexuality is the ground or base, as he insists, for
our capacity to enter into relationships which are life-enhancing,
life-enriching, and provide the possibility for humans to *become*
what God would have them become: namely, fulfilled, integrated,
sharing, and free recipients of the divine love. What is more, he
bravely faces the kind of issue that so often is neglected, when not
completely forgotten: the sexual needs of the disabled, the retarded,
the aging. And he looks honestly and fairly at the better-known
questions: the pre- and extra-marital expression of sex, masturbation, sadomasochism, and the like. His chapter on homosexuality is
both profoundly Christian and utterly realistic. In fact, every subject upon which he touches is illuminated and clarified by his
manner of treating it.

I have been greatly concerned about some of these matters for
many years; and it is a delight to find someone of Dr. Nelson's
learning, insight, and sympathy come out with conclusions that, in
my own inadequate way, I have sought to urge. I mention particularly his discussion of homosexuality where so often fear and prejudice have prevented any open and honest evaluation of the experience of perhaps ten percent of the population, in their attraction to
members of their own gender and with their own remarkable
capacity for self-giving, gracious receiving, and deep love.

But the most important thing is that Dr. Nelson writes as one who
knows *the gospel* and knows it as the en-gracing and healing which
God's enormous generosity makes available to humanity. Far too
much discussion of sexuality and sexual activity has lacked just
such a grounding in a Christian understanding of God. Dr. Nelson
has recalled us to that faith and has shown how in human sexual
life the Love that, as Dante said, "moves the sun and the other
stars," is brought to bear upon our human existence and hence is
able to move *us* too—move us to deepening contacts, genuine participation, and fuller life. And when we go wrong in our loving
and need to listen to St. Augustine's prayer that God would "order
our loving" since we so often exist in "disorder," we have here the

renewed assurance that the God who creates us in love and for love is the God who also redeems us for love and by love.

I hope that this book will be read by many who are not at all expert in theology or ethical discussion, for they will find it eminently readable and enlightening. I hope, perhaps above all, that those who *are* expert will read it—and take to heart what is so winningly, learnedly, and persuasively said in it.

NORMAN PITTENGER

King's College
Cambridge

Preface

CHRISTIAN FAITH ought to take embodiment seriously: "And the Word became flesh and dwelt among us, full of grace and truth . . ." (John 1:14). The embodiment of God in Jesus Christ is, in faith's perception, God's decisive and crucial self-disclosure. But for those who believe in God's continuing manifestation and presence, the incarnation is not simply past event. The Word *still* becomes flesh. We as body-selves—as sexual body-selves—are affirmed because of that. Our human sexuality is a language, and we are both called and given permission to become body-words of love. Indeed, our sexuality—in its fullest and richest sense—is both the physiological and psychological grounding of our capacity to love.

Few would doubt that this is a time of transition in our understanding of human sexuality. The confusion about sexual morals and mores is the more obvious evidence of this. But there is something else. For too long the bulk of Christian reflection about sexuality has asked an essentially one-directional question: what does Christian faith have to say about our lives as sexual beings? Now we are beginning to realize that the enterprise must be a genuinely two-directional affair. The first question is essential, and we must continue unfailingly to press it. But at the same time it must be joined by, indeed interwoven with, a companion query: what does our experience as sexual human beings mean for the way in which we understand and attempt to live out the faith? What does it mean that we as body-selves are invited to participate in the reality of God?

Consciousness of this two-way street characterizes my effort in these pages. Along with that consciousness goes the conviction that our sexuality is a pervasive dimension of our lives not only as individuals in our private, interpersonal relationships, but also in our corporate lives as church and society. The term "sexual theology" in the chapters to follow will carry my suggestion that the legitimate but now too-narrow focus of traditional "sexual ethics" will no longer do.

I believe that such a vision of sexual theology constitutes a needed approach. Yet, I am quite aware that these chapters are genuinely exploratory. The field is still new. André Maurois has reminded us that the need to express oneself in writing springs from an unresolved inner conflict. The writer does not write out of having found an answer to the problem, but rather out of having discovered the problem and wanting a solution. And the solution is not a resolution of the problem so much as a deeper and wider consciousness of the issue to which we are carried by virtue of having wrestled with that problem.[1]

Maurois' insight is real to me. And I hope that the reader will join me not only in the attempt to wrestle intellectually with human sexuality and Christian theology, but also in the willingness to engage more deeply his or her own experience and feelings as a sexual human being who wishes to live out as fully and as faithfully as possible the meaning of the gospel.

Writing a book is a splendid experience in the reality of community and of the gifts of many others—even when the more immediate memory is one of seemingly endless hours at the desk. But the opportunity for those hours is a gift, too, and that occasion came in a sabbatical leave for which I am grateful to United Theological Seminary of the Twin Cities, to The Association of Theological Schools in the United States and Canada for a faculty fellowship, and to many persons at Cambridge University for their hospitality.

Particular stimulation concerning many of the issues in this book
has come from companions in two settings. One is the United
Church of Christ team, under the able leadership of Edward A.
Powers, which prepared the study *Human Sexuality: A Preliminary
Report*. The other is the Program in Human Sexuality at the University of Minnesota Medical School. My colleagues in both of these
groups have enriched my thinking and feeling immeasurably. I hope
that they will recognize their contributions to these pages and for-
give my shortcomings.

Several friends read the entire manuscript and offered both valu-
able suggestions and encouragement in a host of ways: James H.
Burtness (Luther-Northwestern Theological Seminaries, St. Paul),
Beverly Wildung Harrison (Union Theological Seminary, New
York), Eleanor S. Morrison (Michigan State University), James A.
Siefkes (the American Lutheran Church), Gayle Graham Yates
(University of Minnesota), and H. Wilson Yates (United Theological
Seminary).

For counsel on individual chapters I am grateful to Sue Ebbers,
Holt Graham, and Clyde Steckel, all of United Seminary, and to
my other faculty colleagues goes my appreciation for suggestions
concerning the final chapter.

Mary Nelson acceded to the invitation to index the book. But,
with her keen stylistic eye and critical sense for the issues, she did
far more. And to Vivian Freeman goes my thanks for typing assistance.

I suspect that the dedication of more than one book effort to the
same person might smack of double jeopardy for that individual.
Nevertheless, she must endure that risk. Some years ago I dedicated
a book to Wilys Claire, Stephen, and Mary. The latter two are now
young adults whose friendship and wisdom I cherish. Yet with these
pages I particularly want to acknowledge Wilys Claire, and to celebrate with her our twenty-five years together in exploration of these
concerns.

1

The Church and Sexuality:
A Time to Reconsider

AN UNUSUAL PUBLIC CONTROVERSY erupted in England recently. It was precipitated by the announcement of a Danish film producer, Jens Jorgen Thorsen, that he intended to go to that country to make an explicit film about the sex life of Jesus Christ.

For weeks the press covered the debate.[1] Religious leaders and groups quickly expressed their opposition. The Archbishop of Canterbury revealed that church authorities in Britain, Denmark, and Sweden had been in close touch for months. Their concerted alliance had successfully discouraged financial backing for the film in the two Scandinavian countries. With Mr. Thorsen's eyes now on England, the archbishop asserted that he would oppose the making of such a film with every power in his being. Similar statements came from the Roman Catholic archbishop, from the British Council of Churches, and from the Free Church Federal Council.

The issue quickly moved into the political arena. A Member of Parliament introduced a bill which would outlaw the film's production. The Prime Minister assured the country that there existed legal power to refuse Mr. Thorsen's entry into the country on grounds of "public order, public security, and public health."

"There is no doubt," stated the Prime Minister, "that to make a film such as the one I have read about would cause deep offense to the great majority of people in this country, among whom I number myself." While British royalty rarely enter into public controversies, in an unusual step the Queen issued a statement. While the exclusion of the Danish film producer could only be accomplished within the laws of the United Kingdom, she said, "Her Majesty finds this proposal quite as obnoxious as most of her subjects do."

Two church leaders, however, saw the issue somewhat differently. In his diocesan letter, the Bishop of Wakefield said that, while he earnestly hoped that the film would not be made, his fear of the ugly consequences of censorship and the kind of authoritarianism nurtured by moral indignation would not permit him to oppose the producer's entry into the country. Further, wrote the bishop, he would disappoint those who expected him to deny that Jesus was a sexual being. "If he was other than a fully human being then, for me 'the Word becoming flesh' is not wholly true. . . . Jesus was no stranger to sex and its problems. . . . I am convinced that a large part of his moral authority derived from the fact that he had faced the temptations of the flesh and, by grace, had overcome them." Concluding his letter, the bishop declared, "All right, Mr. Thorsen, make your film if you must. But there is nothing you can do that can diminish the majesty and the power of Jesus our Lord and Savior. When you and your film are so much dust and ashes, he will still be King."

Similarly, Dr. Colin Morris, President of the British Methodist Conference, said it was ludicrous to imagine that a faith which had withstood mass martyrdom and the collapse of civilizations would be rocked "by some squalid back-street X film." Urging the church's silent contempt in the face of this publicity stunt, he pleaded for a sense of moral proportion. It was a pity, Morris observed, that the church could not be as united and vocal about other obscenities—injustice and exploitation, the homeless and the dispossessed—situations which comprise "an infinitely greater affront to the spirit of Christ than Mr. Jorgen Thorsen's proposed pornographic project."

An editorial in *The Guardian* summarized the spectrum of reactions to the proposed film. Some reactions seemed to be sighs of despair over this desperate search for a sensationally new angle on pornography. Others were thunderous voices calling for exclusion orders and prosecution for blasphemy. Still others had said it was time for a detailed and genuinely artistic scrutiny of the sexual motivations of the Christ. What would be the result? asked the editor. Would it be a film "destined to plumb the nadir of all that is decadent in post-Christian society"? Or would it be "a deeply sensitive and intensely moving search, enacted in a spirit of rare compassion, for the truest meaning of divinity"? Probably neither. If the film ever appeared, it most likely would be a typical sex film but a vast commercial success because of this massive publicity.

After some weeks, the controversy (and, apparently, plans for the film itself) faded away. Yet, the whole episode constitutes a revealing case study raising issues important for the church. At the most obvious level, we see the exploitation and commercialization of human sexuality so endemic to contemporary western culture. It is one thing to condemn this phenomenon—and it is another to ask why it has occurred.

In addition, the film proposal typifies the "genitalization" of sexuality common today. Thus, the formula for a so-called "explicit" film appears to be this: human sexuality equals sex, and sex equals genital sex acts.

The complex and varied ways in which Christian faith and human sexuality interrelate also emerge in this case study. Beyond the tasteless vulgarity which likely would have characterized this particular film, we must ask, is the notion of Jesus as a sexual person inherently blasphemous, or at least scandalous? Or is "the truest meaning of divinity" humanly experienced in and through human sexuality? Or is neither or these questions accurate?

Further, why can masses of Christians unite quickly and with such feeling over this sort of sex-related issue? And what are the relations of sexual freedom and sexual discipline to the good society? And are issues of sexuality simply less important than the great problems of social injustice such as poverty and racism, or is there some vital interconnection?

If the Thorsen film project is dead, the issues it raised for a few weeks of public debate are very much alive.

The Church as Sexual Community

Christian faith affirms that the church is not adequately understood in terms of *human* community only. More can and must be
said. Whatever else it is, however, the church is also very much a
human community composed of sexual human beings. In recent
decades we have begun to pay more attention to the church as
economic community, as political community, as psychological community, as sociological community. Understanding these dimensions
of Christian corporate existence is important for theology. More
than that, it is important for the life of faith in the body of Christ.
The same must be said of the church as sexual community.

In a variety of ways, human sexuality has achieved an increasingly
obvious place on the church's agenda in recent years, from local
congregation to denominational board. The women's movement,
feminist theologians, denominational gay caucuses, anti-abortion
and abortion-rights advocates, those alarmed by and those hopeful
in the face of changing sexual mores and family styles—these and
others are pressing the church to grapple more deeply with sexual
theology and ethics. Further, one does not have to look hard to
find evidence of considerable suspicion between some church people and some who have been alienated from the church over sexual
issues. On the one side, some are highly suspicious that "sexual
fulfillment" is simply a euphemism for hedonism and sexual license.
On the other side are those who have felt condemned by the church
for being sexual persons and who suspect that its lofty language is
being used to deprive them of their human fullness.

Carl Jung once remarked that when people brought sexual questions to him they invariably turned out to be religious questions,
and when they brought religious questions to him they always
turned out to be sexual ones. Jung's insight bore truth not only for
his patients but also for all of us. Sexual questions have an inevitable religious dimension. The Christian heritage contains not
only a plethora of teachings concerning sexual morality, it also
bears great theological themes of sexual relevance. What we believe
about creation and God's purpose in creating us as sexual beings,
what we believe about human nature and destiny, what we believe
about sin and salvation, about love, justice, and community—all

these and many other basic beliefs will condition and shape our sexual self-understandings.

If sexual questions are also religious questions, so too are religious questions sexual ones. How we experience ourselves and others sexually will condition and affect the style and contents of our Christian beliefs. It is a two-way street. One hopefully obvious example will suffice at this point. If one believes strongly in the inherent superiority of males over females, this will have a significant effect upon one's ways of perceiving God and the divine purposes, one's beliefs about the nature of revelation and scriptural interpretation, one's convictions about the meaning of community, about the nature and mission of the church—and more.

It is the awareness of and the struggling with this two-directional movement which characterize *sexual theology*. In recent years we have become familiar with parallel terms. "Black theology," for example, contends that the existential situation of an oppressed community is the appropriate place for understanding and interpreting the liberating gospel of Jesus Christ. So also, "political theology" and the "liberation theology" stimulated by Third World Christians attempt not only to perceive the ethical implications of Christian faith for human politics; they also take seriously the human political struggle for liberation as an arena for God's continuing self-disclosure. An analogous case can be made for a sexual theology. This is not to claim that sexual theology will provide an all-encompassing approach to the Christian theological task. It is to say, however, that this is another needed approach with which to grapple with the meaning of God's purposes, presence, and action for our lives at this particular time and place in history.

Karl Barth observed that doing theology is much like the attempt to paint a bird in flight. The interaction of the living God with the living and changing human scene, coupled with the limitations and distortions of even our best understandings, makes it impossible to set down once and for all certain immutable and eternal theological formulations. This is patently true of a sexual theology. It is obviously true of the explorations in this book. Yet, explore we must, for there is a growing awareness that the church's task in this area is urgent. It is the awareness of a variety of needs:

the need to recognize that in the very midst of our current sexual chaos and floundering there exists an immense amount of longing for more meaningful and more human sexual relationships;

the need to wrestle with the vastly important insights of recent feminist theology concerning the sexist limitations of much in Christian thought and life;

the need to grapple with the possibility that sexual meanings are more socially-created than biologically-given;

the need not only to understand those whose sexuality is expressed differently from that of the majority, but also to learn from them;

the need for a sexual theology which positively affirms the wholeness of embodied selves, the goodness of sexual pleasure, and the creative significance of sexual self-affirmation in an incarnational theology;

in short, the need to move beyond the traditional confines of "sexual ethics" into sexual theology which takes seriously the human sexual experience in our time and place as an arena for God's continuing self-disclosure at the same time that it takes seriously the implications of Christian faith for our sexual lives.

In looking at various parts of the Christian tradition, we will find it relatively easy to observe how frequently an incarnational understanding of sexuality was lost and how often sinful patterns of domination and submission in human relationships were assumed to arise out of divine decree. But the errors detected in others should remind us that a "definitive" interpretation of God's work in human sexuality is a chimerical quest. Furthermore, as Rosemary Haughton has wisely observed, "over and over again, the mistakes were necessary, in the curious way in which such things work, because it was only by exaggerating, in good faith, some aspect of human sexuality that the real nature of that aspect could be fully seen, and later properly appreciated." [2] Yet, in all of our failures and fresh starts there is also the hope that in some way Christ's gift of human fulfillment might be enhanced in us, and that the church as sexual community might be more faithful to the promise.

Some Assumptions

Already it is apparent that I am using the notion of sexuality as something far more inclusive than specifically genital sex acts and their erotic accompaniments. There is danger in being too broad in definition as well as in being too narrow.

The early Freudian view was far too broad.[3] Particularly in his earlier work, Freud fell into a reductionism which maintained that all human behavior and experience could be considered manifestations of the libido, that life force which ultimately is oriented toward the achievement of sexual pleasure. While this view dominated western psychological thought for several decades, in more recent years social scientists have affirmed more complex and less rigid biologically-determined theories of human motivation. Thus, it has become increasingly common to make the distinction, which I shall try to follow, between *sex* and *sexuality*.

Dictionary definitions of these two terms, however, need some revision for our purposes. According to the standard dictionary, "sex" is either the character of being male or female or it is anything connected with sexual gratification and reproduction, while "sexuality" is said to be the state or quality of being sexual. I shall attempt to be at once more specific and more inclusive in my use of the terms as they refer to human beings and to dimensions of our personhood.

Sex is a biologically-based need which is oriented not only toward procreation but, indeed, toward pleasure and tension release. It aims at genital activity culminating in orgasm. While sex usually is infused with a variety of human and religious meanings, the focus is upon erotic phenomena of a largely genital nature.

Sexuality, on the other hand, is a much more comprehensive term associated with more diffuse and symbolic meanings, psychological and cultural orientations. While it includes sex and relates to biological organ systems, sexuality goes beyond this. To be sure, sexuality is not the whole of our personhood, but it is a very basic dimension of our personhood. While our sexuality does not determine all of our feelings, thoughts, and actions, in ways both obvious and covert it permeates and affects them all.

Sexuality is our self-understanding and way of being in the world as male and female. It includes our appropriation of attitudes and characteristics which have been culturally defined as masculine and feminine. It involves our affectional orientation toward those of the opposite and/or the same sex. It includes our attitudes about our own bodies and those of others. Because we are "body-selves," our sexuality constantly reminds each of us of our uniqueness and particularity: we look different and we feel differently from any other person.

Sexuality is a sign, a symbol, and a means of our call to communication and communion. This is the most apparent in regard to other human beings, other body-selves. The mystery of our sexuality is the mystery of our need to reach out to embrace others both physically and spiritually. Sexuality thus expresses God's intention that we find our authentic humanness in relationship. But such humanizing relationship cannot occur on the human dimension alone. Sexuality, we must also say, is intrinsic to our relationship with God.

The attempt to draw the distinction between sex and sexuality is important and useful. Admittedly, however, it is a difficult distinction to maintain with clarity and consistency. The two terms are interdependent: one (sexuality) includes but also depends upon the other (sex). Moreover, we encounter the linguistic fact that both words have the same adjectival and adverbial forms. Still, it is crucial to bear in mind that *sexuality* involves much more than what we *do* with our genitals. More fundamentally, it is who we *are* as body-selves who experience the emotional, cognitive, physical, and spiritual need for intimate communion—human and divine.

2

Embodiment
in Sexual Theology

LADY BENNERLEY, one of the minor charac-
ters in D. H. Lawrence's *Lady Chatterley's
Lover*, declares: "So long as you can forget
your body you are happy. . . . And the mo-
ment you begin to be aware of your body, you are wretched. So,
if civilization is any good, it has to help us forget our bodies, and
then time passes happily without our knowing it." [1] Lawrence, of
course, was using Lady Bennerley as a foil in his attempt to restore
belief in the basic goodness and importance of human embodiment.
His task, if not altogether successful, was nonetheless vital.

It is a vital task for the church now. Through its Old Testament
rootage in the goodness of creation and through the New Testament's central focus on divine incarnation, Christian theology
ought to have an immensely positive bias toward embodiment.
A great deal of Christian theology, however, has tended to treat
the human body as something other than the essential person. Thus,
the body becomes inherently suspect. It might be redeemable by
the grace of God, but more likely the carnal body is relegated to
the domain of "this world" while the spiritual world is something
qualitatively different. [2]

19

The question before us now is the positive significance of our physical bodies, and hence our sexual bodies, in Christian *theologizing*. The wording is significant. We are not simply asking what theology has to say *about* the body, as if theology were conducted from some superior vantage point by discarnate, disembodied spirits.[3] We are asking what it means that we as body-selves participate in the reality of God and as body-selves reflect upon—theologize about—that reality. Why and how does the Word still become flesh? This is a basic question for Christian theology. Why and how does our flesh become words about the Word? This is a basic question of methodological perspective to be faced at the beginning of any sexual theology.

From the Body to the World

The way we think and feel about ourselves as bodies will always find expression in the way we think and feel about the world and about God. Obviously, this is not a one-directional street; the traffic flows the other way as well. Yet, we can begin with some reflections about this particular direction. If for Christian theology this is not the most fundamental direction, it is surely that to which least attention has been paid.

Sexual theology is body theology. We experience our own concreteness as body-selves occupying space in a concrete world. We experience the world only through our body-selves. Maurice Merleau-Ponty reminds us that, regarding our understanding of the universe, *here* is the key to *there*. "My understanding of my body is the key to my understanding of bodies and places beyond me. . . . I am somehow everywhere by being here."[4] If I were not myself through my body, I could not be anywhere and would not know what it means to be *here*. The body, thus, is always more than just an object. The body is the *means* by which I can know objects, persons, and events.

Our bodies-as-selves give shape to the way in which we feel about the world and about others.[5] If I do not realize the profound sense in which I *am* a body, if in a false spiritualization of my selfhood I deny my embodiedness, I will also tend to minimize the personal significance of activities which I carry on through my body. When my body ceases to be fully personal, my relationships to other body-selves are diminished in their personal meanings. The world becomes external and foreign.

Although our bodies are the agencies through which we encounter the world, it is not easy to know our bodies well.[6] Our bodies are constantly changing, and there are time-lags in bringing our self-concepts up-to-date. Nor is it easy to see many of our important body parts. The genitals and anus are fully visible to us only with mirrors, and the interior organs are beyond the eye's reach. Even when we do inspect more closely some of our body parts, we do so with selective, interpretive mental filters. Certain attitudes about "the dirty body" linger, for a great many of us have been reared to regard the body as a source of sin whose touch we must resist. Culture tells us to master the irrationality of the body. And the very concreteness of our bodies can produce anxiety. They exhibit defect, vulnerability, change, decay. They bear intimations of our own mortality.

Such body attitudes color the "feel" of the world for us. The world "out there" then takes on some of the same confusing and half-known qualities. As psychologist Seymour Fisher puts it, "the world seems to mirror back to us that it is a confusing place—full of mysterious attributes that smack of potential badness. We expect, in a fashion somewhat analogous to our feelings about our bodies, that things out there cannot be clearly grasped or understood." [7]

Thus, bodily boundaries become important to us. We protect our body boundaries with clothing, both for defense and concealment. Anxiety rises when boundaries are in doubt. The parent intuitively holds the screaming child closely, substituting the comforting and restraining enclosure of the parental body for the boundaries which the child temporarily has lost. When life becomes too much we immerse ourselves in hot bathtubs for relief and find the water's warm enclosure reassuring and calming. As individuals and societies we expend enormous amounts of energy defending our social boundaries — measuring property lines with exactness, building fences, spending gigantic sums on military defense systems which exceed rational design.

Societies differ in their ways of boundary setting. Current social psychological evidence suggests that typical individuals from different national or cultural groups have identifiably different ways of understanding their own personal body borders.[8] People who live with constant fear of outside attack develop characteristically protective attitudes toward their own bodies. Likewise, a person's basic distrust in the integrity of his or her own body seems likely to be projected outward as a fear that enemies are constantly threatening attack upon the person's own group, tribe, or nation.

We write the symbols of the body outward upon the world. Thus, during the Middle Ages while both theologians and ecclesiastical administrators in large measure denied human sexuality, Christian architects apparently saw their bodies differently. They went right on building great cathedrals which are richly sexual in symbolism. At least the art historian who has understood a bit of Freud sees this! Without this recognition of sexual symbolism, one such scholar observes, "It would be hard to account for the perennial appeal of Gothic architecture. It may be precisely because of its triumphant sexuality, all masculine with its thrusting phallic towers on the outside, framing the labial doors leading to the enclosing womb of the interior." [9]

In any event, we do move from the body to the world. The way we perceive and feel about our own bodies contributes significantly to the way we perceive and feel about the world.

From the World to the Body

The body-world correlation also moves in the other direction. And here the work of the anthropologists is particularly illuminating. Out of her studies of primitive societies, the distinguished British scholar Mary Douglas claims, "Just as it is true that everything symbolizes the body, so it is equally true (and all the more so for that reason) that the body symbolizes everything else." [10] Thus, views of the cosmic order and of the nature of society are expressed in beliefs and rituals concerning the human body. "The rituals work upon the body politic through the symbolic medium of the physical body." [11] And the functions of the body can represent highly complex social structures. "We cannot possibly interpret rituals concerning excreta, breast milk, saliva and the rest unless we are prepared to see in the body a symbol of society, and

to see the powers and dangers credited to social structure repro-
duced in small on the human body." [12]

Rituals concerning personal hygiene and dirt are a case in point.
Dirt is disorder. It offends against order. And pollution rituals in
various societies say at least as much about world views and understandings of social order as they say about a particular group's
understanding of biology. "For example," Douglas observes, "there
are beliefs that each sex is a danger to the other through contact
with sexual fluids. . . . Such patterns of sexual danger can be seen
to express symmetry or hierarchy. It is implausible to interpret them
as expressing something about the actual relation of the sexes. I
suggest that many ideas about sexual dangers are better interpreted
as symbols of the relation between parts of society, as mirroring
designs of hierarchy or symmetry which apply in the larger social
system." [13]

But such rituals are not limited to primitive societies. In contemporary society we commonly interpret our ideas about dirt as representing sound, scientific notions of hygiene. Yet, our scientific understandings do not go back many generations, and our practices about
dirt are far more ancient. We, too, express through our practices of
cleanliness certain symbolic systems of purity which are very social
in nature. Thus, food in itself is not dirty, but it is dirty to leave
specks of food on one's clothing. Or to leave upstairs equipment
downstairs. Or to put underclothing over outerclothing. Such things
are dirty because they confuse and contradict our cherished understandings and classifications of social order. [14]

The movement from world to body is expressed not only in a
group's views about the social order, but also in its basic religious
views about God and the cosmos. The rituals of holiness in the
Book of Leviticus provide illustration. To be sure, the theological
significance of Leviticus is not exhausted by this particular perspective. The laws of purification meant for the Israelite a divinely-
appointed way of life expressing covenant faithfulness and separation from all idolatry. Granted this understanding, it is nevertheless
important to see also the constant correlations between the religious
perceptions of God's holiness and physical bodies.

In Leviticus, holiness (whatever else it may mean) involves completeness and separation. It means keeping distinct the categories

of creation. Holiness requires correct definition and order. To be
sure, some of the ancient dietary laws were based upon common-
sense health precautions, but this does not adequately account for
all of them. Certain of the "unclean" animals which ought not be
eaten are those which the Israelites believed did not conform adequately to their appointed class, or whose class itself went contrary
to the intended scheme of the world. Contact with those creatures
which were not clearly birds, nor clearly fish, nor clearly four-legged
land animals then disqualified one from approaching the temple.
The abominations described in Leviticus were to be scrupulously
shunned because the obscure and unclassifiable elements which
did not fit the pattern of the cosmos were always threatening to
intrude upon order. They were incompatible with holiness and
blessing.

The threat also extends to those who in some sexual way defy
orderly classification, such as those who appear to cross the sharp-
ly-defined lines of what constitutes male and what constitutes
female. The threat extends to those who are in some condition of
sexual transition, such as the menstruating or pregnant woman.
Furthermore, the polluting rules are different from moral rules.
Pollution rules are unequivocal. They do not deal with a person's
moral intentions or with a careful balancing of rights and duties.
They pay no attention to the particularities of context. The only
question is whether a forbidden contact has taken place. The polluting individual is always in the wrong, regardless of intent or
personal responsibility. Simply by having the wrong condition or
crossing the classification line that person has unleashed dangers
for others.[15]

Bodily boundaries once again illustrate the interaction of body
and world, as the pollution rituals of ancient Israel attest. The orifices of the physical body become particularly important because
they symbolize vulnerability. Matter which comes out of the body
is of the most obvious kinds—spittle, blood, milk, semen, urine,
feces, even tears. When rituals express anxiety about the body's
orifices, anthropologically they appear to express anxiety about the
political and cultural unity of the social group. Douglas observes,
"The Israelites were always in their history a hard-pressed minority.
. . . The threatened boundaries of their body politic would be

Things normal
seem to be filth

well mirrored in their care for the integrity, unity and purity of the physical body." [16]

Thus, our bodies mirror and symbolize our perceptions of the world, and our perceptions of the world feed back upon our understandings of our bodies. By itself, this recognition of the body-world interaction is of basic importance to Christian sexual theology. More specifically, it will provide a vantage point from which to view a variety of issues—from sex role definitions in infants to the sexual needs of the dying.

Body Meanings: Sexuality and Communication

The invention of the wheel, many have claimed, was the most important single event in the development of human civilization. True, the human being is a technological animal. But incomparably more significant for the cultural process was the invention of language and abstract symbols. The human being is *homo symbolicus,* the symbol-making, symbol-using animal. While certain other animals can be taught particular non-instinctive behaviors in response to verbal stimuli—a dog can learn to do tricks in response to its owner's voice—it is human beings who have an extraordinary capacity for dealing with symbols, a capacity unmatched by any other species.[17]

Though there are a variety of ways in which we express our symbolic capacities, language is perhaps the most striking. At this point, reflection upon several characteristics of human language (as distinguished from animal communication) can provide insights into sexuality as "body meaning." [18]

First, speech is culturally determined. The physical potentiality to talk of course, is genetically given. But unlike the animal whose communication repertoire (when unaffected by human training) is rigidly determined by its species genetic code, our own actualization of the physical potential for speech depends on culture. Simply put, it takes a human environment to develop speech.

And the same is true of sexuality. The biological basis of sexuality is genetically given, but our sexuality is never simply biology. It is the way in which we relate to the world as male or as female beings. It is our masculine and our feminine characteristics. It is our attitudes toward our bodies and those of others. It is the affectional orientation we have toward others. As with speech, it takes a human environment to develop human sexuality, precisely because our sexuality is a pattern of meanings.

Second, words are symbols, and the sounds which make up words have in themselves no particular meaning or validity but rather acquire meanings by social consensus.

The same is true of the "sounds" in sexual expression. For example, the mouth-to-mouth kiss has an erotic meaning for us. But there is nothing intrinsic about the kiss which determines that sexual meaning. Such meanings developed in certain (but not all) societies over a period of time. As Edgar Morin contends, "The kiss goes with the eroticism of the face, and both were unknown in antiquity and are still ignored by certain civilizations. The kiss is not merely the discovery of a new tactile sensual pleasure. It revives forgotten myths that identify the soul with breath and symbolizes communion or symbiosis of soul." [19]

Third, human language as distinguished from animal communication is propositional in character and syntactical in structure. Our verbal self-expressions consist of organic units of speech whose meanings are conveyed through word sequences. To understand a word fully, we need the context of the sentence; for the sentence we need the paragraph, and for the paragraph the book.

Something similar must be said of sexual expression. The same physical act can have a whole range of different meanings, depending on the contexts of those acts. Genital intercourse in one setting can be not only immensely pleasurable to both partners but also the bearer of the richest meanings of covenantal love. In a different setting, genital intercourse can be exploitive and dehumanizing. The physical act is the same, but the syntax and context are different.

Fourth, animal communication is basically an instrument of biological survival and need-reduction. Such communications as the sparrow and the deer make are oriented to feeding, mating and breeding, mutual protection and territorial defense. At least presently, we simply lack evidence that animal communication genuinely transcends biological survival needs. It is different with human speech. Except in the most primitive social conditions or in the most extreme situations of danger or deprivation, human speech regularly transcends survival needs—even in the process of meeting those needs. We speak not only to survive but, even more, to express and to transcend ourselves.

And the same is true of sexual expression. The number of occasions in which a wife and husband have intercourse with the intent of conceiving a child is typically an infinitesimal fraction of their total. And even on those "deliberately procreative occasions" the meanings which they bring to the sex act far transcend their felt need to propagate the species.

Thus, as human beings we live in a symbolic world. The existence of language, symbols, and gestures enables us to attach meanings to the acts of everyday life and to interpret the world around us. And these meanings are always in a significant sense social. They arise, they are modified, they are changed through social interaction.[20]

This approach—called "symbolic interactionism" in social theory—throws considerable light on human sexuality. To be sure, our sexuality has a biological foundation: the genitals, the male-female differentiation, the reproductive capacity, the physical possibility of varied forms of intercourse, and so on. But our sexuality is also, and especially, patterns of meaning which are more socially constructed than biologically determined.

Thus, a wide range of sexual meanings exists among different people and often within the same individual.[21] Sometimes sexuality is linked primarily with procreation and child-rearing. But many seldom understand it in this way, and some people never do. (The Trobrianders studied by Malinowski, for example, made no mental connection between acts of intercourse and resultant pregnancy.) Sometimes sexuality means that which is erotic. But erotic meanings themselves vary widely: ecstatic or dirty, exciting or guilt-ridden, submissive or assertive. Or, sexuality can mean love. But love itself has a vast array of meanings to different people. Or, sexuality can be gender identity. But even here the meanings are not completely fixed: the hermaphrodite (whose identification as either female or male is neither evident nor automatic) is the dramatic case in point. Or sexuality can bear strongly religious meanings. It can express the fertility of the land, or the power of the group, or the self's communion with God.

To speak in this way—of sexuality as a highly symbolic dimension of human experience—is to depart from the heavily biological emphasis typical of traditional natural law theory in ethics. There the concepts of "natural" and "unnatural" sexual behavior have clear biological definitions. Certain physical sexual acts (e.g. heterosexual genital intercourse) are believed to be natural, and certain other acts (e.g. masturbation) are defined as unnatural. But such interpretations make unwarranted assumptions concerning a fixed, unchanging human nature. Nor can they do justice to the variety of meanings which might be associated with the same physical acts or to the way in which a sexual expression fits into the larger social context.

Our symbolic interactionist interpretation also differs from the Freudian perspective. Freud's understanding of personality rested heavily on the notion of a closed energy system in which the libido is the one great source of energy. There is a given biological "naturalness" about sexuality. If a person's sexuality does not develop naturally, the energy may be repressed resulting in deviations and neuroses. Or the energy may be sublimated and become the source of extra power for creative or benevolent work. But, according to Freud, the body is never problematic. It is the source of naturalness. Sexual arousal lies in nature. The social world responds to and can give something of a shape to this drive, but it is the biological drive that is basic.[22]

Freud's important legacy lies less in his notions of sexuality and human nature as such than in two other insights. He saw that sexuality was of central importance to both personal and social life—it does not lie on life's periphery. Moreover, Freud saw the sexual dimensions in many forms of behavior which had been thought to be entirely nonsexual. A symbolic interactionist perspective can affirm both of these critical insights. It can also attempt to understand how sexual behavior itself can serve motives and meanings which themselves are not directly sexual. And, it will keep our attention focused on the meanings and symbolic significance being expressed in and through our sexuality. It is our human symbolic capacity manifest in social interaction which gives sexuality its meaning and power.

In some ways, this is a more modest view of sexuality's power than those interpretations which are heavily rooted in Freudian and biological imagery. Present-day exponents of the Freudian-biological approach can be found in both "right-wing" and "left-wing" varieties. The former attributes to sexuality such power that, without strong societal regulation, order will collapse, moral decay will prevail, and civilization will decline. The left wing, on the other hand, sees sexuality as the great liberator, the powerful central drive which would be the chief means of creative self-fulfillment if it were not twisted and repressed by society and church. But both of these viewpoints overlook a more likely possibility: "that the significance of sexuality is exactly in proportion to its perceived significance." [23]

A symbolic interactionist interpretation of sexuality is a congenial tool and companion for a Christian sexual theology. It is compatible with important biblical perspectives on human nature. Our human nature, in the dominant biblical view, is not static and fixed. It is not merely read off our biological constitution. Rather, as human beings we are human *becomings*, historical and dynamic. So too, our body meanings, while dependent upon biological foundations, are never automatically given by our physical constitutions. The process by which we become sexual seems to be less a natural unfolding of biological tendencies than a social learning process through which we come to affirm certain sexual meanings in our interaction with significant others.

Biblical theology affirms that we are thoroughly social. We are created by God in community. This is true of our body meanings. We are born into historically-created "sexual worlds." Various groups and institutions convey certain sexual meanings to us—the family, the church, the legal system, the medical world, and the advertising industry among them.

Biblical theology asserts that we are not only created in community but also for community. That is our intended destiny. Communities exist by shared symbols, language, communication, and meanings. And that is of the essence of our sexuality. More than

mere biological drive, it is a symbolic medium, a means of communication, a potent sign of our need for communion.

A biblical posture welcomes the symbolic interactionist contention that sexual meanings are not absolute but rather are historically
and culturally relative. After all, "the Protestant principle," rooted
in the first injunction of the Decalogue, reminds us that God alone
is absolute, and hence no finite truth ought to make an infinite or
absolute claim.

In simpler societies there may be considerable agreement about
what constitutes sexual reality and what are appropriate body
meanings. It is not so in a complex, pluralistic society such as ours.
There is a massive variety of sexual meanings—increasingly ambiguous, often contradictory, always changing. As a community of faith
and nurture, the church is called upon to teach and transmit those
sexual meanings it finds consonant with Christian faith.

As community of faithful inquiry and transformation, the church
must also be open to fresh experiences of God's presence and truth
in the very midst of our current sexual confusion and searching.
A symbolic interactionist perspective also assists us at this point.
For example, most accounts of sexual "deviance" assume that the
social norms which define normality and abnormality are absolutely
real and unproblematic. Thus, the major question is "how did this
person become a sexual deviant?". But if we assume that the social
meanings of sexuality (and sexual deviance) themselves are relative, then the important question shifts: why is this certain sexual
expression considered deviant? how do we account for the social
meanings which have led to the labeling of this as deviant? how
do we evaluate these meanings? [24] And these are appropriate questions of which a transformative church is not afraid.

If bodies are meanings, if human sexuality is a richly symbolic
language, we need to press more directly the question of the relation of the body-self and theology. For, theology is our language
about the meanings of God's relationship with the world.

Theology as Body Language

In the Christian West, theology has too often been a disembodied enterprise. It has been understood as preeminently a ra-

tional discipline, a matter for the head. There have, of course, been exceptions. In certain medieval mystics and, later, in the evangelical movement emotionally-felt religious experience was accorded a primary place. Among major theologians, Frederich Schleiermacher stands out as one who believed feeling to be foundational to Christian faith. Even in most of these and other exceptions to an excessively cognitive theology, however, there continued to lurk a deep suspicion of the sexual body.

It is time to rethink—and to reexperience—our approach to the theological task. Four interwoven themes might assist us in seeing the significance of the sexual body to Christian theology. They are: feeling, desire, communion, and incarnation.

Feeling. The poet W. B. Yeats claims, "We only believe those thoughts which have been conceived not in the brain but in the whole body." [25] Indeed, the person who is out of touch with his or her feelings is out of touch with reality, as psychiatry amply testifies. If I cannot feel injustice, I cannot really perceive injustice even if I have learned from others how to name it and what it looks like.

But feeling is not simply emotion. One can experience emotions (as in some noncommitted, superficial sexual experiences) without experiencing feeling. Feeling includes the emotions, but it also has a spiritual and rational core. Charles Davis has emphasized this: "Feelings . . . are responses springing from what we are. They are the eros of our being when that being is aroused by its interaction with reality. . . . Feelings are bodily responses that are animated by intelligence and spiritual affectivity or, conversely, embodied intelligent and affective responses." [26]

Feelings, then, are neither antirational nor irrational. Let us consider feelings as the wholeness of human response to the realities experienced by the person. To be sure, simply an emotional response can be a denigration of reason. It can mean irrational excess. Likewise, however, an excessively cognitive response can be a falsely cold, objective, computer-like suppression of the self's affective dimensions. The feeling response to reality involves both cognition and emotion. It is the willingness to respond with as much of the totality of the self as one is able. It is the openness to both spontaneity and discipline. It is the capacity to be deeply aroused by what we are experiencing.

Feeling is inseparable from the body-self. The term body-self points to the unity of the person. It is the refusal to be split into mind over body or heart over head. It is the refusal to locate true selfhood in only part of the self. The notion of feeling, then, is one way of pointing to the unified response of the body-self. And unified response means listening to the messages from all dimensions of the self—the mind, the heart, the spiritual senses, the genitals, the viscera.

Desiring. Under the impact of certain European theologies (e.g., Barth and Nygren) we have been conditioned by doctrines of revelation which, in their more extreme forms, make the human being into receptor only—a passive, waiting vessel who can only respond to the divine initiative. But this is to impoverish the erotic dimension of knowing, the intimate connection between desire and knowledge.

The ancient Hebrews knew better when they occasionally used the verb "to know" *(yādáh)* as a synonym for sexual intercourse. The sexual act at its best is the union of desiring and knowing. If I desire another sexually without wanting to have deep knowledge of the other, without wanting to be in a living communion with the partner, I am treating the other merely as object, as instrument, as means to my self-centered gratification. But in the union of desiring and knowing, the partner is treated as a self, the treasured participant in communion.

This insight is suggestively invoked by John W. Dixon Jr.: "To know and to desire are parts of the same act. We know with the same flesh that desires, and the attempt to know outside desire falsifies the knowing, which would be no more than a private fate were it not that we also falsify the known. We desire with the same flesh that knows, and the attempt to desire without knowing impoverishes the desire, which would be no more than a private failure were it not that we thereby impoverish the desired." [27]

Thus, the image of the passive self totally pliable before God not only truncates the fullness of the body-self but also impoverishes the God to whom we would respond. To speak of the erotics of knowing God is neither essentially blasphemous nor necessarily an invitation to the distortions of fertility religions past and present. Rather, it is a testimony to a true dimension of communion. It is sensed in the lament of a Hebrew in exile:

> As a doe longs for running streams,
> So longs my soul for you, my God.
> My soul thirsts for God, the God of life;
> When shall I go to see the face of God?
> (Psalm 42:1-2, *The Jerusalem Bible*)

Desire as an expression of the body-self is an intrinsic element in our openness to God. Not to desire is not to receive, and not to receive is not to know. But, conversely, to desire can mean to know, and to know can mean to love.

The Old Testament's Song of Songs and its treatment in Christian history is instructive at this point.[28] It is a Hebrew love song celebrating the richly sensuous love between a woman and a man. One of the ironies in the long chronicle of biblical interpretation, however, is that few parts of the Bible so patently clear in their original intent have caused so much difficulty as this. Embarrassed by the possibility that sexual love could have such a prominent place in the canon, churchly interpreters brought the allegorical method to the rescue. Hence, from the third to the nineteenth centuries, the dominant explanation of the poem held that this was an allegory of the prayerful communion of the religious person and God. "Indeed," William Phipps observes, "the Song came to be reckoned as one of the most important books by sexually ascetic Christians because allegorical sermons on it showed how the dishonorable libidinous drives could be pommeled and sublimated." [29]

Origen's treatment of the Song was typical. Utilizing Plato's distinction between sensual and spiritual loves, he declared: "There is a love of the flesh which comes from Satan, and there is also another love, belonging to the spirit, which has its origin in God; and nobody can be possessed by the two loves. . . . If you have despised all bodily things . . . then you can acquire spiritual love." [30] In his lengthy commentary on the Song of Songs, Origen perceived it as a pure and spiritual drama of the inner soul in union with Christ. Even so, he warned that reading the Song was potentially dangerous and should be done only by older persons no longer troubled by sexual desires.

However, in ways that Origen and many others through the centuries could not comprehend, a handful of contemporary theologians have affirmed that human sensual love can be a vital dimension in the relationship with God. Dietrich Bonhoeffer describes the wholehearted love of God as a *cantus firmus* to which the other melodies of life, passionate sexual love importantly among them, provide the counterpoint. Of the Song of Songs, he says, "It is a good thing that the book is included in the Bible as a protest against those who believe that Christianity stands for the restraint of passion." [31] And Charles Davis speaks of the self-transcending power of sexual love: "The erotic dynamism of bodily love is not an arbitrary and somewhat bold and dangerous symbol, but an intrinsic element in the movement of an embodied person in openness toward the plenitude of reality, toward God." [32]

Communion. In its deepest experience sexuality is the desire for and the expression of communion—of the self with other body-selves and with God. Acknowledgment and celebration of the sexual dimension in our relationship with God thus is important if we are to overcome the commonly-felt subject-object dichotomy in religious experience.

Communion does not mean absorption, however. The fundamental differences between the finite, sinful self and God are not simply dissolved. But polarity must be distinguished from dichotomy. Polarity is the creative difference and creative tension between elements bound together in communion. Dichotomy means fundamental distinctions which are not resolved and which preclude communion. The inability to overcome the sense of dichotomy between the body-self and God results in the fading of an experiential awareness of divine immanence. God is no longer experienced, when this happens, as vital indwelling presence, permeating and giving life to the relationships and the basic stuff of everyday life. When God is only object over against subject, immanence recedes. And when immanence fades, even God's transcendence becomes less real.[33]

In authentic sexual communion dichotomy is overcome while polarity remains. The body-self is united with the beloved partner.

The physical intertwining of selves is accompanied by an emotional and spiritual intertwining. But this communion retains its polarity. It is an experience of unity but not unification. Each self respects the other's identity, not confusing it with its own wishes or fantasies. In the ecstasy of mutual giving and receiving, uniquenesses and creative differences remain. But such sexual communion furnishes more than an analogy for the human communion with God. If God is the in-betweenness of self and self, the occasion itself is the communion with God. And it becomes that which nurtures such communion in other types of human experience.

God's knowledge of us and our knowledge of God and of ourselves and the world in and under God is the subject matter of theology. Knowledge itself is communion and not possession. In a true sexual relationship with the beloved, I do not possess my partner. The same is true in the knowing relationship with God. It is a sad but obvious tendency of religious groups throughout history to substitute knowledge as possession for knowledge as communion. When this happens, the founder's participation in mystery seems too elusive, even too compelling, to survive. Then the cultic practices necessary to any religious group become solidified as possessions, and the doctrines call for the believer's submission to correct definitions.[34] But true knowledge is communion. Whether in sexual intercourse, or in the self's intercourse with God, or in the two experiences as one, it is a matter of participation rather than possession.

Incarnation. The body is instrument of communion. The body is language. As such, the body is not merely the necessary physical substructure through which the spoken and written word must come, as if the body were only vocal cords or fingers on typewriter keys. The body can be word itself—as Christians recognize in Jesus Christ, the Word made flesh.

The incarnation of God in Jesus Christ is, in the eyes of faith, the unrepeatable, unique, and sufficient revelation. This One is the norm of God's presence, the measure of our humanity. Paradoxically, however, it must also be said that in another sense God's incarnation is sufficient only if it is non-unique and repeatable. If the body of each of us is to be, in Arthur Vogel's fitting term, "the body-word of love," it will be so only if and always when the immediacy of God is present.[35] Christian faith is an incarnational faith, a faith in the repeatable and continuing incarnation of God. God is uniquely known to us through human presence, and human presence is always embodied presence. Thus body language is inescapably the material of Christian theology, and bodies are always sexual bodies, and our sexuality is basic to our capacity to know and to experience God. We have come full circle.

The case for a sexual theology rests on the assumption, therefore, that sexuality cannot adequately be considered merely as a sub-theme of moral theology or ethics. True, we must and will continue to ask what Christian theology has to say about the sexual body. But we must also (and at the same time) ask what it means that as body-selves we participate in the reality of God. Those acts and relationships which constitute the material of theology itself are inescapably intertwined with our sexuality—in our sin and in our salvation, in our dualistic alienations and in the possibility of our resurrection and human wholeness.

3

Sexual Alienation:
The Dualistic Nemesis

Body Alienation

IN A CULTURE drenched with an emphasis upon "the body beautiful" and inundated with sex it may seem odd to speak of the pervasiveness of alienation of the body from the self. Yet, a closer examination reveals unmistakable signs of the split. We experience the dualism of self and body. A *dualism,* like a dichotomy, is the sense of two different elements which may live together in an uneasy truce but are frequently in conflict. They are essentially foreign to each other. This is different from *duality*—or from its parallel term, polarity—in which two harmonious elements essentially belonging together are yet distinguishable and may exist in creative tension.

True, the line between duality and dualism, between polarity and dichotomy, sometimes seems hazy. Everyday language reveals this. One might argue that to speak of my body as an object or possession of the self—"I have a body," "my body," the body as "it" —does not necessarily signal a problem of dualistic division or alienation. This is simply everyday language for distinguishing the parts that are essentially me. It is possible. But our ordinary language still betrays the dualistic threat. It is far easier, for example, to speak of "the personality" as identical with the self than it is to speak of the body and the self as one. "I am a personality" simply sounds more "natural" than "I am a body." If my personality (mind, spirit, emotions) becomes disoriented, then surely *I* am disoriented. It seems somehow different with the body. Ordinary language *does* betray the problem.

The dissociation of self from body is seen most dramatically in its psychiatric manifestations. Psychiatrist Alexander Lowen describes the loss of feeling in the body, with accompanying sensations that the body is strange and unreal, as typical in the first stages of a psychotic episode. To know who one is, the person must also be aware of his or her own facial expressions, body movements, postures, and body feelings. "Without this awareness of bodily feeling and attitude, a person becomes split into a disembodied spirit and a disenchanted body. . . . The complete loss of body contact characterizes the schizophrenic state."[1] Contrarily, the healthy self senses unity. The body as expression of selfhood is alive, vibrant, charged with feeling. However, as Lowen observes, "The first difficulty that one encounters with patients in search of identity is that they are not aware of the lack of aliveness in their bodies. People are so accustomed to thinking of the body as an instrument or a tool of the mind that they accept its relative deadness as a normal state."[2]

In addition to psychiatric manifestations, there is also a physiology of the self-body dualism. In days of public awareness of psychosomatic ailments, it does not surprise us when a medical school dean estimates that between sixty and seventy percent of those persons currently appearing at physicians' offices and clinics have no organic origin connected to their complaints. Yet, they are physically suffering, even though the root of the ailment is not in a virus but in the emotions.

Body alienation can be experienced as self-alienation in a variety of ways even by those who never darken the psychiatrist's door or for whom psychosomatic illnesses are seldom a problem. Two examples will suffice: the effects upon the patterns of our thinking and upon our perceptions of our sexuality.

The alienated body produces a mind detached from the depth of feelings. It becomes narrow and controlling, machine-like in observation and calculation. While this is more prevalent among males in our society (for reasons which we shall examine later), it can affect persons regardless of gender. And certain patterns of self-deception seem to come in the wake of our losing the vital sense of embodiment.

It is common to regard thinking as opposed to feeling. We contrast the thoughtful, rational individual with the impulsive one. What we forget, or are unable to experience deeply, is the emotional basis of thought. Of course, we can make a decided effort on appropriate occasions to think objectively, consciously attempting to detach personal feelings from our reflection. At other times we are aware that our thinking is highly subjective and colored by our feelings. On still more rare occasions we experience times of creative thinking and recognize that it seems to depend on the interplay of reason and feeling, it seems to occur when the body is unburdened and most alive. But a considerable amount of body alienation in our culture seems to be manifested in our thinking, as is evidenced by some of our literary products. Bernice Slote thus writes of twentieth century poetry, describing "its intellectual complexity, its concentration into cubicles of wit, its wasteland erogation of possibilities, its lack of physical joy, . . . (a) rigorously honed intellectualism in which the old worship of the soul has been replaced by the worship of the mind, but in which the same sort of exile is imposed on the body." [3]

Dichotomized thinking also seems to emerge from mind-body dissociation. The fragility of our sensed identities links with resistance to the complex and often contradictory emotions which come from bodily feelings. We become resistant to ambiguity and seek simple, single reasons for things. Our conceptual worlds become populated with dichotomies—me/not me, male/female, masculine/feminine, heterosexual/homosexual, black/white, smart/stupid, healthy/ill, good/bad, right/wrong. [4]

If the mind is alienated from the body, so also is the body from the mind. The depersonalization of one's sexuality, in some form or degree, inevitably follows. The body becomes a physical object possessed and used by the self. Lacking is the sense of unity with the spontaneous rhythms of the body. Lacking is the sense of full participation in the body's stresses and pains, its joys and delights. More characteristic is the sense of body as machine. It is the phenomenon experienced by both the ascetic and the libertine (and both of those temptations in any of us). The ascetic experiences the body as a dangerous, alien force to be sternly controlled, even crushed into submission. It is "the lower realm," whose experiences and pleasures cannot be integrated into the moral self. For the libertine, the body becomes the instrument of sensuality. It is driven in a restless pursuit of pleasure. It is detached from the ego's vulnerability and capacity for self-surrender. Rather, it becomes an instrument of the partner's domination, a tool which wards off love.[5]

Psychiatric testimony underscores the connection between body alienation and promiscuous sex. Few of Rollo May's patients seem sexually repressed in their behavior; most have many partners. "But what our patients do complain of is lack of feeling and passion. . . . So much sex and so little meaning or even fun in it!"[6] Similarly, Alexander Lowen observes the striking amount of body alienation in his patients, wherein genital excitation is felt as a strange, disturbing force to be discharged. "This results in a compulsive sexuality which is nondiscriminating and devoid of affection. . . . (But) when the body becomes alive, compulsive sexual behavior and promiscuity cease. Sexuality assumes a new meaning for the patient."[7]

To the extent that we reject our bodies we become uncomfortable in talking about ourselves as *body*-selves. True, we will share with a close companion news about a medical condition or a dysfunctioning organ, particularly if these do not involve our immediate sexual capacities. Even then, however, we tend to speak as if the body function in question were a thing, an object separate from the real me, a once-useful part of the machine whose operation is now impaired. Where the more directly sexual aspects of body life are concerned, there may even be a loss of the capacity to verbalize at all. In their research John Gagnon and William Simon have discovered that throughout adulthood most people remain unable to talk about their own sexual activity, even to their spouses in the midst of arousal or to themselves in fantasy. The incapacities for such speech not only inhibit genuine sexual pleasure but also further cement the alienation of body from mind. "What is impressive is the enormous control that silence retains in the sexual area." [8]

When the body is experienced as a *thing*, it has the right to live only as machine or slave owned by the self. That to a significant degree this is the experience of countless ordinary people and not only psychiatric patients and subjects studied by sex researchers might be underscored by an imagined test.[9] Suppose on Sunday the minister were to announce as the day's text Romans 12:1, "I appeal to you therefore . . . to present your bodies as a living sacrifice, holy and acceptable to God . . ." Would "bodies" be interpreted by most hearers as the entire self (as Paul intended)? Probably not. Would the mood conveyed by that text be the prospect of wholeness, joy, ecstasy? No, more likely it would be heard as the injunction addressed to the mind or the spirit to engage in the dreary duty of disciplining and controlling one's body, imposing upon it from outside an alien willpower.

The problem of this dualistic alienation is further complicated by the fact that an oppressed or rejected body (whether for reasons of the ascetic within us or the libertine) becomes a nemesis. It seeks its revenge. We do not kill the body, we consign it to hell. And "hell consists of the dead who cannot accept their death," and so the body's ghostly influence continues, but in ways little understood by or integrated into the self.[10] Deprived of eros, the body can become the champion of thanatos.

Alienation is the root experience of sin. It is always triadic in experience and manifestation. It involves alienation experienced within the self, of which thus far I have been speaking. It also, and necessarily, involves alienation from the neighbor. And, most fundamentally, it is alienation from God. At this point, consider the manifestations of body alienation expressed outward toward "the neighbor"—our human companions as individuals and groups, and the natural world as well.

What we reject in ourselves becomes projected outward. The figure of the devil most often represents what we will not acknowledge in ourselves, and in the late Middle Ages when demonography became highly developed it was clear that the devil represented the sexual body. In male form it was the lustful Pan, with satyrs as attendant demons. In female form it was the witch. In both, it was the magnified and distorted image of the erotic.[11]

In our less dramatically symbolic present age we continue to project outward the alienations within. Fear of the body finds expression in our daily patterns of human interaction. We distance both emotions and bodies from our relationships. Much of our lives is conducted with calculated disembodiment with rigid formalities regulating those socially-permissible public contacts—the handshake, the polite kiss, the elbow grip—even though athletes may be granted a temporary reprieve from such constraints following the crucial play of the game.

Separation from the neighbor is frequently undergirded by the dualism which treats the spirit as free and immortal but the body as mortal and corrupted. With this assumption, only part of the self is acceptable. If we are acceptable at all, it is not because of our concreteness but because of our transworldly divinity. But then the neighbor, too, is only of transcendent value. I then love that person as another occasion to experience God. However, if the other is only that, he or she loses particularity and value. John Fenton aptly declares, "Non-bodily theologies are anti-self, anti-neighbor, anti-society, and anti-world." [12]

Herbert Marcuse links bodily repression with repression in the social order. Reinterpreting Freud from a Marxist perspective, he argues that bodily repression in an exploitive economy has led to the stripping from sexual love of its playfulness and spontaneity. Love has become primarily a matter of duty and habit, with the blunting of sensuality its inevitable result. Under the bourgeois-capitalistic system, productivity, achievement and individual strength have become the chief virtues, and "the performance principle" a prime value. Drawing on elements from both Marx (the transformation of alienated people into things) and Max Weber (the psychological-spiritual need to perform and produce), Marcuse finds that alienation from society and alienation from one's own sexuality go hand-in-hand. Our sexuality is intended to be diffused throughout the entire body. The body as a whole should be the source of sexual pleasure—in responsiveness, feeling, giving, and receiving. Under the pressure of the performance principle, however, our sexuality becomes genitalized, identified with specific "sex acts." [13]

Even if one does not accept Marcuse's blend of Freud and Marx at all points, his general conclusion is both defensible and significant: there *is* an important link between the alienation of self from neighbor in a highly competitive society, on the one hand, and the alienation of self from body through "the performance principle," on the other hand. In our society, there is an exaggerated estimation of the virtue of competent sexual performance in genital intercourse. (Witness the typical linguistic identification of "having sex" and engaging in coitus.) Corresponding to this, there is an underdeveloped understanding of sexuality as that which is diffused throughout the entire body and enriches all relationships. Rather, as William Masters and Virginia Johnson contend, "Sex, like work, becomes a matter of performance. There is always a goal in view—ejaculation for the man, orgasm for the woman. If these goals are achieved, the job has been satisfactorily performed. . . . Sex, for them, is not a way of being, a way of expressing identity or feelings or a way of nourishing a commitment. It is always a single incident, an occasion, an accomplishment. . . . (But) usually, goal-oriented sex is self-defeating. Sex interest is soon lost as the result of performance demand." [14] Indeed, most of the street-word synonyms for intercourse reflect the technological mind's goal orientation rather than caring, sensitivity, and responsiveness. Body alienation does not nurture eroticized, sensitive persons who can love sexually; it produces technically competent, genitally-focused individuals who "make love."

The competitive ethos finds its solid grounding in the pervasive male sexism which affects us all. Men and women struggle against each other, often unconsciously, in patterns of dominance and submission. Women compete with women for male acceptance which society teaches them is essential for their self-worth. Men find emotional intimacy and tenderness with men threatening to the masculine, heterosexual image. Spouses find it difficult to speak honestly with each other about their sexual needs and anxieties, and performance fears invade their sexual loving.

In the larger social network and in our links to the natural world the "undead" body also works its revenge. Later we will return to these issues in greater detail. At this point we must simply remind ourselves that much of the world's violence cannot be adequately comprehended apart from its connection to "machismo," that hyper-masculine image of toughness and power. We cannot understand white racism without recognizing its sexual dimensions. We cannot fathom our ecological dilemma without seeing how the dichotomy of spiritual and sensual becomes the split between humankind and the earth.

Most basically, body alienation is alienation from God. For a variety of reasons many have become convinced that in God's eyes human sexuality is at best a regrettable necessity. Not only has sexuality nothing intrinsically to do with our relationship with God, it can only get in the way. In part we are reaping the fruits of the ladder mysticism of late Greek thought, which had such an impact upon the church. To the scale of being there corresponds a scale of loving. On the lower rungs of the ladder, the soul can love God through creatures, but on the highest rungs, the soul loves God for the sake of God alone. "The soul becomes a solitary, uncon-taminated virgin, contemplating a God who is the same." [15] In part we are reaping the fruits of our fear of the material and of the inability of Protestant orthodoxy to deal with the category of crea-tion. Nature is dissolved in history, and creation in eschatology. Then the body and its sensations, which *seem* to belong to the natural world more than to history, are religiously suspect.[16]

If through our religious socialization we have been taught that our sexuality is an impediment to the life with God, guilt may be attached to sexual feelings, often in unrecognized ways. But, in the vicious circle of things, hostility toward God may then enter—hos-tility because of God's rejection of that which seems (even in the face of much we have been taught) to be inevitably part of us.

The technical formulations of theologians, both for good and for ill, do have an impact on the church at large. If some years ago certain theologians shocked numerous Christians by declaring the death of God, some people recognized the partial truth in what was being said. Truncated *ideas* and *images* of God must surely die. Indeed, God is transcendent and radically beyond us. Indeed, God is revealed in history. But God is also and at the same time the radically immanent One, infusing nature, expressing divinity in embodiment, rejoicing in sensual love. Why these latter dimensions of the divine life are still foreign to many, and perhaps at some level to all of us, presses us to look more closely at the history of our body alienation.

A History of Sexual Dualisms

The Christian culture is not the only one to have had problems with sexual alienation and dualisms. It is an unfair oversimplification to assume that only the Christian West has been thus afflicted while so-called primitive cultures and Eastern civilizations have escaped.[17] For example, among the Manus of New Guinea sex was degraded and rigidly controlled. And the frank sexuality of Hindu art says little about the day-to-day sexual life of the Hindus, which has been governed by strict caste-based rules and prohibitions. Further, in Buddhism, even more explicitly than in many strands of Christianity, the rejection of sex and bodily expressiveness is counted essential to the attainment of freedom. So, the problem is not unique to the Christian story. Nevertheless, this is our story, and with this we must deal.

The individual histories of our sexual alienation undoubtedly are as complex and as varied as each of us is unique. Yet, there are two major common threads: spiritualistic dualism and sexist dualism. The two threads intertwine and mutually sew the fabric of alienation in both history and in the individual, but they can be singled out for identification.

Spiritualistic dualism has its roots in the body-spirit dichotomy abounding in Greek philosophy and culture at the beginning of the Christian era. Hence, the term *Hellenistic dualism* is also appropriate. Or, Jacques Maritain's word *angelism* likewise fits—the angel as the bodyless mind. Earlier Greek culture was significantly different in this respect. It did not view the immortal spirit as a temporary prisoner in a corruptible, mortal body, nor did it see the good life as an escape from the flesh into pure spirit. Quite the opposite, it saw the erotic experience as a basic key to the eternal.

At the close of the Greek Classical Age, however, a body pessimism had set in. Plato gave it lasting articulation. In the *Phaedo* (speaking through Socrates) he writes in praise of "the man who pursues the truth by applying his pure and unadulterated thought to the pure and unadulterated object, cutting himself off as much as possible from his eyes and ears and virtually all the rest of his body, as an impediment which by its presence prevents the soul from attaining to truth and clear thinking." Further, Plato adds, "It seems that so long as we are alive, we shall continue closest to knowledge if we avoid as much as we can all contact and association with the body, except when they are absolutely necessary; and instead of allowing ourselves to become infected with its nature, purify ourselves from it until God himself gives us deliverance." [18] This was the dualism which was to infect Christian understandings of the self, in spite of the holistic view of body-spirit unity and the person's psychosomatic oneness typical of Hebraic experience.

Sexist dualism is the second major root and expression of sexual alienation, intertwined with and at least as important as spiritualistic dualism. It was present in Israel of the Old Testament as well as in the early Christian church. It was the subordination of women —systematically present in the institutions, the interpersonal relations, the thought forms, and the religious life of patriarchal cultures. Hence, the term *patriarchal dualism* is appropriate, also, or simply the contemporary word *sexism*.

The alienation of spirit from body, of reason from emotions, of "higher life" from "fleshly life" found both impetus and expression in the subordination of women. Men assumed to themselves superiority in reason and spirit and thus believed themselves destined to lead both civil and religious communities. Contrarily, women were identified with the traits of emotion, body, and sensuality. Their monthly "pollutions" were taken as a sign of religious uncleanness and emotional instability.

Rosemary Radford Ruether characterizes both the pervasive manifestations of sexist dualism and its intricate interconnection with the spiritualistic dichotomy: "The psychic organization of consciousness, the dualistic view of the self and the world, the hierarchical concept of society, the relation of humanity and nature, and of God and creation—all these relationships have been modeled on sexual dualism. . . . The male ideology of the 'feminine' that

we have inherited in the West seems to be rooted in a self-alienated
experience of the body and the world, projecting upon the sexual
other the lower half of these dualisms. . . . it is always woman
who is the 'other,' the antithesis over against which one defines
'authentic' (male) selfhood." [19]

The Unfolding of the Story

A number of historians have traced the development of both
dualisms in a variety of ways and in considerable detail. Yet, the
story deserves retelling, for it is an important part of our self-
understanding. I shall try to capture only its most significant expressions and developments.

Pre-Christian Hebrew life exhibited a minimal amount of spiritualistic dualism. To the Hebrews sexuality was a good gift from
God. Indeed, their scriptures commonly called a person "flesh"
rather than "spirit." Marriage was highly valued, though especially
for procreative more than companionate reasons. Even so, the Song
of Songs, as we have seen, celebrates the companionate and sensuous love of a betrothed or married couple in a most delightful way.

Yet, body-denying influences gradually crept in. In part this
seems to have come through the effect of Persian beliefs which
correlated salvation with sexual restriction. But the historical situation of the Jews itself was of no small importance. Vern L. Bullough
contends that the greatest period of sexual repression occurred following the return from the exile. "The most logical explanation for
the changes in attitude seems to lie with the Jewish attitudes toward
themselves. When Judaism seemed threatened, when the Jews, both
as a group and as individuals, were insecure, their sexual attitude
was the most repressive. When there was a greater feeling of security, attitudes were more tolerant." [20] Feelings about the individual
body and about the social body do appear to be closely tied
together.

If spiritualistic dualism was minimal in earlier Hebrew history,
however, sexist dualism was present throughout. The culture was
clearly male-dominated. While this generalization, unfortunately,
holds true, it is not without exception. The Old Testament does
contain critiques of patriarchy. In passages such as Genesis 2 and
3, the Song of Songs, Ruth, Jeremiah 31:15-22, and Hosea 4:14,

sexual mutuality is celebrated as the norm. In addition, female imagery is occasionally used for God, and Israel refrained from absolutizing its patriarchal life as a theological assertion.[21] Nevertheless, patriarchy was dominant. Women were viewed as property in the legal codes, valued for their procreative sexuality, but to be secured and disposed of by men. Women were effectively disenfranchised by Israelite religious law: "the people of Israel" was exclusively the congregation of adult males. Extramarital sex was dealt with by a double standard. Economic rights were a male preserve, and sons were heirs. The sexual emphasis was upon male potency and the life-bearing power of semen; the male genitals were of great importance and were to be protected. In short, while angelism was not a pronounced fact of Hebrew life, sexist dualism was.

Greece was to exercise a towering influence upon Christian sexual thought and practice, although that influence came preeminently from the negative rather than the positive side of Greek sexual interpretation. The picture is decidedly schizophrenic in this sense. On the one hand, until the late Classical Age, sexuality and sensuality were highly honored. The Greek gods were thoroughly sexual beings. The Greeks not only accepted but cultivated the human body as a source of admiration and pleasure. The grace of harmonious motion in nude male athletes expressed the conviction that the training of the body was the training of the soul. Homosexual as well as heterosexual expression was affirmed, though the ideal homosexual relationship was a non-orgasmic bond between an older man and a young man. Religion and sexuality were intimately intertwined. For all the celebration of bodily life, however, early Greek culture was patriarchal and androcentric, with a double standard for the two sexes.

It is striking that a profound, spiritualistic dualism arose in Greek culture. Principally after the death of Alexander the Great it became powerful. Platonism perceived the soul as timeless, changeless, and immaterial. The senses were of no account in knowing the real world, and because sacred love dealt with the beauties of the soul while profane love dealt with the body, the true state of existence was devoid of any physical sexual activity. The ascetic ideal was celebrated, and with it the renunciation of marriage and family, the downgrading of earthly ties, and the emphasis upon pure contemplation as the good life.

While the Greek world was experiencing political failure and their thinkers turning to otherworldly preoccupations, Rome's power was growing. Contrary to much popular opinion, the sexually excessive behavior of the Romans at the time of the empire has perhaps been exaggerated. With certain exceptions, they remained a rather moralistic people, emphasizing the importance of marriage and children and hostile to sexual behaviors regarded as deviant. But the Roman world in the centuries immediately preceding the Christian era also underwent a dramatic change. Stoicism became its reigning ethical philosophy, celebrating passionlessness as the supreme virtue and holding the expression of visceral emotions to be a vice. Seneca, the Stoic philosopher and a contemporary of Jesus, taught that the sign of true greatness was the achievement of the state in which nothing could possibly disturb or excite one. To the Stoic sex was not bad in itself, but passion was greatly suspect, and the only justification for marriage was procreation.[22]

Such were the major sexual inheritances of the Christian era. If Morton Scott Enslin's comment does not tell the whole story, nevertheless it carries considerable truth: "Christianity did not make the world ascetic; rather the world in which Christianity found itself strove to make Christianity ascetic." [23]

Jesus himself did not proclaim any new sexual ethic. In fact, he explicitly disowned such an intention, and his recorded comments on sexual matters are few. Yet, his contributions were of inestimable importance and are all the more striking because of their contrast with the prevailing spirit and practice of the time.[24] Jesus explicitly condemned infidelity and divorce as interruptions of the Creator's intended one-flesh union of woman and man. He insisted upon the supreme importance of love and forgiveness in sexual matters as well as in every other area of life. Not of the least importance, in both teaching and example Jesus insisted upon the fundamental equality of the sexes. His consistent concern for the oppressed helps us to grasp his striking teaching about divorce:

women were profoundly oppressed when treated as property to be disposed of by male decree.

In Paul we meet "the apostle of love." We also meet one whose writings on sexual matters are marked by ambivalence. As a Jew, Paul affirmed a highly positive view of creation. As a Christian, he proclaimed the liberation of the whole human being in Jesus Christ. But as a child of patriarchal times he was conditioned by sexist dualism, and as a "Greek" he was not untouched by spiritualistic dualism.

Paul's letters emerged out of the context of a licentious cultural climate. His concern for sexual purity through dissociation from the idolatrous practices of the pagans is clearly understandable. Yet the evidence is strong, contrary to unfair interpretations of Paul, that he did not heavily embrace Hellenistic dualism. Speaking to this issue John A. T. Robinson asserts that the concept of the body *(soma)* forms the keystone of Paul's theology: "It is from the body of sin and death that we are delivered; it is through the body of Christ on the Cross that we are saved; it is into His body the Church that we are incorporated; it is by His body in the Eucharist that this Community is sustained; it is in our body that its new life has to be manifested; it is to a resurrection of this body to the likeness of His glorious body that we are destined." [25] Further, when Paul contrasts "flesh" *(sarx)* with spirit, it is a mistake to read this as unvarnished Greek dualism—the immortal soul over against the corruptible body. More typically, Paul uses "the mind of the flesh" to refer not to sensuality as such but to the denial of human dependence on God and a return to reliance on the law as the means of salvation.[26]

Undoubtedly, Paul's great positive contribution to Christian sexual theology lies in the manner in which he elevates the sexual union in marriage as a parable of the "great mystery" which symbolizes the union of Christ and the church. This involves a remarkable psychological understanding of intercourse as an act which is not simply a pleasurable genital function but rather one which can engage the whole person in ways which express a unique mode of commitment and self-disclosure.[27]

Yet, there is ambivalence about it all, and there are negativistic elements which were eagerly seized by later and much more dual-

istic Christian theologians. Paul clearly prefers the single state and
tolerates marriage as a begrudged necessity. The most favorable
interpretation is that he is here simply reflecting his vivid eschatological awareness: since the end of the age is near, Christians should
live in keen anticipation, on tiptoe, undistracted by earthly cares
and pleasures. But that the preaching of the kingdom's imminence
ought automatically to take precedence over all else, including
marriage, is too simple an answer. It makes sense only if one has—
at least to some extent—imbibed something of Hellenistic dualism
wherein pure love for God by its very nature must divorce one
from earthly loves. Thus, for all of Paul's Hebraic understanding of
the unity of the body-self, he was not consistent. When he interpreted marriage as a regrettable concession to human weakness, an
unavoidable remedy for the highly sexed, a lesser of the evils but
still an evil—Paul was a Hellenist.[28]

Paul's teaching and example regarding women likewise is per-
vaded by ambivalence. Clearly he valued certain "sisters" as colleagues in the church's leadership, yet their leadership was not
equal to that of men. To his lasting credit is his ringing declaration
of the radical equality of all persons in Christ—"neither male nor
female" (Gal. 3:28). Yet, at the same time Paul could readily invoke
those traditions of sexist dualism which insisted upon woman's
subordination: they should keep silence in the church, and while
men ought not to cover their heads since they are the glory of God,
women should be veiled for they are the glory of man. At this point
it simply appears that Paul was operating with a futuristic eschatology which did not have a transformative effect upon social relationships in the present time. In the eschaton—the new age in Christ
—there will be equality and mutuality according to God's original
and primordial will. But until that new age arrives, Paul apparently
is content to endorse the inherited patterns of sexual inequality so
that "decent order" might be maintained in church and society.[29]

It is only fair, however, continually to remind ourselves that
particular biblical statements about human sexuality are inevitably
historically conditioned. Specific injunctions cannot legitimately be
wrenched from their historical context and applied in a mechanical
manner to the late twentieth century. Our essential scriptural guidance must come from the larger perspectives of biblical faith. It

must come from the Bible's basic understanding of the human person in the light of God's presence, action, and purposes.

The Church Fathers in the first five centuries after the New Testament era were far less ambivalent about the sexual body than was Paul. By and large, they were simply negative. This does not mean that most Christians of that period felt and believed similarly —we simply do not know. Most of the writings from this formative period come from males at the top of the church's hierarchy, with few extant writings from ordinary priests and still fewer from the laity.[30]

The Fathers were little concerned with a systematic theology of sexuality. Theirs was a much more practical interest—the purity of Christian life in a licentious, pagan environment. Still, they had to develop theory in order to give practical advice, and in doing so they reflected the increasing impact of spiritualistic dualism. Tertullian represents the more moderate position, declaring against the heretic Marcion, "We do not reject marriage, but simply refrain from it. Nor do we prescribe [single] sanctity as the rule, but only recommend it . . . at the same time earnestly vindicating marriage, whenever hostile attacks are made against it as a polluted thing, to the disparagement of the Creator."[31] Jerome displays the more extreme dualism. He could accept marriage, reluctantly, only because from marriages virgins were born: "I praise marriage and wedlock, but only because they beget celibates; I gather roses from thorns, gold from the earth, pearls from shells."[32]

Since the Fathers could not Christianly speak of two different creations, one spiritual and good, the other material and evil, they typically assigned sexuality not to the good order of creation but to the results of the Fall. Given this, the image of God could not reside in the whole person but only in the individual's unfallen or spiritual state, divorced from the body and its sexuality. The net result was the hierarchical view of virtue characteristically found in the writings of the Church Fathers. Martyrdom was the highest goal of Christian aspiration. Virginity and celibacy came next on the ladder, while the lowest rung was occupied by the state of marriage. Even within marriage, however, there was a hierarchy of goods. Since sex was always a danger to true Christian piety, the highest form of marriage was the dedication of spouses to each

other in total sexual abstinence. Lower was the marriage in which
spouses had intercourse but only for the sake of procreating children and then as a conjugal duty not to be enjoyed as pleasure.
Least good was marriage in which the sexual union was enjoyed.
Thus, in the patristic literature spiritualistic dualism had won
the day.

Of all the Church Fathers, Augustine deserves special comment.
His imposing theology was to set the stage for many centuries of
Christian thinking, including thought about sexuality (with which
Augustine himself had a long and personal struggle).[33]

Augustine was deeply troubled about the problem of sexual lust
and was almost exclusively concerned about the genital aspects of
human sexuality. Our subjection to the lust of "concupiscence," he
believed, is a direct result of the Fall. One of the Fall's clear marks
is that the genitals are no longer under our voluntary control, and
our insatiable search for self-satisfaction (concupiscence) though
evident in all spheres of life is particularly evidenced by the genitals' disobedience. Since Augustine sees a clear link between original sin and concupiscence, every sex act is not only directly connected to original sin (for which each of us is responsible) but also
binds us more firmly to it.

In this interpretation every act of intercourse is inherently lustful. Augustine does give a marvelously accurate and vivid description of lustful, unloving sex, but, fatefully, he sees no power
in love to transform the sex act in any significant way. There is
something inherently suspicious about this act, for in the moment
of its consummation both reason and will are overwhelmed, the
partners out of control. Augustine could not fathom the mutual loss
of the wife and husband to the ecstatic medium of their shared
love, nor could he see sexual love as both analogous to and expressive of the self's communion with God. To the contrary, sex
was the bestial appetite of lust, and for a couple to copulate for
any purpose other than procreation was debauchery. If, however,
procreation was its single aim, intercourse was good, for then it was
being used for its ordained end. In *this* sense, compared to the radically anti-body, anti-sex Manicheans with whom he debated, Augustine had a pro-sex attitude. Yet, the cloud over even procreative sex

could not be lifted, for single-mindedness about procreation still would not dissolve the inherent lustfulness of every act of intercourse, and hell itself could be described as "the burning of lust."

During the Early Middle Ages we can find little systematic theological reflection on sexuality in the Western church. It is the "penitentials" which give us the best clues to the minds of the church's leadership. These handbooks for confessors, with descriptions of penances appropriate for particular sins, reveal a continuing emphasis upon the procreative use of sex. The Stoic mistrust of pleasure is still strong. Yet, here and there in the penitentials is evidence of a growing appreciation of the possibility that sexuality might have some positive role in Christian personhood.

The High Middle Ages (approximately the eleventh to fourteenth centuries) saw a new flowering of systematic theology and with it more systematic reflection on sexuality. By this time the church also had jurisdiction over the legal regulation of marriage. Marriage was elevated to a sacramental character because it symbolized the union of Christ and the church and because it was an ecclesiastical institution for procreation. But the divorce between the interpersonal dimensions of marriage, on the one hand, and sexuality, on the other, continued. While intercourse did not arouse the intense theological reactions characteristic of the Church Fathers, to the medieval theologian it was still the marital duty of procreation and not to be enjoyed. The rationalistic and legalistic mind-set was still too strong in that era's theology for sexual expression to be perceived as a unique means of mutual fulfillment and sensuous self-giving love. The greatest medieval theologian, St. Thomas Aquinas, laid down a three-fold standard for the moral judgment of sexual acts: they must be done for the right purpose (procreation), with the right person (one's lawfully-wedded spouse), and in the right way (heterosexual genital intercourse).[34]

Unfortunately, the sixteenth century's Protestant Reformation did not overcome the reigning spiritualistic dualism in Christian thought on matters sexual.[35] While the Reformers' approach was largely practical, they reintroduced a major theological emphasis which carried sexual implications: the emphasis upon justification by grace rather than by virtue or works of the law. This led both Luther and Calvin to undercut the cult of virginity and the notion of meritorious sexual celibacy, and hence marriage was lifted to a new level of theological affirmation.

Nevertheless, ambivalence about sexuality remained. Luther himself was a curious mixture of the radical and the conservative in this regard. Marriage, he believed, is an honorable estate ordained by God for all (with the very few exceptions of those who can remain virginal for the kingdom). It is to be commended with enthusiasm as a great divine gift in which the relationship of husband and wife can be a heavenly school of love. Yet, Luther also saw marriage as a necessity because the power of the libidinal drives is so strong that few can resist sex. Hence, in spite of his eulogies of marriage, Luther could also term it an "emergency hospital for the illness of human drives."

A positive affirmation of sexuality evaded him. Every sexual act recapitulated the sinful effects of the Fall, and no "marital duty" could be discharged without sin. Luther's hearty realism about the strength of sexual urges (undoubtedly strongly felt in himself) made him less willing than many others to condemn those whose sex expression was not entirely monogamous. In any event, sexuality was always married to lust in the fallen human being. If lust at times was a mad and raging animal that must be allowed to run its course, regrettably that must be. Yet the strange work of God is this: in a married couple's sexual desire, however corrupted it remains, they find God's pardon and permission, for through marital intercourse the divine will propagates the race and restrains human vice.

John Calvin's differences from Luther were largely matters of emphasis, with one major exception: companionship, rather than procreation and the restraint of lust, was God's chief intention for marriage. To Luther the wife tended to be the bearer of the husband's children and the provider of his sexual relief. While Calvin still subordinated the woman in status and expressed his own share of sexist dualism, he argued that she was to be her husband's inseparable companion in life and work. (He did not, of course, argue that the *husband* was destined to be his *wife's* inseparable companion in life and work.)

Calvin was less pessimistic about sex than was Luther. If Luther principally sought to confine the raging power within marriage, the

Geneva reformer believed that sex could have constructive effects. Thus he rejected any false prudery about marital sex and insisted on mutual agreement between spouses concerning their sex acts. But Calvin, too, continued some of the traditional suspicion of sexuality, and spiritualistic as well as sexist dualism was present in his writings on the subject. His attempts to control the sexual drives led him into moralism and legalism on the subject. In the final analysis, sex was not really to be enjoyed by the spouses; it was to be kept within the rigid bounds of "delicacy and propriety."

Though modest, there were some Reformation advances in lessening the massive spiritualistic dualism of early Christian centuries. In regard to the subordination of women, however, there were some retrogressive tendencies. Prior to the Reformation, unmarried women had theological blessing to be independent of men—living as nuns and making their own contributions to the life of the church. Now for Protestants the housewifely ideal was given divine sanction, and it was that ideal which saw the woman principally restricted to children, kitchen, and church (in German, "the three-K mentality"—Kinder, Küche, Kirche). While Calvin believed that he saw the woman positively, as the lifelong companion of the man, it was she who was his companion, his "helper," his "support." She was to contribute "thoughtfulness and tranquility" while the man was to furnish "wisdom." [36] Furthermore, the Reformers turned to the Old Testament patriarchs for their model of the Christian family. If the great Hebrew kings furnished the appropriate pattern for "the godly prince" of Europe in the sixteenth century, so also the households of Abraham, Isaac, and Jacob (except for their polygamy) should be family images for Reformation Christians. But such patterns not only perpetuated the submission of wives to husbands; they also gave the father an almost magisterial authority in regard to disciplining "his" children. [37]

In Roman Catholic thought no major changes in official teachings about sexuality emerged from the sixteenth century to the mid-twentieth. In the late medieval period, William of Occam had given impetus to a certain style of moral theology: teaching moral duties according to a negative interpretation of the Ten Commandments rather than in regard to the positive virtues. This negative framework applied to the teaching of sexual morality as well, and over the centuries the church's moral manuals came to be dominated by the delineation of sexual "thou-shalt-nots." Procreation continued as the only legitimation of sexual activity. Further, the medievalists' prominent distinction between acts "in accordance with nature" and acts "contrary to nature" was diligently maintained. The former type of sexual act preserved the procreative possibility; hence, a sexual sin in accordance with nature was a lesser violation of the moral order than was that sin contrary to nature in which procreation was impossible. The lesser violations (though still serious sins) included fornication, adultery, incest, and rape. Acts contrary to nature included masturbation, homosexual acts, and bestiality.[38] The curious conclusion to which such reasoning could lead is that masturbation is a greater moral evil than is rape.

In the centuries following the Reformation, the most significant Protestant development was the increasing awareness that sexual intercourse had values quite independent of procreation. In the seventeenth century, for example, the Anglican ecclesiastic and theologian Jeremy Taylor spoke to the relational values of physical sexuality: "to lighten and ease the cares and sadnesses of household affairs" and "to endear each other." [39] From the Puritan side, poet John Milton—in spite of his pronounced subordinationism regarding women—could express the conviction that the sexual union of spouses could be a prefiguring of the heavenly realm. And in his depiction of the heavenly vision in *Paradise Regained,* the sensuous and the spiritual are blended together in a manner reminiscent of ancient Semitic imagery.[40]

That in the Christian tradition there are positive sources of insight in regard to our sexual salvation is evident in the preceding survey. But, obviously, my accent has been upon the negative. At this point it is important that we face honestly those elements of our common tradition which have contributed to the sexual alienation we presently experience. In spite of the church's gradually growing valuation of the place of the sexual relationship in marriage and in spite of its striving toward a single standard of moral integrity, the pervasiveness of both spiritualistic and sexist dualisms can be read in bold type on the pages of our Christian past.

Yet, until the recent work of feminist theologians, it was spiritualistic dualism which received the lion's share of attention in histories of Christian sexuality. For one thing, it seemed easier to understand why this particular dualism had made its inroads. The typical interpretation—valid as far as it went—was this: The more unified view of selfhood and more positive view of sexuality characteristic of the Hebrews did not have a chance to become rooted adequately in the Christian community. The Hebrews were one people with a cultural unity expressing both faith and morality. But the Christian church had the more complex task of relating to many cultures as it attempted to become a universal community. Beginning as a small group expecting the imminent coming of the kingdom, a group which could afford a large measure of indifference to secular society, it then became the religion of a world empire. As such it tried to maintain its integrity in a Hellenistic world, borrowing from, adjusting to, and interpreting through the thought forms and values of that cosmopolitan world. Thus, the church, as its own blends of thought became increasingly rooted in its life, failed to develop the positive understanding of sexuality which a biblical view of life implies.[41]

Such an interpretation has validity. But it is incomplete. It does account for some of the lasting impact of spiritualistic dualism. Yet, what it leaves unspoken is the fact that sexist dualism has been closely interwoven with angelism throughout the centuries. Indeed, the alienation produced by man-over-woman has both nurtured and given persistence to the alienation of spirit-over-body.

A Further Look at Sexist Dualism

Women are identified with body, and men with spirit. The connection between the two dualisms is painfully obvious. Women are perceived as lacking in the capacity for autonomy, for rationality, for will power. Dependency and irrationality, passivity and sensuality (all characteristics of repressed bodiliness) are assumed to be their defining characteristics. And the alien woman then becomes the model for the perception of other subjugated groups, classes, castes, and races.[42]

It is true that alienation is sin, and at its root there remains something mysterious and inexplicable. Yet, we can understand, at least in some significant part, why our alienation takes certain forms. Why has the dichotomy of man-over-woman arisen, and what gives to it its stubborn persistence?

At the outset, the possibility that there are biologically-given differences between men and women which will account for this phenomenon must be raised. Yet, the available research strongly indicates that this is not the answer. The evidence comes from a variety of disciplines:

● From her anthropological studies, Margaret Mead concludes: "Many, if not all, of the personality traits which we have called masculine or feminine are as lightly linked to sex as are the clothing, the manners, and the form of headdress that a society at a given period assigns to either sex." [43]

● Psychiatrist Judd Marmor puts it this way: "As one moves up in the evolutionary scale . . . one finds that inherited instinctual patterns become less complex but more subject to modification by learning. This development reaches its apogee in human beings, who are born, not with complex instinctual adaptive patterns, but with relatively unfocused basic biological drives. The direction these drives take in human beings and the objects to which they become attached are subject to enormous modifications by learning." [44]

● John Money's research at the Johns Hopkins Gender Identity Clinic has dramatically indicated the immense power of social and psychological influences upon a person's sense of being either female or male, not to mention traits of "femininity" and "masculinity." Even the basic gender difference is not simply biologically-given. If (as has happened) a child has been reared as a member of the other sex, that child will continue to experience himself or herself as a member of the "wrong" sex throughout life, regardless of that person's biological construction. Money concludes that "sex differences are relative, not absolute. They can be assigned however we wish, as long as we allow for two simple facts: first, that men impregnate, women menstruate, gestate, and lactate; and second, that adult individuals cannot alter the nuclear core of their gender schemes." [45]

• A major review of the available literature on psychological similarities and differences between the sexes by Eleanor Maccoby and Carol Jacklin concludes with a similar judgment. There are a few identifiable differences in average men and women, but only in two areas. In intellectual skills women tend to exhibit higher verbal abilities and men higher abilities in mathematical and visual-spatial tasks. And, on the average, men seem to have a biological basis for greater readiness to learn aggressive behavior, though this does not mean greater aggression *per se*. On the whole, however, no discernible differences appear to exist between men and women even in areas wherein they are commonly believed to be present: analytical abilities, self-esteem, suggestibility, achievement orientation, nurturing capacities, social orientation, and the like.[46]

If inherent biological and genetic differences do not adequately account for sexist dualism, we must turn elsewhere. Several plausible and overlapping theories deserve reflection.

One possibility has to do with the awesomeness (and hence fear) which men have felt about the biological powers of women.[47] While the common prejudice, buttressed by Freud, holds that the woman envies the man's strength, and particularly his penis, a persuasive argument points in quite the opposite direction. Throughout history, men have harbored feelings of inferiority because of the special powers which women seem to have, especially the capacity for pregnancy and giving birth. Historically, if women were seen as creatures with special supernatural gifts, two types of responses appeared open to men: adoring the woman as divine or treating her as demonic. Both have occurred, and both have found ample expression in Christian theology.

Fear of the demonic is evident in the Church Father Tertullian, who called woman "the gate of Hell." Pettus Damiani, an eleventh century monk, described women as "bait of Satan, by-product of paradise, poison in our food, source of sin, temptresses, whores of lust, sirens, and chief witches." [48] The *Malleus Maleficarum*, written as a handbook for the persecution of witches, portrayed women as inherently defective and perverse, and, after the Fall, doubly prone to the demonic. This fate was escaped by men because of the maleness of Jesus, according to the authors, two fifteenth century Dominican inquisitors.[49] The other side of the picture, the worship of woman, is best illustrated in the cult of Mary. With its emphases upon both virginity and motherhood, Mariology accents two common strands in the persisting male attitudes toward women: purity and the capacity to produce children for their men.

A second and related hypothesis is likewise connected to the male anxiety in the face of women's sexual power. In this suggestion, the oppression of women is linked with the transition of tribal societies into urban societies.[50] In the early tribal society people considered themselves part of nature, imitating the biological processes in their environment. Women held a place of coeminence with men, for their fertility was essential to the ongoing life of the tribe; sexual creation was primary inasmuch as the family was coextensive with all other institutions.

However, the break from the kinship tribe—the courage of Abraham to leave his tribal home to establish a new nation—required an important psychological development. The bondage to nature must be broken and a new basis of society realized. For the Israelites this new basis was Law and Covenant, the primacy of legal over biological power. But this struggle to break with the earlier biological consciousness led men to project that very consciousness upon women. It was women, now, who were the biological beings from whom men must be separated and in relation to whom men must be superior. Thus a series of ritual taboos arose which marked women, particularly during menstruation and childbirth, as "unclean." According to Herbert W. Richardson, "Through these taboos, the male not only separates himself from the sexuality of the female, but separates himself from his own instinctive sexuality. He attains, in this way, a more-than-sexual identity . . . a new definition of himself: as one created not in the image of any biological thing, but as a being sharing in the covenanting-legal power that rules the universe." [51]

A third and related theory focuses upon the man's more direct sexual fears of the woman, especially in intercourse itself. The notion of "castration anxiety" is psychologically commonplace and relevant: the penis must enter the vagina, literally be engulfed by it in coitus, and this may arouse subconscious castration fears. In addition, however, men feel threatened in other ways. For inter-

course to be achieved, the man must "perform." He must produce
and maintain an erection, and the threat of impotence is ever
present. But in this sense, the woman never "fails," and in some
strange biological sense she always "wins" in the sex act. The male
organ is reduced to flaccidity and, for a time, to incapacity, while
the woman is capable of sustained sexual activity. Anxious and jeal-
ous, the man retaliates with assumptions of his own superiority.
Indeed, the anxiety he feels in face of his partner's sexual power
threatens to make him impotent, but by the transformation of that
anxiety into aggression he can perform, he can dominate, and he
can penetrate.

The plausibility of such theories as these, all finding the roots
of sexist dualism somehow located in man's anxieties in the face
of woman's sexuality, is enhanced when one reflects on the psychic
strata of our sexual history. Rosemary Ruether has identified three
psychic layers, all not equally pronounced in any given historical
period, but all present.[52] One is the notion of women as quasi-
property, as servants, and as permanent dependents of men. This
is "primary patriarchy" in which it is assumed that women can
never grow up to become autonomous persons. The second layer
identifies woman as body in the sense of carnality and evil. Now
the servant becomes the witch, for the body is demonically alien
to men who have identified themselves primarily as mind and spirit.
Here, Hellenistic dualism dramatically interlaces with sexism. In
the third psychic stratum woman is the spiritualized ideal. She is
pure, and at once both mother and virgin. Now it is she who is the
guardian of religion and morality in the private sphere of the home,
though "the real world" (which belongs to men) lies elsewhere.

In addition to these broad theories and historical overviews
concerning sexist dualism, particular facets of our Christian heritage illuminate its entrenchment and its continuing power. One
example from the Roman Catholic side and a second from the
Protestant past will illustrate.

The manner in which biological misinformation can become
ensconced in religious doctrine is the first case in point. Our accurate knowledge of certain major biological facts about reproduction
is a relatively recent acquisition. It was not until 1827 that the
mammalian ovum was clearly observed and recognized for what it

was. By 1879 scientists had observed the penetration of an egg by a spermatozoon of a starfish. But only in the present century has reproductive and genetic science clearly demonstrated the biological contributions of the female as well as of the male to the creation of offspring.

However, Christian sexual thought, in this instance through Roman Catholic tradition, has been deeply colored by Aristotle's primitive biological theories.[53] Aristotle analyzed the body as a union of form and matter. The mother (*mater*, matter) supplied the raw material, while the father contributed the soul. The female, observed the philosopher, was a rounded and sloppy creature, close to the earth and to water, lacking in the capacity to create form out of matter. If all went well in the procreative act, the male would master the female and impose his form upon her matter. But, if his vitality were low, a plump and shapeless daughter would result instead of a formed and angular son.

Aristotle's views gained their most significant and lasting entrance into Christian thought through Thomas Aquinas. To the latter as to the former, males are endowed with natural superiority. Women are ordained to be passive, and men to play the active and forming role. In women sexual appetites predominate, while men are inherently more rational and stable. Aquinas borrowed directly from Aristotle's biology and from that philosopher's definition of women: the female is a "misbegotten" or "defective" male. Nature always intends to produce males, so a woman is a man gone wrong. Thus, Aquinas could say, "Man is the beginning and end of woman, just as God is the beginning and end of every creature." [54] So embedded in Western thought was the notion of the man's superior biological function in reproduction, that four centuries after Aquinas early microscopists were picturing spermatozoa as containers with homunculi (miniature, fully-formed males) sealed up inside.

Turning to the Protestant side of our heritage, we have already noted the Reformers' continuing suspicion of sexuality as such. What remains to be observed is the manner in which that was linked with a pessimism and subordination in regard to women. Thus, Luther could say, "We can hardly speak of her without a feeling of shame, and we surely cannot make use of her without shame." [55] And Calvin declared, "Let man exercise authority with moderation, let woman be satisfied with the state of subjection and not take it amiss that she is made inferior to the more distinguished sex." [56] If the Reformers were not always consistent in these expressions, such attitudes were, nevertheless, unmistakably present.

We have seen that the Reformers' attacks on the cult of meritorious virginity and their elevation of the spiritual status of marriage also meant that the innovating and formative influence of women in the Catholic monastic communities was removed as a Protestant possibility. At the same time, something else occurred in Reformation thought and practice which, though not deliberately calculated to subordinate women, had this effect. It was the distinctive Protestant shifts in the understanding of God, and the results of this in ecclesiastical practice.[57] Doctrinal teaching virtually abandoned any strong emphasis upon God's immanental presence (so characteristic of late medieval mysticism). Rather, divine justification of the human sinner meant that the Wholly Other God worked through extrinsic historical acts quite independent of human cooperation. It was the God "whose inscrutable judgments were symbolized by a renewed emphasis on the doctrine of predestination and a preference for the Word over sacrament as the chosen means of God's saving presence among us." [58] Further, the imagery and language about God much more heavily reflected the patriarchal patterns of the Old Testament, in contrast to the vocabulary of medieval experiential theology to which women had made significant contributions.

Parallel with these theological shifts came certain ecclesiastical practices which implicitly reinforced traditionally masculine over feminine values. The Protestant Reformers, understandably reacting against serious abuses in the church, embarked upon an iconoclasm in both practice and theory. There was an attack upon things physical in the church—relics, stained glass, crucifixes, images of the Virgin. As Eleanor L. McLaughlin observes, "The mood was one of distinction, analysis, criticism, rather than integration and rediscovery of wholeness." [59] Ulrich Zwingli's campaign against music in the church illustrates the point. Lest the true worship of God be marred by those emotions and fleshly feelings which music elicits, he declared, let the church organs be smashed and the singing of chorales forbidden. The Reformation mood was heavily and traditionally "masculine."

The Continuing Costs of Sexist Dualism

The price of our continuing experience of sexist dualism which must be paid by women is most immediate and most profound. Mary Daly's description makes the point.[60] One cost is the tendency toward psychological paralysis. Through their internalization of an identity which is other-than-the-norm, women frequently experience immense anxiety over social disapproval should they attempt to express a positive self-image and a new consciousness of self-worth. The mechanisms of social control in such instances quickly come into play: "ridicule, insults, instant psychoanalysis expressed in such comments as 'penis-envy,' 'man-hater,' or 'unfeminine.'"[61]

Related to this is the phenomenon of "feminine antifeminism." Many women have identified with the male power structure. Some find comfort and security in the traditional, submissive role. A few have risen to outstanding achievement in a "masculine" field and discourage the competition from other women who would follow them. Thus, some women view as threats those others who would challenge the male power structure.

False humility is a price which many women feel forced to pay. Based upon the internalization of traditional male opinion and norms, such false humility internally counsels the woman to fear success and never to rise too high in achievement. Guilt feelings are induced over any significant challenges to the male ego.

Emotional dependence is closely related, and its manifestations are both numerous and varied: the fear of going out in the evening without male accompaniment; rigidity in following rules and orders; seeking the advice of the man before making important decisions; the stifling of intellectual creativity.

Coupled with these profound psychic and emotional costs are pervasive social and institutional ones. Job discrimination, lower pay for commensurate work, discrimination in educational opportunities and ecclesiastical positions, economic penalties in credit and Social Security—these are but a sampling of a long list.

The "sexual revolution" in recent decades has begun the quest to overcome spiritualistic dualism. But, as we have already seen, many of these trends only perpetuate the dualism in altered ways. Women presently encounter this in a unique manner. For centuries subject to a sexual double standard, many are now claiming a single standard of sexual morality for all persons. Yet, if women are urged to adopt typical male attitudes toward sexuality, if they are to learn a casual and physical orientation toward sexual expression, if they are encouraged to take up the quest for orgasmic experience divorced from the integrity of the person, then the mind-body alienation will continue. Rosemary Ruether thus concludes, "however much women are exhorted to learn the same casually physical view of sexual experience, the continued power relations between men and women assure that they will be more the victims in the process." [62]

While women have been the chief victims of sexual dualism, the costs to men are heavy as well. One cost of male dominance is hyper-rationalism and its counter side, the truncated development of the affective life. Many men simply do not "feel" very well. The high value placed upon technical reason, classification, and systematization tends to make them neglect the senses and the emotions as instruments of perception. Further, this pattern frequently causes men to ignore realities which do not seem to fit into the current analytical scheme, as was dramatically illustrated by administration officials and others during the Vietnam War. [63]

Fundamental to such narrowed rationalism is the male psychology of dominance and control. In the typically masculine value system talking is valued over listening, competition and conflict over incremental growth, self-confidence over humility, decisiveness over thoughtfulness, charisma and dynamism over long-term credibility, an aggressive approach over a persuasive one, and tangible rewards over the more internal satisfactions. [64] Dominance and control are evident in this constellation of values, and this combined with the fear of emotion makes interpersonal intimacy difficult for large numbers of men. Competition is injected into situations which do not call for it. [65]

As an adjunct of this syndrome, violence becomes a manifestation of masculinity, with immense costs to both individual and group. [66] A certain code of masculinity is purchased at the price of suppressing tenderness and self-acceptance. Socialized toward a deep fear of homosexuality and toward a self-respect based in considerable measure upon sexual potency and conquest, the young man is torn by both cultural demands and fears about his own sexual strength. The implications for social violence are unmistakable.

The masculine orientation to sex tends strongly toward genital-centeredness. There is an inordinate male concern about their genital size, a factor not unrelated to the "bigger is better" pattern of masculine cultural values. Largeness of body build generally seems evidence of masculinity and the ability to control. But this, in turn, nurtures self-conscious, mechanical perspectives about sex and leads to the diminution of capacities for self-giving, tenderness, ecstasy, and play.

Genitalization of male sexuality means loss of whole-body erotic sensitivity. Many men have been reared to think of their bodies as fortresses in need of defense. Anything that tries to penetrate the body's boundaries is dangerous. But this in turn delimits the capacity for psychic intimacy, for intimacy seems to involve the willingness, at least in some degree, to give up the rigid differentiation between one's own body and that of another.[67] The result is "psychic celibacy"—the tendency to keep women emotionally and mentally at arm's length, even when there is genital sex expression.[68]

Genitalization also means the heightening of the dominant-aggressive images of sex expression in men. Germaine Greer notes that the common street words for the penis are "tool" names, and for intercourse they are "poking" words—images which are instrumental, technological, and controlling.[69] Obsession with genital prowess then perpetuates a double standard in sexual ethics. The sexually-experienced man who insists on the importance of his bride's virginity may well be prizing her sexual ignorance for his own security; she will be easier to lead and control, and she will not make comparisons. Further, her virginity assures him that he is the winner in one more competitive game.[70]

The costs of male sexism to women should be painfully obvious. The costs to men are present, too, and the toll taken upon the social and institutional fabric is beginning to be recognized. Most fundamentally, however, sexist dualism is a No spoken to God. It violates the divinely-created equality of persons. It is a refusal of God's invitation to the life of faith which by its nature calls for risk and trust, acceptance and dependence. Dualistic sexism as initiated and sustained by men betrays an anxious and self-defeating kind of works-righteousness. It is a secularized quest for justification, for proving one's worth and acceptableness as a man through achievement and performance.[71]

The Need for a Religious Answer to Sexual Alienation

In the face of both alienating dualisms, spiritualistic and sexist, the key question is, From whence is our salvation? Where, in the midst of death, is life? Where, in our illness, is healing to be found?

Philosophy can assist us. The crucial limitation, however, is that only *rethinking* the problem of dualistic alienation is insufficient.[72] It assumes that the problem is "out there," and if a solution can be formulated the problem can be solved. The fact of the matter, however, is that *we* are the problem. The issue lives in us.

Nevertheless, philosophical insights can lead part of the way. While, unfortunately, philosophy to date has given precious little attention to sexist dualism, the discipline has been concerned about the spiritualistic variety. Thus, Marcel and Sartre are so convinced of the intimate union of mind and body that they find it only appropriate to say, "I *am* my body." Yet, there is a persisting paradox. Not only do I experience my body as me, but I also experience it as other than me. My body imposes limitations upon "me," and it has processes which continue of their own accord whether "I" will them or not. And, as Richard Zaner remarks, "Most of all, my body is the embodiment of that most foreign of all things—death. In some sense, I, too, die; my body takes me with it . . . "[73]

Thus, some philosophers in attempting to overcome the Cartesian dualism of mind versus body, can describe the problem with insightful helpfulness; we experience both identity of mind and body, and we also experience otherness, separateness. Beyond the articulation of the problem, however, there seems to be no solution on the rational level alone.

Psychoanalytic theory and practice appears a more hopeful answer. Regarding Hellenistic dualism, Freudian theory illuminates the various forms of projection utilized by the alienated self, and in therapeutic practice assists the individual to recognize repressed urges and integrate them more constructively into the conscious self. Yet, Freudian theory itself is freighted with a biological naturalism about human sexuality which ultimately undercuts its social and personal dimensions (see Chapter 2).

Regarding patriarchal or sexist dualism, psychoanalytic theory also shows its limits. Freud himself believed that women were inherently defective because they lacked the male genital characteristics necessary for normative humanity. Thus, the woman's psychic development was fated to be a frustrated quest to receive from males the potency of which nature had deprived her. The major Freudian revisionists, however, were more helpful. Alfred Adler revised Freud, observing that "penis-envy" was not the reflection of an ontological deficiency in the woman but rather the envy of male power and social domination. Karen Horney went further in her reconstruction. Beneath the rationalizations of male misogynism she found male envy of and revenge against women who appeared more central to the procreative process than did men. Outside of the Freudian tradition, Carl Jung had a more positive view of women, and he constructively pointed toward the ideal of the androgynous personality—uniting in one individual the "masculine" and "feminine" characteristics. But if Jung refused to see woman as naturally deficient or as the embodiment of sensuality, he still fell prey to another cultural stereotype, the "spiritual feminine." Thus, for him masculinity remains ego and intelligence, while femininity is unconscious creativity and intuition, and the stereotypes are not finally overcome.[74]

But, it can be argued, psychological theory is not inherently bound to dualistic sexual assumptions. And that is true. Further, some of its presently-available insights into the inner dynamics of both alienation and reconciliation are invaluable. We shall draw upon them time and again. Still, the psychotherapeutic process of healing at its best not only utilizes the creative human powers of restoration but also points beyond their limits and distortions to the ultimate human need: the grace of God. From a Christian perspective this divine love, continually enfleshed in human experience, is ultimately and utterly necessary if the dualistic nemesis of our sexual alienation is to be overcome.

4

Sexual Salvation:

Grace and the

Resurrection of the Body

S IN IS ESTRANGEMENT; grace is reconciliation."[1] Salvation, in its original meaning, is healing. It is the reuniting of what has been torn apart and estranged. It is the recovery of a center and a wholeness in that which has been split asunder. It is the overcoming of alienation within the body-self, between the person and the world, between the person and God.

Salvation is sexual. This does *not* mean that we are saved by our sexuality. We are saved by the grace of God—God's unearned, healing, life-giving love. But "sexual salvation" *does* mean that we are given new life not in spite of the fact that we are sexual body-selves but precisely in and through this entire selfhood which we are.

The focus for this chapter is not on salvation generally, the incredibly broad and rich dimensions of divine grace and human healing. Rather, the focus is more particularly on the healing and augmented wholeness we experience both in and through our sexuality, those dimensions of us which have been wounded and divided by spiritualistic and sexist dualisms. Our concern is the process and meaning of the resurrection of the sexual body.

Three attitudes toward sexuality have appeared most commonly in Christian thought.[2] The Medievalists typify one of them: control by reason and will. After all, is it not our experience that we can more easily master other appetites than we can master the sexual? We can come to terms with our greed. We can repress or sublimate our aggression. But our sexual desires seem to leap up at inconvenient moments, revealing to us our animal state, taking possession of us with forces we do not understand. Instead of being our own master, at times we seem to become our own monster. Thus, we seek to control our sexuality for higher purposes through reason and will power.[3]

But self-control easily slips into bodily mortification—the death of the flesh. In reaction to this, a second attitude emerges. Over against the stringency of "the Apollonian," some would have us exalt "the Dionysian" within us. This may be the oldest attitude of all, though it is forever being rediscovered. Sexuality, it is said, has been artificially repressed. We must throw off the social masks, reclaim our inner forces and feelings, and in this way be united with a cosmic vitality. While there are many secular advocates of the Dionysian, there are articulate Christians as well. But, curiously, the members of this school do not seem to regard sexual expression and sexual love as truly personal.

Then there is a third attitude: sex is unimportant. It is simply there. This is the approach of detachment in some form or another. Sexuality is neither divine nor demonic. Jesus demythologized sex, and we can have freedom over our sexuality, too, only if we can "take it or leave it." Indeed, we must be able to laugh at sex or we shall be humiliated by it, for it is an irrational, impersonal force which threatens to turn even the best of us into caricatures of ourselves.[4] Odd and laughable, sexuality becomes almost inconsequential.

If there are hints of truth in each of these orientations, there also is something basically amiss. A common thread unites persons of each of these apparently widely-differing views. Dan Sullivan says it well: it is "the unyielding determination to locate sex somewhere—or anywhere—outside the human self, the authentic 'me,' that inner core of personhood which makes humanity distinctive. In this one crucial respect there is no difference between the Christian Fathers' conviction that sex is a 'beast in the belly,' and Norman Brown's that it is 'Christ in me.'" [5] And, if sexuality is still experienced as being outside of and apart from the authentic self, there is still alienation.

To Christian faith, however, alienation is never the last word. The Apostle speaks with power of both alienation and reconciliation. Of the former, he exclaims, "Wretched man that I am! Who will deliver me from this body of death?" (Romans 7:24.) It is not inconsistent with the Gospel to alter Paul's words at this point: "Wretched person that I am! Who will deliver me from this *death of the body?*" Then, with him we can continue, "Thanks be to God through Jesus Christ our Lord!" Because fear is at the root of our alienation, merely an intellectual understanding of the problem will not release us. But the Gospel does not announce salvation through correct understanding. Rather, it comes through the gracious love of God received in human openness and trust.

It is quite possible that the term "salvation" may not be particularly helpful to many contemporary Christians. In spite of its widespread traditional use in the church (and perhaps because of it), the term is fraught with numerous associations which may mislead rather than assist. We need then to be flexible and pluralistic in vocabulary, as, indeed, the Bible is. Different nuances will attach themselves to different words, and that is all to the good. A variety of polar concepts thus can be used, bearing common meanings with different shadings: sin and salvation, alienation and reconciliation, fragmentation and wholeness, death and life, law and gospel, death and resurrection.

The experience of the new life is a relational reality in which the miraculous and the everyday stuff of life are interwoven. The incarnation of God, the divine presence in and through human flesh, is always a miracle. We celebrate its decisive and normative occurrence in Jesus Christ. We also celebrate faith's conviction that God's incarnation continues to occur. The resurrecting power is beyond our own. It is the mysterious creativity and renewal of life itself, God's power in our midst. And the miracle of the body's resurrection is all the more awesome because it occurs through human gestures, human words, human touch and caress, human intimacy.

We experience new life of the body-self as a gift. A dead body cannot raise itself, nor can we lift ourselves by our own bootstraps. It is the eternal paradox of life and of the gospel that our own strenuous and strident efforts to possess renewal seem to shut us off from it more completely. This is inevitable, for the self who so strives to be changed is the very self who is organized by means of a dualism, which itself must be challenged and overthrown, not simply confirmed by effort. The latter is the trap of both sexual ascetics and libertines who, in trying to overcome the alienation of their bodies, only seem to establish it more firmly since their weapon is the dualism which has nurtured the alienation in the first place.[6]

The miraculous dimension in sexual salvation lies not in the fact that it is necessarily dramatic, which it may not be, nor that it interferes with the "natural world" (if by that we mean an external structure working according to its own laws). It is in our discovery of what we really are. As H. A. Williams declares, "The discovery is miraculous because the previous organization of our being provided no vantage point from which we could have seen what now we do see. Our new vision has come to us. It has arrived from we know not where."[7] To be sure, there is a paradox here. Significant change in the body-self does not usually occur without effort, risk-taking, courage, and pain. So Paul counsels, "work out your own salvation with fear and trembling." But the point is that the effort, risk, and will are expended within the context of a creative Power for change which is neither our invention nor possession: "for God is at work in you . . ." (Philippians 2:12-13).

The experience of reconciliation of the body-self surely is not the exclusive possession of any sect or creed, Christian or otherwise. In point of fact, because both sexist and spiritualistic dualisms have so plagued Christianity, many people have left the church to seek the wholeness of their sexual humanity elsewhere. And, for our own understanding we must draw on the experiences and insights of numerous non-Christians who have realized something genuine of that sexual salvation to which we point with Christian symbols. But those of us who find ourselves within the church, both by fate and by free choice, will use also those faith symbols which for us best express that universal and gracious Reality which the words themselves cannot possess but in which they meaningfully participate.

Within the experience of sexual salvation there seems to be a double movement. It is not simply a temporal sequence, though there are elements of that. Yet, Christian experience throughout the centuries has found articulation in two distinguishable and complementary dimensions of reconciliation. Again, these have been given different names bearing different nuances: justification and sanctification, God's power over us and God's power within us, gift and response, acceptance and growth, forgiveness and fulfillment. We can begin with the reality to which the first term in each pair points.

Grace and the Sexuality of Jesus

That we experience God's gracious justification or acceptance in and through Jesus Christ has profound sexual implications. "The Word became flesh." Jesus was a sexual being. And here is God's affirmation of our own sexuality.

Nevertheless, the most common Christological heresy is still the docetic heresy, spiritualistic dualism applied to Jesus. It is the conviction held in varying forms by countless Christians past and present that Jesus Christ could not have been fully human, that God (acting in proper taste) would not have expressed the divine Spirit through human flesh, and that in Jesus we see true God but only in the *appearance* of a human body. Unfortunately, the record is clear: for the most part the church has presented Jesus as sexless. Because the human body is vitally and spontaneously sexual, many Christians in their dualistic alienation have been offended by the radical implications of the incarnation. And, to deny Jesus sexuality in one way or another "for most people today is about the most effective way of saying that he was not fully human." [8] The Victorian within still winces at the thought that the incarnation might be "a tale of the flesh."

Yet, the gospel has always had elements of scandal about it, and it has never shied away from offending the tastes of the respectably righteous. On this particular issue, however, theologians have been slow. Until recently it was more often the writers and artists who wrestled openly with the question of Jesus' sexuality—D. H. Lawrence, Nikos Kazantzakis, the rock opera *Jesus Christ Super-*

star, and the like. If their conclusions were not altogether persuasive, at least they sensed, with an urgency greater than that of most orthodox Christians, that what is at stake in this question (as in every Christological issue) is the possibility, meaning, and nature of human salvation.

In recent years, however, several theologians have voiced their positive beliefs on the matter. A considerable part of the concern is the realization that sexuality appears to be intrinsically and not accidentally related to one's capacity to love. Thus, John Erskine writes of Jesus, "His character renders it for me utterly impossible that his youth and manhood could have been unmoved by warm, human emotions. . . . If he really took our nature upon him and was human, then he had our equipment of sex." [9] Similarly, Tom F. Driver observes, "The absence of all comment [in the Gospels] about Jesus' sexuality cannot be taken to imply that he had no sexual feelings. . . . I cannot imagine a *human* tenderness, which the Gospels show to be characteristic of Jesus, that is not fed in some degree by the springs of passion. The human alternative to sexual tenderness is not asexual tenderness but sexual fear." [10] Likewise, psychiatrist-theologian Jack Dominian reflects upon the necessary connection in Jesus between self-acceptance and genuine openness to others: "This response was unhampered by any need to reject, deny, or condemn any part of himself, hence of others. . . . Although the evidence is extremely limited, it is hard to see how such total self-acceptance and availability could have been present without including full awareness of his sexuality." [11]

William Phipps has been the most vigorous in pursuing the question. He argues that while Jesus' celibacy is a possible interpretation, his marriage is much more probable. The evidences, he believes, are multiple. The Gospels do not record Jesus as having stated either that he was born of a virgin or that he himself was a virgin. Nor does the book of Acts indicate that those closest to him knew of any special virginal conditions about him. In addition, while Jesus was sharply critical of certain aspects of Judaism, he was thoroughly Jewish in most respects, and that faith-culture rejected celibacy both in theory and in practice. Since we have no information about Jesus' life between his ages of twelve and thirty (the customary time for Jewish betrothal and marriage), it is likely that he followed prevailing Jewish custom and married as a young man. Indeed, his delight in women and his understanding of them seems to contrast markedly with the style of an ascetic, as is apparent when one compares Jesus' manner and personality with that of the Essene ascetic John the Baptist. Phipps concludes that the notion of a celibate savior is not the product of the apostolic age but rather grew out of Christianity's later contact with Hellenistic dualism.[12]

The conclusion remains, I believe, highly debatable. It is possible, to be sure, but the arguments from silence are not convincing enough to make it probable. In any event, Jesus' marriage is not the crux of the issue. His sexuality is, and the virtue of at least pressing the possibility of marriage is to help us take his *fully* human nature with greater seriousness. Even if his celibacy remains probable, the possibility of genital expression and, most likely, the temptation toward it need affirmation. If we are offended at the thought that Jesus was ever inclined toward a fully sexual union, such offense might simply betray the suspicion that sex is unworthy of the Savior because it is unworthy of us. But we need not project our own alienation upon him. If he at times was so inclined, we can well assume that he did not think of it as a temptation toward something intrinsically tainted and suspect, but rather as a temptation to turn aside from a growing conviction of his compelling vocation toward a unique role in God's kingdom.[13]

John A. T. Robinson quite appropriately links the issue of Jesus' sexuality with the question of the manner of his birth.[14] A non-physical interpretation of the Virgin Birth story still leaves unresolved the manner of Jesus' conception, and Robinson, together with several other biblical scholars, raises the possibility of an irregular sexual union. This question, like that of Jesus' marriage, remains debatable, but this line of inquiry should not be rejected out of hand because of its supposed impropriety. At the very least, it should prompt us to view God's incarnation in Jesus of Nazareth in a fresh and scandalous light, a perspective that is hardly out of character for a gospel which proclaims that the divine love is often a surprising affront to our assumptions of human righteousness.

In addition, we might need to take another look at the debates

of Nicaea and Chalcedon.[15] On those occasions there was a persistent worry that any insistence on Jesus' full humanity would lead
to a denial of his divinity. The fears of Athanasius and Cyril led
them to insist that the Word *became man* but did not come into
a man. "And they were prevented from understanding that men
like Theodore and Nestorius really were arguing (as we can now
see) for a genuine and deeply *personal* union of God and man in
Christ—however inadequate their vocabulary. . . ."[16]

Thus, the issue of Jesus' sexuality is not simply a curious historical debate. Nor is it an inappropriate sort of "prurient interest."
If the docetic heresy, though early condemned by the church, continues to linger in current Christian mentality, this suggests something about our own salvation and possibilities for wholeness. For,
if we are not really sure about the full humanity of the one whom
we call Truly Human, we can only be confused about what authentic humanity might mean for us. If we try to take Jesus with utter
seriousness and yet uneasily retreat from thoughts of his sexuality, or
even recoil with repugnance, it is also likely that we shall either
deny much of our own sexuality or else find considerable difficulty
integrating our Christological beliefs into the reality of our lives as
body-selves.[17]

But the Word did become flesh. Logos, Cosmic Meaning, was embodied, and our own embodiment has been given definition and vin-
dication in Jesus Christ. What is at stake—and here the Nestorians
were right—is whether or not it is possible, however partially we
may experience it, that there be a genuine and deeply personal
union of God and our embodied selves. If we deny the radicality
of God's incarnation in Jesus, we may well persist in a vain attempt
to be more spiritual than God. The possibility of our own full
humanity, after all, decisively hinges upon "the humanity of God"
(to use Karl Barth's fine phrase). That humanity of God is an unexpected scandal, and the issue of Jesus' sexuality is an important
place to test our commitment to it. In those central symbols of
incarnation and resurrection Christian faith affirms that God embraces fleshly, bodily life. God invites us to do so.[18]

Justification as God's Acceptance of Our Bodily Life

Grace is "God's generosity in personal action."[19] It is not a supernatural "something" which God gives to us. Rather, it is a gracious personal relationship, the gift of the accepting personal Presence itself. Gregory Baum puts it well in saying that "the author of reality is on our side. The ground of being is not far away, hostile or indifferent to us: the deepest dimension of the total reality facing us is for us. There is no reason to be afraid of the world . . . for the ultimate root of all being protects and favors human life. Despite the suffering and evil in the world . . . we are summoned to believe that the ultimate principle of reality is love itself." [20]

God's radical, unconditional, and unearned acceptance of us is a fitting contemporary translation of justification by grace. In his powerful sermon, "You Are Accepted," Paul Tillich evocatively states, "It strikes us when our disgust for our own being, our indifference, our weakness, our hostility, and our lack of direction and composure have become intolerable to us. It strikes us when, year after year, the longed-for perfection of life does not appear, when the old compulsions reign within us as they have for decades, when despair destroys all joy and courage. Sometimes at that moment a wave of light breaks into our darkness, and it is as though a voice were saying: 'You are accepted. *You are accepted,* accepted by that which is greater than you, and the name of which you do not know. Do not ask for the name now; perhaps you will find it later. Do not try to do anything now; perhaps later you will do much. Do not seek for anything; do not perform anything; do not intend anything. *Simply accept the fact that you are accepted!'* If that happens to us, we experience grace." [21]

When we have experienced that kind of acceptance, even momentarily, we know that everything is transformed. Though recognition of this frequently has been neglected in Christian theology, God's word of acceptance is addressed to the total and sexual self, not simply to a disembodied personality. We might extend Tillich's language in this manner: You are accepted, the total you. Your body, which you often reject, is accepted by that which is greater than you. Your sexual feelings and unfulfilled yearnings are accepted. You are accepted in your ascetic attempts at self-justification or in your hedonistic alienation from the true meaning of your sexuality. You are accepted in those moments of sexual fantasy which come unbidden and which both delight and disturb you. You are accepted in your femininity and in your masculinity, for you have elements of both. You are accepted in your heterosexuality and in your homosexuality, and you have elements of both. Simply accept the fact that you are accepted as a sexual person! If that happens to you, you experience grace.

An incarnational, non-docetic understanding of acceptance takes seriously its enfleshed mediation. Such grace can be mediated by words of Scripture and tradition. It can be conveyed through the church's liturgy. Yet, in regard to sexual acceptance, tradition and liturgy at times are more alienating than gracious, and Scripture is frequently interpreted docetically. So the gracious Word often becomes flesh in ways not usually labeled religious. It is mediated through sexual communion in ecstasy and playfulness with the beloved partner. It comes as healing through "the laying on of hands"—the spontaneous hand of a friend on one's shoulder. Such grace is mediated by parents when the child receives (as in breast feeding, sensitive toilet training, physical expressions of affection, and appropriate sex education) a sense of the trustworthiness and goodness of his or her own body rather than a legacy of mistrust and shame. Grace comes through human agency in struggle and judgment as well—as when the Women's Movement gives a woman new self-respect and power born from her pain, and when in judgment on distorted masculinity it opens a man to new ranges of emotion and bodily self-acceptance.

Thus, beyond the dualistic alienations we experience the gracious resurrection of the body-self. I really am *one* person. Body and mind are one; my body is me as my mind is me. Beyond the imprisonment of rigid sex roles I am freed to be a *person*. And in such resurrection I discover that I belong intimately to others and intimately to the world.

We live in grace, but we also continue in sin, and the experience of radical acceptance and God's resurrection of the body is never unambiguous. Reinhold Niebuhr thus declares, "The element of sin in the experience is not due to the fact that sex is in any sense sinful as such. But once sin is presupposed, that is, once the original harmony of nature is disturbed by . . . self love, the instincts of sex are particularly effective tools for both the assertion of self and the flight from self." [22] In our experience of sexuality there is often a bewildering confusion of elements. If in our estrangement we never utterly lose our original unity, so also in the gracious experience of acceptance and reunification, estrangement is not totally or permanently conquered. The glorious oneness I experienced begins to disintegrate as body and mind once more compete for the title of being me. And the glorious liberty of the children of God once more submits to old and fearful assumptions as men and women imprison themselves and each other in dominance and submission.

Thus, to speak of—and to celebrate—God's radically accepting love does not require us to engage in a romanticized idealism about human perfection under grace. Nevertheless, when we are open to the divine acceptance, in some measure everything *is* transformed. If the old fears and sexual dualisms do return, still we are not the same as before. "Grace aims at fulfillment," as Harold Ditmanson rightly affirms. "It is the operative power of God's personal action, moving us toward that which God intends us to be. The purpose of creaturely existence is that each of God's creatures achieves the fullest excellence of which its nature is capable. Any thwarting of fulfillment, therefore, is really a wrong against the basic purpose of creation itself." [23]

This affirmation leads us to grace's second dimension: sanctification. If that traditional word is less than intelligible to many modern ears, contemporary equivalents are appropriate: growth, fulfillment, God's empowerment toward our greater wholeness. To explore what this might mean sexually, I have selected several facets of our bodily experience: growth in self-acceptance, in sensuousness, in knowing, in freedom, and in androgyny. While each of these is an expression of love's fulfillment, a fuller discussion of love will await the next chapter.

Self-Acceptance

It is not always easy to accept love—either from others or from ourselves. On the issue of self-love Christian ethical reflection has been notably divided over the centuries, a matter we shall look at in more detail later. At this point I want to consider some of the dynamics of self-rejection and self-acceptance in the sexual person's growth toward greater wholeness.

Among the related psychodynamics are shame and guilt. These are constructive signals of residual moral health in many instances. If we willfully violate the personhood of another and do not experience shame and guilt, there is something wrong. But what of these emotions when they are directed at ourselves because of our bodies and our sexuality as such? One psychiatrist, Alexander Lowen, declares that guilt frequently "arises when a negative moral judgment is imposed on a bodily function that is beyond the control of the ego or conscious mind. To feel guilty about sexual desires, for example, makes no biological sense. . . . If this desire is judged morally wrong, it means that the conscious mind has turned against the body." [24] To be sure, some sexual desires are an appropriate reason for guilt. The point of concern, however, is when guilt and shame are felt simply because of any kind of sexual desire. That is rejection of the body-self.

Another psychiatrist, Theodore Isaac Rubin, observes: "Indirect self-hate . . . is pervasive and global because it affects every aspect of personality or character structure. . . . Neurotic states such as martyrdom, masochism, self-effacement, symbiotic and overwhelming dependency, grandiosity, aggression, despotism, perfectionism, sadism, vindictiveness, withdrawal, resignation are all functions of self-hate." [25] If initially this sweeping conclusion sounds a bit extreme the psychiatric evidence on closer examination is quite compelling. Indirect self-hate is a rejection of one's actual self: who we are actually, in emotional health and neurosis, in wholeness and estrangement, in grace and sin. The idealized image of the self, on the other hand, is the shining illusion of impossible perfection. We can use such an image to protect ourselves against our feelings of fragility. But because the image is unattainable, hurt pride and self-hate emerge together with resentment of others and then more attempts to achieve "glory."

In sexual activity this works-righteousness syndrome becomes performance anxiety. "Performance involves self-consciousness, self-judgment, fear of self-hate and fear of derision from other people. In performing I split myself into two people, the one doing the performing and the one watching the performance and also watching audience response." [26] But such self-conscious splitting, watching, and judging both nurture my anxiety and undermine my integrated communion with the other. I make myself feel less in order to perform better.

Lowen summarizes the results of self-rejection: "I would suggest that the common denominator in all neurotic behavior patterns is a diminuation of the sense of self. This includes a loss of feeling of identity, a reduced awareness of one's individuality, a decrease in self-expression, and a diminished capacity for pleasure." [27] Christian teaching too often has had enormous difficulty distinguishing between creative self-love and selfishness. Too frequently they have been equated without the realization that egotism and selfishness arise from inadequate self-acceptance rather than from too much of it. As a result the familiar polemic against selfishness can undermine, unwittingly, that self-acceptance which is integral to genuine faith and outgoing love. Women in particular have suffered, socialized into derivative identities and nurtured in the supposed virtue of giving without receiving. The all-too-frequent result is the tendency to cling to self-negation as if too much affirmation and success would depress them. This is one of the tragedies of sexist dualism.

But self-acceptance is related to the ability to say No. Those of either sex who feel driven to accede to all requests and demands of others are expressing a consuming anxiety about their basic acceptability. The ability to say No at the appropriate moment is the ability to resist the forces of depersonalization which surround us. It is essential to our humanity and our being-for-others.

Self-acceptance thus carries with it the ability to distinguish between feelings and desires, on the one hand, and genuine needs, on the other. We know that we ourselves are the source of our feelings and desires, and we can accept that. We also know that some of our desires do not represent humanly fulfilling needs. Thus we can distinguish between those which can be fulfilled with constructive and enriching effects for ourselves and others, and those which if acted upon might impoverish and destroy. But, whatever our desires, they do not embarrass us in such a way that we need to push them out of consciousness, for to do that is to make them demonic. Instead, we can recognize them for what they are; we can name them and thus take the compelling power out of them.[28]

Genuine self-acceptance is basic to humility. Authentic humility is not self-deprecation. It is realistic self-appreciation founded upon the experiential conviction of divine acceptance. It is the security of self that does not compulsively demand narcissistic support and constant affirmation from others. In contrast, self-rejection feeds upon illusions about the self's competence and virtue, often manifesting a need to be universally loved and admired. But such illusions mask a curious combination of arrogance and self-hate, pretense and anger.

Humility is a basic acceptance of the body-self. The physical bodies of most of us fall far short of the ideals portrayed by the advertising industry. Lumpy where they should be slim, skinny where they should be firm, wrinkled where they should be youthful, they are, nevertheless, us, "warts and all." And they are graceful bodies because they have been graced.

Self-acceptance thus personalizes the body. There is psychological evidence that creative thinking, depending as it does upon the free flow of unconscious ideas, best occurs when the body is most alive and unburdened.[29] The body's personalization thus expresses itself in the mind. The intimate links with the emotions are also very real. Depression, for example, is frequently connected to the lack of body integration with self.[30] When we are in touch with our bodies we are aware of bodily tensions and their causes, and when depressive patients become attuned to their bodies, depressive tendencies often are eliminated. This does not mean the elimination of sadness or anger. Rather, it means a deep awareness of what gives rise to these feelings, how they can best be expressed, and what steps can be taken to cope with them.

This suggests that self-acceptance gives rise to the spontaneity of the body-self. Wooden, mechanical behavior is born of the need to comply rigidly with dictates heard from within and without the self. But when we receive the security not to demean ourselves, we do not deaden any aspects of ourselves. Our resources of energy and time are not dissipated in useless rituals or in the search for illusionary fulfillment. They are available for feeling and acting with spontaneous aliveness.[31]

Self-acceptance thus brings with it a profound sense that I am the body which I live, and in consequence I will not tend to minimize the personal significance of the activities which I carry on through my body.[32] This gives shape to the style of my relationships with others. A positive awareness of my bodily basis of selfhood gives the confidence that I have a real self with which to relate to others. This diminishes the desire to shift responsibility for my life to them, or to be absorbed by them, or, conversely, to absorb them and impose my ideas on them. I am I and they are they. We are unique selves interested in communication and communion, not in conquest or dependency.[33]

The resurrection of the body in self-acceptance seems to bring with it a new openness to the world itself. In John Woolman's words, "The world smells different!" Paul's theology of the resurrection is instructive here.[34] In his understanding, resurrection has both continuity and discontinuity with the body. Flesh and blood *as we know them* cannot inherit the kingdom, it is true. But the resurrected state will *not* be bodiless. Interpretations of Paul's view which put all of the emphasis on discontinuity with the flesh simply ignore one whole side of his position. There will be a new body which we can only dimly comprehend now. And this is corroborated by Paul's hints about the destiny of the material universe. "It is not to be scrapped as of no permanent significance. For it is in Christ that all things exist, and God's plan for the fulness of time is 'to unite all things in Christ, things in heaven and things on earth.' " [35] Thus, the material universe is not to be seen as emptiness or illusion. Rather, the story is one of a transformation of the material world so that it is no longer in bondage to decay but attains the glorious liberty of God's own children. And this sort of transformation of the world *as we experience it* can begin now with the resurrection of the body in that new self-acceptance made possible by God's grace.

Sensuousness

In reflecting on sensuousness as another mark of growth in sexual wholeness through God's grace, another comment on the Song of Songs is appropriate. It is a sensuous poem of love, celebrating in an unparalleled biblical way the joys of erotic communion. One interpreter writes, "Love poetry is carnal knowledge, a hymn to the beauty of the body and the goodness of creation, to the sheer joy of bodily existence and its pleasures. In love the body is a means of grace, and the graceful forms of the body are a means of love." [36]

The Song is a particularly significant commentary on graceful sensuousness, for in its lines there is a striking absence of the alienating dualisms. In contrast to Hellenistic, spiritualistic dualism, the lovers in this poem embrace their sexuality joyously and shamelessly. Their nakedness before each other is cause for delight. Their desire for each other sexually is treated not as judgment but as promise of fulfillment. And, in contrast to accounts of sexist dualism, the Song displays a notable absence of male domination and female subordination. Mutuality and cohumanity are evident. Unlike the woman in the other garden, Eve, the woman of this erotic garden has an identity which is not derived from the man, nor is her sexuality defined by its procreative function. She has her own autonomy. She is the man's full equal—in work, in initiative, in identity.

It is true that the Song borders on the idyllic. "And in a curious reversal of the mythic and the historical, the prehistorical Genesis saga gives a more profound and realistic portrayal of the human sexual story; while the Canticles, which is a real historical tale of two lovers, borders on sexual myth with its celebration of eroticism which knows no sin, no prohibitions, no disobedience, no betrayal." [37] Nevertheless, the Song of Songs stands as an important and unique scriptural portrait of sensuousness. It is the sensuousness made possible by grace. Though Yahweh is not mentioned by name, surely the divine Presence is in that erotic garden, else the dualistic alienations of sexism and spiritualism could not be so markedly transcended.

As we have seen, however, much in the Christian tradition has been highly suspicious of such eroticism. If to many earlier theologians sexual desire was inherently mated to lust and hence to sin, numerous contemporary Christians are wary for similar reasons. The celebration of sensuality, they seem to believe, is a dangerous invitation to depersonalized sex, sex unredeemed by love, and sensual hedonism which seeks sexual pleasure for its own sake only. Neither do I welcome such results, but the fears of sensuality and eroticism as such are misplaced.

For one thing, it is a gross oversimplification to regard impersonal sexual acts (which appear to be done only for pleasure and without love for the partner) simply as expressions of animal sexuality. The British psychologist W. R. D. Fairbairn provides an important corrective at this point. The erotic dynamism of the human self, he contends, is something which intrinsically aims not primarily at the pleasure of the senses, but "at something more commensurate with its source in the whole person, namely, union with the other person as person." [38] Even in impersonal sex what we see is not merely animalistic sexuality but rather "desperate lunges, by an ego already torn apart under the pressure of various conflicts, at reestablishing some emotional links with the world. . . . Eroticism and perversions, which to the onlooker—and even to the subject—may seem anonymous and mechanical, the result of a blind, obsessive alien instinct, are in fact efforts of the shattered self to salvage something—almost anything—of natural emotional relationships." [39] Fairbairn concludes that only when the individual's deprivation of love becomes relatively unbearable does the libidinal drive lead to hedonistic and mechanical relationships.

The affirmation of sensuality is not an inherently dangerous invitation to depersonalized sex. In point of fact, it seems to be quite the opposite: the unloving suppression of the self's erotic needs eventually nurtures aberrant sex. Mary Calderone, the dean of American sex educators, underscores this: "The price paid by individuals, both as children and as adults, for the ignorance and fear inflicted upon them by the society because of their normally occurring erotic behavior is very high, whether in terms of eventual sexual inadequacy in marriage, or of compulsive behavior such as promiscuousness (heterosexual or homosexual), sadomasochism, fetishism, voyeurism, exhibitionism, or repetitious recourse to hard core pornography for the only sexual reactions many sexually crippled individuals are able to achieve." [40]

Christianly speaking, the issue has elements of the gospel and law problem. While law is good and necessary, it can be misused to suppress the erotic and hold it in check by rigid disciplines buttressed by fear. But the unintended result is frequently the very sexual compulsiveness which is so dreaded. The approach of gospel may well be a trusting affirmation of love's sensuousness. Such trust is grounded in the confidence that our Creator has so designed the self's erotic dynamism that it is intrinsically aimed not at impersonal sexual hedonism but at personal sexual communion.

Sensuousness suggests that there is a *physiology* of grace to which we ought to give attention, along with the psychology of grace. Once again we can speak of the graceful body. In a non-theological sense, this is the quality of a person whose body is free from chronic tension, whose movements are spontaneous and yet coordinated and effective. In spite of their apparent contradiction, both spontaneity and self-control are present. Self-control implies self-possession, the attribute of those persons in touch with their feelings and in command of their movements. Since their motility is not constricted by chronic muscular tensions, they differ from the controlled and compulsive individuals whose behavior is a reaction to their tensions. Current bioenergetic therapy thus seems to demonstrate that the freer persons become in their movement the more self-control they gain.[41] Theologically speaking, this is one of the marvelous paradoxes of incarnated grace—that spontaneity and self-control merge in the sensuous body.

Growth in sensuousness also means an increased capacity to give and receive pleasure. Pleasure is more than simply good feelings. It is the union of bodily, emotional, mental, and spiritual feelings in ways that the person experiences markedly positive sensations about the self. While the source of pleasure may well be outside the self, it is the self who *feels* pleasure. We can imagine a continuum of feelings in the body. On the positive side of that continuum there is movement from the sense of ease, relaxation, and harmony—to greater awareness of softness, vibrancy, and buoyancy—to an excitement which is lively and graceful—to the explosion of ecstatic pleasure.[42]

Pleasure involves a distinct sense of happiness and, in its more intense moments, self-transcendence. In the climax of sexual communion, orgasmic pleasure can reach the heights of ecstasy in which the body-self feels profoundly unified, taken out of itself into another, yet intensely itself. There is a self-abandonment, a willingness to risk the depths of experience. In pleasure of whatever sort, the will seems to recede and the ego surrenders some of its control over the body. Self-conscious deliberation is replaced by absorption into feeling. A psychiatrist observes, "Pleasure cannot be possessed. One must give one's self over to the pleasure, that is, allow the pleasure to take possession of one's being. Whereas the response of pain involves a heightening of self-consciousness, the response of pleasure entails and demands a decrease of self-consciousness. Pleasure eludes the self-conscious individual, as it is denied to the egotist. To have pleasure one has to 'let go,' that is, allow the body to respond freely." [43]

This seems dialectically related to a variety of qualities which are important to our human wholeness. Creativity is one. "Without pleasure, there can be no creativity. Without a creative attitude to life, there will be no pleasure. . . . Pleasure in living encourages creativity and expansiveness, and creativity adds to the pleasure and joy of living." [44] Ego strength is another related quality. Psychologically, it strongly appears that "the strength of the ego determines the intensity of the sexual drive and . . . the amount of sexual pleasure and satisfaction influences the strength of the ego." [45]

There is also the dialectical relationship between commitment and pleasure. We experience pleasure in the full commitment of mind and body to worthwhile activity, and the pleasure experienced in that process enhances our commitment to the activity.

And commitment is a dimension of love. Love is necessary for pleasure, but the reverse is also true. Love involves the commitment which makes pleasure possible. Our work is never pleasurable without some commitment to the task and to those persons involved in and affected by our work. But such work commitment becomes a burden and onerous duty (even if willingly borne) without the experience of pleasure. So also in interpersonal relationships, the amount of pleasure is directly proportional to the amount of commitment and feeling which we invest in the relationship. Love gives it security. Love is the promise that the pleasure of today will also be tomorrow's.

In sum, the gospel's eternal paradox is characteristic of pleasure: the one who directly searches for it as the major goal will never find pleasure as fully as the one who is willing to let go—in creativity, commitment, and love.

Yet, a cloud of churchly suspicion still hangs over pleasure. While many theologians and ecclesiastical groups have rejected the anti-sex extremes of early Christian history, and while they now pronounce sex to be holy, they still leave the subject of sensuous pleasure largely unexplored and largely unaffirmed. But why does this suspicion linger, particularly if we are to renounce spiritualistic dualism and if we are to affirm that the primary purpose of sex is loving communion?[46] The persisting worry about boldly affirming sexual pleasure seems directly related to the fear that it will become self-indulgent and destructive of the personal communion of love for which intercourse is intended by God.

But this assumption needs to be challenged, and Francois Chirpaz's phenomenology of sexual pleasure assists us. Chirpaz observes that while sexuality receives its full meaning in the deep interpersonal relationship it can give, in everyday experience sexual desires often are not immediately *inter*personal. At such times we simply seem to feel sexual desire as such. But this has to do with the reality of our body-selves. The desires awaken "the thickness of one's flesh." "In sexual pleasure one experiences a coincidence with one's own body. My body is completely close, identical with me." It is the "fleshly closeness of the self to the self." "In pleasure, the body . . . is revealed in thickness . . . the density of being human, the heaviness of being material . . . [but] this density is not a weight to bear because in it the reverberation of pleasure becomes so much the greater. Only here does pleasure take all its fullness. . . ."[47] In sensual pleasure, then, I enjoy and love my bodily self and in this experience realize the coincidence of self and body. Dualism is overcome in reunion.

As John Giles Milhaven emphasizes, it is precisely this momentarily-healed self who is able to experience the depth of communion with the partner. Such communion, though it is possible to some extent even in moments of our greater estrangement, realizes new dimensions when it comes in moments of our healing. For, when in bodily pleasure I experience once again my essential unity, I can be that much more open to the other. There seems to be a spontaneous movement from my own enjoyment of myself to my enjoyment of my partner, and in this spontaneity there is something of a miracle of transformation. It is not that my conscious altruistic motives *direct* me to enjoy my partner's pleasure as well as my own. It seems truer to experience to say that in my own experience of body-self reunion I simply, and miraculously, experience reunion with the beloved other.[48]

Then the giving and receiving of sexual pleasure enhance the pleasure itself and facilitate greater body-self harmony. Interper-

sonal communion nurtures self-communion, and this is spontaneously expressed in the desire for interpersonal communion. Such
sensual pleasure is a gift of divine grace. This sensuality is God's
invitation to reunion—with both self and the loved companion. And
in this reunion God is experienced, whether there is consciousness
of the divine name or not.

Closely related to pleasure, play is also a form of sensuousness.
It is the realm of the child, and of the child within the adult. Play
involves the ability to let the mind wander without inhibitions, the
ability to let the body be free and loose. In our society men find
this particularly difficult because of their "masculine" self-image
and its pressures toward control, competence, and the rational work
ethic. But, "to play is to learn to trust that the environment will not
wound or maim and to relax long enough so that one's own vulnerability can be enjoyed." [49] Playfulness involves the devaluation
of control as the prime element in the activity. It is often unstruc-
tured. It is egalitarian, not authoritarian. It values and depends on
cooperation, openness, and freedom.

Play and pleasure are mated in sensuous sexuality. Sidney Callahan writes, "Play is intimately related to culture, contemplation,
and through human sexuality to human wholeness and healthy
equilibrium. With sexual play, pleasure must be the mainspring of
activity; pleasure is a means of recovering and enjoying . . . [our]
unconscious dimensions . . . which are not tapped in rational, pur-
posive activity like work or abstract thought." [50] She perceives the
irrational dimension of our sexuality as intrinsic to play, and also
to our own humanness. While we have been conditioned to fear
the irrational aspects—frivolity, pleasure-loving, purposelessness, violent desire and violent release, passive surrender to the involuntary
—these elements of sexual play are immensely important. For, it is
"joyously human to actively accept and cooperate with forces beyond human mastery. A lover can welcome eroticism and passion
just as a mother in childbirth can consciously and exultingly welcome the expulsive waves arising from within." [51]

Faith affirms that the capacity for such sexual play arises from
grace. I am open to trust and spontaneity, to surrender and to the
involuntary, only as I am able to trust my beloved and my own
body-self. But this ability to trust is not an achievement. It is a gift.

Growth in sensuousness is also marked by the diffusion of the erotic throughout the entire body. If the narrowing of sexuality's focus to the genitals is a mark of alienated sexuality, its diffusion throughout the body reflects its sanctification. Herbert Marcuse, Norman O. Brown, and Alan Watts are particularly suggestive at this point. Each of them acknowledges a debt to Freud, whose notion of "polymorphous perversity" (an unfortunately misleading term) referred to the diffusion of the erotic throughout the infant's body. But each of these three writers in contrast to Freud believes that such diffusion needs to be recaptured by the adult as well.

Marcuse contends that we all long to experience the entire body as a source of sexual pleasure once again. If Wilhelm Reich believed that human happiness is linked to the genitalization of sexuality, in Marcuse's social philosophy such genitalization is reactionary. It leaves the body desexualized and thus susceptible to economic and political exploitation.[52]

Norman O. Brown goes further. "The adult sexual perversions, like normal adult sexuality, are well-organized sexual tyrannies: they too represent an exaggerated concentration on one of the many erotic potentialities present in the human body." [53] Brown envisions a truly non-repressive civilization in which sexuality would be undifferentiated. Not only would the individual's entire body then possess the capacity for sexual awareness and pleasure, but also the sharp distinctions between male and female would pale.

It remains to Alan Watts to characterize with greatest sensitivity some of the possibilities of sexual diffusion. He is here speaking about *maithuna,* an Oriental ideal of sexual love, but his words are germane to western Christians: "It is not quite correct to say that such a relationship goes far beyond the 'merely sexual,' for it would be better to say that sexual contact irradiates every aspect of the encounter, spreading its warmth into work and conversation outside the bounds of actual 'love-making.' Sexuality is not a separate compartment of human life; it is a radiance pervading every human relationship, but assuming a particular intensity at certain points. Conversely, we might say that sexuality is a special mode or degree of total intercourse of . . . [persons] and nature. . . . [In regard to the man-woman relationship] the psychic counterpart of this bodily and sensuous intimacy is a similar openness of attention

to each other's thought—a form of communion which can be as sexually 'charged' as physical contact. This is the feeling that one can
express one's thoughts to the other just as they are, since there is
not the slightest compulsion to assume a pretended character. This
is perhaps the rarest and most difficult aspect of any human relationship. . . . Yet this is quite the most important part of a deep
sexual relationship, and it is in some way understood even when
thoughts are left unsaid. . . . To unveil the flow of thought can
therefore be an even greater sexual intimacy than physical nakedness." [54]

The resexualization of the entire body, the movement away from
the genital tyranny in relationships, the eroticization of the world
so that the environment's deliciously sensuous qualities are felt—
these things are possible, faith affirms, by the grace of God. To the
extent that I can accept my acceptance, experience my body-self as
one, and know that my sexuality is richly good, to this extent my
sexual awareness and feeling inevitably expand beyond a narrow
genital focus. Then I will be less fearful about recognizing and celebrating the erotic dimensions in a whole variety of my interpersonal
relationships. I will be able to perceive the sensuousness of shared
personal communication, and of the environment's movements,
shapes, sounds, and smells.

This sensuous diffusion thus undergirds our capacities to experience beauty. Sexuality is that living and flowing energy which
invites us into communion with other realities in creation. Philip
Sherrard writes as a specialist in eastern Christianity, where (in
spite of some of its other dualisms) the affirmation of God's self-
mediation through the material world and its beauty has been particularly strong. Sherrard believes it no accident that there is little
in western Christian literature about a positive view of sexuality,
and correspondingly there is little about beauty, especially that of
the human body and of nature. With the exception of a few authors,
most seem closer to the spirit of Tertullian in believing that natural
beauty ought to be concealed "since it is dangerous to those who
look upon it." Ultimately (as even the negative instances demonstrate), our awareness of creation and its beauty is a sexual awareness. "Indeed, there is an intimate, unbreakable link between sexuality and a sense of beauty. . . . So much is this the case that it

can be said quite categorically that those who have no living awareness of their sexuality have no sense of beauty." [55]

Knowing

We think with our bodies as well as with our minds. This is inevitable, for the self is essentially one being. As the alienated body nurtures certain patterns of the mind, so does the reconciled body.

Tillich's distinction between "ontological reason" and "technical reason" suggests one way in which the body-mind connection can be seen. Ontological reason is "the structure of the mind which enables the mind to grasp and transform reality." By contrast, technical reason deals much more narrowly with the cognitive realm and within that area with "only those cognitive acts which deal with the discovery of means for ends."[56] Both types of reason are necessary, he argues, but under the conditions of estrangement the depth of ontological reason is lost and technical reason becomes dominant.

There is, then, an important distinction between that type of knowing which is participation in reality, communion, and awareness of mystery, with that type of knowing which is possession, control, technique, and means to ends. When the divorce between these modes of knowing occurs, as it frequently does, it is not only a divorce in our mind but also (and quite fundamentally) in our sexuality. The split between those two modes is a split born of sexist dualism. Knowledge as possession, control, and technique has become a way of knowing socially identified as "masculine." Men are supposed to achieve, compete, control, win. Women are supposed to nurture, respond, care, relate. When technical reason becomes dominant and determinative, we see not simply the picture of the alienated reason but also the picture of the alienated body-self. It is the healing of the body-self into a more androgynous whole which affords a return to ways of knowing that are also participation and communion. But before we examine androgyny more closely, consider several other facets of knowing and sexual growth.

Increased reconciliation of the self and the sexual body is likely to make one's patterns of knowing less predictable, more creative and imaginative. Already we have seen some psychiatric evidence that indicates the vital connection between the body's aliveness and spontaneity with that of the mind. The same connection can be seen in the relation between institutional socialization and sexuality. Social theorists describe the manner in which society is formed by a series of institutions—families, schools, religious groups, economic organizations, the military, government, and so on. Persons are socialized by and into these institutions into certain roles and patterns of self-understanding, behavior, and thinking. Institutions tend to place a premium upon patterns of individual thought and action that are predictable and which serve the institution's purposes.

This is quite understandable. We need institutions, and institutions need harmony and coherence on the part of their members. But institutional patterns also need to be challenged, changed, and transformed with regularity, and the "one-dimensional person" who has been so thoroughly socialized by the group is not likely to rock the boat. Yet, as Urban T. Holmes contends, "Contact with our sexuality in any depth opens the self to aspects of our inner life which have not been conditioned by the social structures, since institutional control of sexuality is notoriously superficial. Hence, the person in touch with this runs the risk of living out of a self-understanding that is not predictable in terms of the society as a whole. This is risky and threatening." [57] It can also be significantly creative.

The reconciliation of the body-self also has an important effect on our tolerance of ambiguity. Each of us is a complex unity, comprising within ourselves an immensely varied mix of feelings, goals, needs, purposes, and patterns, not all of which are congruent and harmonious. Insofar as we try to earn our ultimate acceptability, insofar as we try to justify ourselves by our own purity (with whatever definition of purity we might hold), we will be threatened by the ambiguity within. We will be prone to insist on utter consistency, clarity, singleness of definition and motive. We will tend to project outward onto others our inner contradictions, but we will not recognize that we have done so because of alienation from the feeling body.

But reconciliation with the body brings a fresh and more accurate recognition of our feelings. The more we internalize the body-self's acceptance, the more we can "own" the complexity of motives, goals, and needs which comprise who we are. To own these does not necessarily mean to approve them all. It does mean that we will live with greater honesty, with more empathy toward those who differ from us, with less need to project onto others, and with more trust in the One who accepts us in spite of who we are. And such is the invitation to grow toward that which we might yet be. Again, Mary Douglas' anthropological studies of purity rituals in various societies force her to a conclusion of no small importance for a theology of grace: "There is hardly any pollution which does not have some primary physiological reference. As life is in the body it cannot be rejected outright. And as life must be affirmed, the most complete philosophies, as William James put it, must find some ultimate way of affirming that which has been rejected." [58]

Finally, our ways of knowing are always wedded to the ways of our loving, and love is always an affair of the body-self and not just the mind. "Reason," as Daniel Day Williams observes, "will be informed by the loves of the reasoner, and distorted by the corruption of . . . [those] loves." [59] And as Martin Buber has reminded us, our love for another person opens the door to a whole new dimension of knowledge which can never be found without it. But love and sexuality can never be separated, for both are the impulse toward communion. Thus, it also makes eminent sense to say that reason will always be informed by the sexuality of the reasoner—distorted by its alienation and directed and enriched in that sexuality's reconciliation.

Freedom

Sexual growth in the context of divine acceptance is growth into freedom. The psychologist Abraham Maslow, speaking of love and sexuality in "self-actualizing people," furnishes helpful clues. The subjects whom he studied in this regard "were loved and were loving, and are loved and are loving." [60] Here are his characterizations of their sexuality:

● They enjoy genital sex wholeheartedly, far beyond the possibility of the average person, and yet specific sex acts do not play any central role in their philosophies of life. "In self-actualizing people the orgasm is simultaneously more important and less important than in average people."

● The sex act itself may bring on mystical experience at times, yet on other occasions may be experienced lightheartedly and playfully.

● There is "a healthy acceptance of the self and of others. . . . Their talk about sex is considerably more free and casual and unconventional than the average. . . ."

● Such persons clearly recognize their sexual attraction to others, but they are less driven to secretive affairs precisely because their own marriages are profoundly satisfying.

● "They made no really sharp differentiation between the roles and personalities of the two sexes. . . . These people were all so certain of their maleness or femaleness that they did not mind taking on some of the cultural aspects of the opposite sex role."

● "[Another] aspect of the healthy love relationship that was very clear in my subjects . . . [was] fun, merriment, elation, feeling of well-being, gaity."

● "[Still another characteristic was] the affirmation of the other's individuality, the eagerness for the growth of the other, the essential respect for . . . [the partner's] unique personality."

This rather remarkable portrait of freedom and responsiveness in sexual expression is obviously grounded in the sense of security in the persons here described. Maslow himself makes a powerful statement about grace (though in secular language) in his concluding statement: "I have suggested that self-actualizers can be defined as people who are no longer motivated by the needs for safety, belongingness, love, status, and self-respect because these needs *have already been satisfied.*" If his wording sounds too optimistic and lacking in the recognition of our continuing sin, we can nevertheless affirm the truth toward which he is pointing. Even the partial and incomplete healing of the body-self, by divine grace, does nurture something of the freedom which Maslow has described.

Christian faith knows that freedom always depends on trust. Contemporary psychiatry is teaching us that trust in one's own body is essential to personal health. Alexander Lowen has described many of his patients in terms of their fears. They are afraid to feel the depths of their sadness. They are afraid of their suppressed panic or terror or rage. To confront these fears the patient must let go of control and thus learn that they are not as threatening as they seem. Lowen comments, "Letting go of ego control means giving in to the body in its involuntary aspect. It means letting the body take over. But this is what patients cannot do. *They feel the body will betray them.* They do not trust it and have no faith in it. They are afraid that if the body takes over, it will expose their weakness, demolish their pretentiousness, reveal their sadness, and vent their fury. Yes, it will do that. It will destroy the facades that people erect to hide their true selves from themselves and from the world. But it will also open a new depth of being and add a richness to life compared to which the wealth of the world is a mere trifle." [61] To this secular statement of grace I would add only this: when our trust in God is a trust with the body as well as the mind, the body can become the means of our liberation.

Androgyny

The word "androgyny" literally means the union of the male (*andro*) and the female (*gyne*) in one human personality. Its literal meaning, however, is misleading. More accurately, the term means the bringing together of personality characteristics traditionally or conventionally thought of as masculine with those thought of as feminine so that such characteristics are creatively present in the same individual.

Grace aims at the fullest possible development of each human self. Descriptions such as autonomous and dependent, rational and emotional, initiating and nurturing, cognitive and intuitive, assertive and receptive have been split apart into gender stereotypes. But the growth and development of full personhood requires both sets of traits.

It is important to recognize what androgyny is not. It is neither hermaphroditism nor bisexuality. The former is an abnormality in which the physiological sexual characteristics of both male and female are found in the same individual. The latter refers to the

psychic orientation of those who in their adult lives feel a strong
genital attraction for persons of both sexes. Androgyny is neither.
   Granted, the term itself is not free from difficulty. To some it
suggests the virtual erosion of maleness and femaleness and the
creation of some third kind of "unisex" being. Others might object
that the term does not adequately express the plurality of ways in
which individuals, regardless of their sex, can find their own indi-
vidualized humanness. We can use the term as a helpful one, however, even if it may be susceptible to misunderstanding at points. In
our present state of sex-role consciousness, androgyny is at least a
necessary transitional concept pointing toward "the transformation
of past role expectations into more humanized ways of being." [62]
   A biblical vision of redemption points to a human liberation
beyond oppressive sex roles. True, sexist dualism unfortunately is
present in the Bible, as we have seen. But there is also present a
strong "prophetic non-patriarchalism." [63] The Exodus narratives
powerfully convey the basic theme of freedom from all forms of
human oppression. "Of special interest are the women who nurture
this revolution: Hebrew midwives, an Egyptian princess with her
maidens, and Hebrew slaves, mother and daughter, unite to defy
Pharaoh, the male oppressor. Alone they take the initiative that
leads to deliverance." [64]
   Further, Israel's understanding of God has implications for human
androgyny. "Unlike fertility gods, Yahweh is neither male nor female
but Creator and Lord who embraces and transcends both sexes." [65]
And in the New Testament, Jesus' whole message and ministry declares the liberation of all human beings. The roots of his teaching
are not in the rigid Judaism of the centuries immediately preceding
the Christian era, a time when ritual restrictiveness had led to the
cultic degradation of womanhood. Rather, his roots were in the
prophetic Hebraism of earlier centuries. And it was the great prophets who not only decried the injustices of their societies, including
the oppression of women, but who also used the semantics of the
feminine as well as of the masculine in speaking about God.[66]
   The Russian theologian-philosopher Nicolas Berdiaev was pressing the implications of androgyny for Christian faith as early as
1914. Years before our present consciousness of this possibility he
declared that there is a fundamental androgyny of the human being

created in the likeness and image of God. Nor have the sex roles of
the world destroyed this. "In fact, 'in the beginning' it is neither
man nor woman who bears the divine similitude. In the beginning
it is only the androgyne . . . who bears it. The differentiation of the
sexes is a consequence of the fall of Adam." [67] Now, in our estrangement we have an unassuageable desire to recover our lost unity.
Men are drawn toward the feminine principle in women, and
women toward the masculine in men. "It is by means of this femininity that the male-human can once again be integrated to the
androgynous source of his nature, just as it is through this masculine
principle that the female-human can be . . . integrated to her lost
androgynous source. But the reality of these personalities can only
be revealed through love. . . . Ultimately it is in God that the
lover meets with the beloved, because it is in God that the personality is rooted. And the personality in God, in its original state,
is androgynous." [68]

But other theologians are uncomfortable with the notion of
androgyny. Derrick Sherwin Bailey, for example, argues that the
myth of the androgyne excludes genuine meeting and communication between man and woman. It denies the reality of sexual antithesis and complementation. Its goal is simply an undifferentiated
unity, and its motivation is narcissism or self-love.[69]

Bailey is right, of course, that sexual *antithesis* is denied. Indeed,
that is the positive vision of androgyny—that the dualism which has
undercut the growth of unique persons and which has infected the
man-woman relationship with distorted stereotypes be transcended.
But Bailey's other charges need answering.

Is androgyny really fueled by narcissism? Does my partner become simply a means for my own healing, a tool used in my own
quest for reunification? I believe that the dynamics of pleasure, discussed earlier, provide a clue. There is an element of truth in the
charge, but it is not the whole story. Just as I am drawn to my
partner sexually not simply out of love but also (and sometimes
principally) because of my own sexual desire, so also I am drawn
to my partner not only because of the other's unique worth but also
(and at times primarily) out of my own incompleteness and need
for reunification. But then something happens. The miraculous does
occur. Self-love is not erased, for it has positive worth. But self-love

is expanded and transformed by love for the other. The attraction fueled by my incompleteness becomes an expression of love in which the beloved is cherished for her or his own sake.

But does androgyny exclude genuine meeting and communication between a woman and a man? Does it deny complementation? Quite the opposite. Herbert Richardson's interpretation of "psychological bisexuality" speaks to the point.[70] In his use of the term, *psychological* bisexuality does not mean an individual's genital attraction to members of both sexes. Rather, it means the process by which men and women begin to identify with something in each other. The growth of this possibility can be seen historically. The separation of sex from love in earlier societies—the notion that women and men could not really be genuine friends nor could they converse meaningfully with each other—led to the strong tendency for the two sexes to define themselves as contrary beings. In a modern society where intimate conversation between women and men is possible, there is also the possibility for the person of one sex to identify with the self-feelings of the other by a process of empathetic imagination. "Women become 'masculinely feminine' and men become 'femininely masculine.'" [71] While male socialization in our society tends to shape men toward the objectification and conquest of women, when empathetic identification occurs the aggressive aspects of sexuality are lessened and the partner is seen as friend and equal. Nothing in the woman's world is totally foreign to the man, and nothing in the man's world alien to the woman. The sexual relationship then can become much more fully integrated into the personhood of the partners. Empathetic identification nurtures the growth of androgyny and with it genuine meeting and communication.

Because of sexist dualism the feminine in men and the masculine in women are suffering. The ancient Greeks knew that their gods Apollo and Dionysus belonged together. Apollo personified the detachment and objectivity which we conventionally call masculine. Dionysus embodied the feminine traits of proximity and union. But the two were equally honored in the high temple at Delphi. The ancients seemed to know that "without Dionysus, Apollo leads to the neglect and abuse of basic human needs, to the destructive manipulation of nature, and to a severe alienation from the earthy, maternal life-source of our own natures. Dionysus without Apollo leads ultimately to the obliteration of reason and culture." [72] Psychically, this means that if we neglect the open, receptive, sensitive parts of ourselves we become progressively more rigid, sterile, and compulsively involved in meaningless action. Similarly, if we fear the thrust of energy and the focused goal, our lives become stagnant.[73]

The social ideology of androgyny is egalitarian. Gayle Graham Yates has perceptively compared it to the two other major ideologies or paradigms present in the Women's Movement.[74] The feminist paradigm evolved historically from those women who sought the privileges, rights, and opportunities which were valued by men. Its values have been essentially male values. The women's liberationist ideology, on the other hand, is antimasculine. Its insistence is upon separation from men, and its goal is the dominance of women in society and in value formation. The androgynous ideology is different from either. The characteristics and values of neither traditional sex role are assumed superior to the other, either implicitly or explicitly. The goals for change are neither integration of women into a male model, nor segregation with female superiority, but rather pluralism and diversity within the unity of the sexes and of gender values.

Yates' depiction of androgynous sexual expression is illuminating: "Regarding sexuality, the androgynous view transcends and comprehends the feminist and the women's liberationist views. Recognition of the root humanness of sexuality implies that the avenues of its expression should be open alike to women and men, and that the particulars of physiology and the feelings of female and male alike should be authenticated. . . . Sexuality is a wellspring of human nature. It has female and male courses, but the determination of its expression can be made and sanctioned by females and males together. The principles governing sexual choices can be human standards." [75]

Because we are social selves, the increased realization of androgyny in individual lives will have effects throughout society—predictably, augmented justice for women, and quite possibly, a diminution of institutional exploitation and violence. And also because we are social selves, personal change will be facilitated by social change—alteration of sex role images conveyed by the media, changes in laws, policies, and in the patterns with which various institutions treat the two sexes. Yet, change within the self is not totally dependent upon what happens in the social environment. In a basic sense we do not have to *become* androgynous, for we essentially *are*. We simply need to accept the power to become actually what we are essentially—unique individuals, female and male, each with the capacity to be both firm and tender, receiving and giving, rational and intuitive, diffused in awareness and focused in thinking, flexible and strong—like the duet in which two instruments skillfully blend into harmonious oneness.[76]

The image of the duet is significant, for while the harmonious blend is present there are still two instruments playing. Yet, when genuine artistry is present, one is less aware of the separateness and individuality of violinist and pianist than of the beautiful interplay between them. Likewise, the so-called masculine and feminine traits are not dissolved into undifferentiated unity in the self. It is more accurate to speak of the internalization of polarities or the compresence of dualities. This is not a matter of inner dichotomy or polarization or dualism. Psychotherapist June Singer puts it this way: "Androgyny is not trying to manage the relationship between the opposites; it is simply flowing between them. One does not need to ride the rapids, one can *become* the rapids." [77] And in this process new energy is released.

Moreover, if we accept the fact that essentially we are androgynous, that each of us has a variety of capabilities and psychological tendencies that fall into both of the categories which society calls masculine and feminine, then to ask, "Which of these is predominant in me?" is to ask the wrong question. We might better ask ourselves, "What capacities within me, what gifts that I have been given, are called for in this particular situation?" We can learn to use our varied characteristics appropriately, and to blend our different energies into the best mix for the most creative response to the situation at hand.

Growth in the realization of our androgyny seems to bring with it fresh realization of our unity with other persons and with God. Accepting the polarities within ourselves, we can respond more concretely to other persons as unique individuals. And we can also sense more vividly the polarities embedded in our experience of the universe and of God. The Sky Father and the Earth Mother are one God. The Transcendent and the Immanent are One.

In living with the polarity of the feminine and the masculine within each of us, in a sense we also live with the New Testament polarity of the present age and the age of fulfillment. In Paul's great vision of the unity of all—"There is neither Jew nor Greek, there is neither slave nor free, there is neither male nor female; for you are all one in Christ Jesus" (Gal. 3:28)—we encounter the eschatological mystery. But God's gracious possibility is that we can, at least in part and at least in moments of our healing, live proleptically—allowing that eschatological vision to invade and transform our present existence. That is the possibility of realizing the androgyny which is at the essential core of each of us as unique sexual selves.

Our salvation—including our sexual salvation—is incompletely realized. Yet it is real. Because we are not yet whole, the unhealed parts of our sexuality will continue to hurt us and others. But the first and last word of the gospel is grace; grace as forgiveness and acceptance, grace as growth toward fulfillment and empowerment for new life. The Word is made flesh and our flesh is confirmed.

5

Love and Sexual Ethics

Sex as the Language of Love

CENTRAL TO THE image of God in which we are created is the will to communion.[1] We are social beings through and through. We are nurtured into our humanness in community, and we have some deep, often unarticulated, sense that loving communion is our intended and ultimate destiny. The positive ethical claim upon us, then, is that we are to become what we essentially *are*. We are to realize in our actions and in our human becoming that communion of love. The negative side of this—sin—is not fundamentally the breaking of moral codes or the disobeying of laws, though it may involve that. More basically, it is the failure to become what we are. It is the estrangement, the alienation, which inhibits fulfillment and destroys communion.

Our sexuality, as we have seen, is not one restricted or compartmentalized segment of our lives. It is at the center of our response to life. It is the way in which we are in the world as embodied selves, female or male, with certain affectional orientations, with qualities socially defined as "masculine" and "feminine." It is a basic way in which we express both our incompleteness and our relatedness. It is God's ingenious way of calling us into communion with others through our need to reach out and touch and embrace— emotionally, intellectually, physically. Sexuality thus is never accidental or peripheral to our possibility of human becoming. It is basic and intrinsic to that possibility. It is both the physiological and psychological grounding of our capacity to love. And if we meet God most truly as the "beyond in our midst," as the One whose continuing incarnation is expressed through creaturely relationships, then our sexuality is a sacramental means for the love of God.

Communion depends on communication, and human communication depends significantly on language. Recall (Chapter 2) how languages are cultural products. They are socially developed and they constantly change. Human speech, as distinguished from animal communication, is aimed more at self-expression and meanings than simply physical survival. This is true of our sexuality in general and of specific sex acts in particular. As human beings we have sexual capacities and needs, as do animals. But our sexual acts are never simply acts of instinct, nor are they ever simply geared to species survival. Our organic drives and urges are never separable from the search for meaning and the quest for communion.[2]

To understand sex as a particular form of language yields some important ethical insights. For one thing, it presses us to try to understand *every* sexual act (and not just sex acts of a certain prescribed kind) as an expression of the human search for meaning and belonging. To say this does not give moral justification to any and every sexual act. It is, however, to say that even those we might judge deviant or unnatural or oppressive or cruel are still human attempts to find belonging and love.

Further, verbal languages are always contextual in their operation. The meaning of a word depends on its context in the sentence, the sentence in the paragraph. It is also true of sex as a language form. An older, simplistic ethical formula would have us judge the morality of a sexual act in essentially external and physical ways: the right organ in the right orifice with the right person. The more appropriate questions, however, ask about the nature and quality of personal communication which are intended in a sexual act, the kind of communion which that act actually serves, and how all of this fits into the broader social fabric.

Sexual acts have special characteristics which make them emotionally powerful as a form of language. Such acts are heavily dependent on touch, and touch is an intimate receptor of communication, contrasted to distant receptors such as the eyes. We give and receive touch with the skin, and the skin delimits our physical bodies, so touch and identity seem particularly related. And adult sexual acts link us back to the earliest tactile pleasure and oral-anal-genital sensations of infancy and childhood. In so doing, they seem to gather up our personal histories in the present moment. All of this gives force to sex as language.[3]

More than simply language as such, sex for human beings is a language of love. We are humanly created in and for community, in and for communion, in and for love. In one sense, this is the ideal. In another sense—even in our estrangement and distortions—it remains descriptive of the actual situation, as I argued in Chapter 4. For however broken we might be, the image of God is never utterly destroyed. We never, even in our most "inhuman" moments, lose the need and the desire for love. Our sexual acts, in one way or another, will always express that fact.

Toward the Integration of Sex and Love

In spite of all that I have just said, the *conscious* connection between sex and love is essentially a modern discovery.[4] All human ideas and understandings have their histories and hence are historically relative. This is clearly true of the conscious link between sex and love.

This perceived connection took centuries of human history to develop on any wide scale. The emergence of human "self-consciousness" is usually dated beginning around the thirteenth century in the West. By this is meant the gradual development of the empathetic ability—learning to experience the other's point of view, and hence to see oneself as the other sees one. Such self-consciousness is important for the development of "sexual love."

In the practice of "courtly love" the late Middle Ages added something essentially new to sexual relations—the notion of romance. Of course, people had fallen in love before, but an understanding and conscious experience of romance was new. Courtly love was marked by three characteristics: that love was seen as ennobling and not sinful; that the beloved was seen as superior to the lover; and that the quest of love was always uncertain.

But this type of love was impossible in marriage—at least at that time. In marriage love was taken for granted and not freely given. In marriage the woman (the beloved) was inferior to the man. And marriage lacked exhilarating quest and furtive fulfillment. Thus, courtly love became a cult of adultery. Historian Roland Bainton contends, however, that after courtly love had emerged in Europe the path was broken open to find the unity of romantic love and sex in marriage.[5] In France the pioneer was Christine of Pisa, a fourteenth century woman who rebelled against the denigration of members of her sex and in her writings articulated the delights of wedded love. About the same time in Italy Francesco Barbaro lauded the romance of married sex and vehemently decried the practice of family-arranged marriages which, in effect, denied the emotions of those about to be wed. In England, the sixteenth century poet Edmund Spenser wove romance and marriage together in his poetry (and, apparently, in his life), with the conviction that love is the key to all reality.

The point here is a double one. Courtly love opened up the possibility of love's integration with sex on a conscious level. By that same token it also opened up to consciousness the sexual experience as a vehicle of communication, so that people more than ever before came to experience the sex act as *meaningful*.

If the conscious possibility of integrating love's meaning with sexual expression arose in the centuries following the Middle Ages, it is likely that the modern period has added another dimension—psychosexual intimacy. Only in the modern period have we had literature that has *typically* exposed the author's inner feelings and self-consciousness. So also, in the modern period love began to be experienced as a unique form of self-consciousness. To tell the beloved how you felt meant to describe how you were aware of *yourself* in the beloved's presence. "In modern time, love becomes— for the first time in human history—the experience of psychological intimacy." [6]

Some scholars identify Shakespeare with an important advance

in the connection of love with sex. While he undoubtedly shared
with others of his time many ambiguities about sexuality, he also
went beyond them. His writings portray a new sensitivity to the
meaning of wholeness in sexual love.[7]

The Puritans and Quakers took things a step further. They came
to believe that the *primary* purpose of marriage was communion,
and, likewise, the *primary* purpose of sexual expression was communion. Procreation then became "a non-essential good." It was an
added blessing, but marriage and sex were not dependent on procreation for their legitimation.

The notion of romantic marriage is part of a larger social revolution in the West which, beginning in the seventeenth century, also
led to the development of the capitalistic economy and the demo-
cratic state. It was a basic reordering of the traditional ways in
which persons were understood to relate to each other. Before that
time, the more usual assumption had been that people must adapt
to society. With that revolution, however, it became commonly believed that social institutions could and should be changed to meet
human needs. That applied to marriage and the sexual relationship.

Herbert Richardson has summarized this broad historical development with the observation that there are four general ways in which
the relation between sex and love can be perceived.[8] One is to
separate rather than unite them, by focusing each on different persons. Thus, in ancient Greece and modern Japan men quite typically
have focused the orgasmic and procreative elements of sex in marriage, but have expressed the unitive quest for love and romance
outside of marriage. Or, the two drives can be directed at the same
person but remain essentially separate. Thus it appears that Victorian spouses expressed themselves sexually to each other and also
loved each other, but did not genuinely link the two; sex was seen
as a biological need, and "love" was higher. Or, sex can be re-
nounced altogether in order that one might love more fully, as does
the celibate monastic. But the fourth way is to envision the radical
union of sex and love. That is now our possibility. Indeed, that is
now part of our "nature," a human nature which is not simply biologically-given but also and significantly is historical and evolving.

To summarize: humanity's image of God is at once constant and
changing. We are created for love and community—that is constant.

Our sociality cannot be escaped—it is the essence of our humanity. This inescapable mark stamps the whole sweep of history, in its abuses as well as in its fulfillment. On the other hand, as any one of us experiences the essence of our humanity we also experience change. Its possibility and its meaning can deepen in our realization, or it can be denied and distorted. But on a more corporate and historical level there is also change. In relatively recent history, to a degree unknown previously, we have become capable of sensing the connection between our created destiny for community and our sexuality. Because human consciousness is what it *now* is in our culture, even at those times when we refuse to affirm it we are *capable* of affirming this: sex is intended to be a language of love.

The Meanings of Love

Surely, love is not the only ethical norm for Christians. But I believe that it is our central norm, and inescapably so. It is the Bible's supreme way of articulating God's purposes for and actions toward humankind. It has been Christians' paramount description of their experience in meeting the divine presence in Jesus Christ.

Yet, the word itself is slippery and even dangerous. From the torturers of the Inquisition to paternalistic slave-owners to dominating husbands and fathers, in gross and subtle ways people over the centuries have dehumanized other people in the name of love and frequently with the sincerely-felt conviction that they were indeed acting in disinterested love.[9] So also, "love" has been invoked to justify sexual expressions of all sorts: "if you love each other, it's all right." In one sense that claim is profoundly true—since love is the central meaning and purpose of our sexuality, it is also the measuring standard and justification for any particular sexual act. But everything hinges upon the content given to the word, so to that inquiry we must turn even though the question deserves a volume rather than a few pages.

Love is both the process and the reality of communion—it is that relationship of reunion with God, with the creaturely neighbor, with the self. Tillich puts it well: "[Love] is the moving power of life . . . which drives everything that is towards the unity of the separated. . . . The power of love is not something which is added to an otherwise finished process, but life has love in itself as one of its constitutive elements. It is the fulfillment and the triumph of love that it is able to reunite the most radically separated beings, namely individual persons." [10]

It is commonplace and useful in Christian ethics to utilize the classic distinctions in speaking of love. *Epithymia* (or *libido*) is the desire for sexual fulfillment. *Eros* is aspiration and desire for the beloved. *Philia* is mutuality and friendship. And *agape* is freely offered self-giving. Useful as these distinctions are, they are misused when they are interpreted as signifying four different and separable loves. Rather, they appropriately point to different dimensions of the rich unity of love—dimensions which can be disjoined only at the expense of serious distortion.

Unfortunately, that distortion has plagued Christian thought, causing endless confusion about human sexuality. It has been most commonly expressed by posing a sharp contrast and opposition between agape and eros. A generation ago, Anders Nygren formulated the most influential contemporary statement of this sort.[11] God's love, he argued, is sheer agape, and hence this becomes the paradigm of that distinctively Christian love to which we are called. Such love is spontaneous and unmotivated by its object. It is the initiator of the relationship and indifferent to the value of its object. It is value-creating: "God does not love that which is already in itself worthy of love, but on the contrary, that which in itself has no worth acquires worth just by becoming the object of God's love." [12]

Nygren postulated a fundamental opposition between divine love and human love, especially human sexual passion. Human love is by nature possessive and egocentric. *Christian* love, however, transcends this because now divine love flows through the human receptacle, a love which has nothing to do with desire, longing, and sexual fulfillment.

Sadly enough, this divorce between agape and eros has been affirmed in one way or another by numerous contemporary Christian thinkers, even folk of widely differing theological outlooks. The results have been several. Human emotions, desires, and sexual feelings have remained unintegrated into Christian understandings of selfhood. The manner in which our sexuality underlies and informs all of our loving has been left unappreciated and unclarified.

The positive functions of both desire and self-love have been misunderstood and denigrated. And countless Christians have been deprived of constructive guidance and burdened with needless guilt.

Yet, the sharp contrast between agape and ordinary human love is not supported in the Greek Bible. There is no separate word there for sexual love. "Agape" is used to describe the divine love, the intimate friendship of David and Jonathan, and the sensuous love of the Song of Songs alike. Nor does it appear that "eros" and its cognates were deliberately avoided by the biblical writers simply because these words referred to sexual desire in pagan literature.[13]

In short, this persisting dichotomy between agape and eros in so much Christian interpretation cannot be justified or explained by careful biblical and historical scholarship. The more likely reason for its pervasiveness is simply the pervasiveness of our experience of the alienating sexual dualisms. The connection of the agape-eros disjunction with spiritualistic dualism is most obvious. Plato's split between spiritual love and vulgar (bodily) love, the Stoics' definition of virtue as freedom from all passions, Augustine's division between heavenly and earthly loves—all of these have left their mark.

But patriarchal dualism is just as much present and may even underlie the Hellenistic variety. Beverly Wildung Harrison contends that "sexism is the most basic paradigm, and most fundamental dynamic, for the inherited evaluative dualisms reflected in language at every level. . . . That is because biological dimorphism is surely the first, and most universally experienced. . . . I assume that physiological substrate must, in fact, enter in and inform our basic experience of duality so deeply and pervasively that we can hardly detect its impact."[14] The problem is that we then move from our perceptions of life's dualities into supposed dualisms. We move from distinctions and differences to subordination and subjection. And (predominantly male) theologians and ethicists get involved with dualisms of concepts which they assume to be fundamental and irreconcilable: eros *vs.* agape, self-regard *vs.* self-sacrifice. These become seen not as polarities within a basic unity, but rather as irreconcilable ways of living and loving. Like the two sexes, they are utterly different, and one must dominate the other.

But what if the definition of love reflects more of our gracious healing than the distortions of our alienation? As we move toward an androgynous mode of being human, we also move toward the possibility of celebrating polarity without dichotomy, toward affirming duality without dualism. For we sense in our own body-selves that oneness and unity is utterly basic. We sense that dichotomies cannot do justice either to God or to humanity, either to the divine love or to our own. Significantly, Reinhold Niebuhr (whose great contributions to Christian thought themselves were not unmarred by the agape-eros disjunction) wondered in one of his last writings before his death about the "mystery that the Christian faith is consistently embarrassed by all efforts to relate love to eros." He continued to recognize how easily the sexual impulse can become distorted, but he had begun to believe that it might also become sacramental and that sensual love might be "a seed pod of a more universal love." [15]

The different dimensions of love need each other for love's wholeness. Sexual desire, epithymia, for example, needs eros if sex is to have its intended meaning. Rollo May has said of our tendency to split the two, "We are in a flight from eros—and we use sex as the vehicle for the flight." [16] And what is eros? "Eros is the drive toward union with what we belong to—union with our own possibilities, union with significant other persons in our world in relation to whom we discover our own self-fulfillment." [17] Eros draws and attracts us. Unlike sexual desire divorced from eros, eros does not simply seek a reduction in tension nor is it just a quest for sensations. It expresses a constant desiring, a forever reaching out, a quest for communion with another, with beauty, with knowledge, with goodness. If sex without eros loses meaning and becomes a "need-pleasure," eros without epithymia loses its passion and power. Sexual desire without eros is primarily a fact about ourselves. United with eros it becomes a fact about the Beloved. As C. S. Lewis puts it, "It becomes almost a mode of perception, entirely a mode of expression." [18]

I believe, in addition to our humanly-directed expressions of epithymia and eros, we can justifiably speak—and we need to speak —of the erotic *and* sexual dimensions of our love for God. For, if sex without eros loses meaning and direction, it is also true that eros without epithymia loses its passion and power. And a love for God devoid of passion and power does little to gladden either the human or the divine heart. (We shall return to this in the last chapter.)

Sexual desire and eros also need philia—mutuality and friendship. For example, a marriage without libido and romantic attraction is less than full, at best, and most likely has become a marriage of convenience. But sexual and romantic attraction without genuine friendship is also an invitation to disappointment and distortion. Without the equality of friendship, without shared interests and concerns beyond their own relationship, without the deep sense of their cohumanity, a marriage will most likely stagnate and very probably succumb to the sexist patterns of domination and submission.

Further, in the relation of friends apart from marriage it is a mistake to see the bond between them as philia alone, uninformed and unaffected by sexual dynamics and erotic desire. To be sure, there may be no desire for genital expression at all. But the lack of "sex" does not mean the absence of sexuality and its power. These are still two body-selves who rejoice in each other's physical presence, and the closer the friendship the more likely physical touch will be important to "being in touch." Nor is eros absent in deep friendship. If such virtues as benevolence, good will, caring, and courtesy can (and should) be unrestricted, by its very nature friendship is selective. In a rich friendship, eros is always present —as one is drawn to the other as a particular, desirable, yearned-for companion.

Agape is not another kind of love. Nor is it, as Tillich rightly notes, a dimension strictly comparable to the other three dimensions of our loving. It is the transformative quality essential to any true expression of any of love's modes. If we define Christian love as agape or self-giving alone—without elements of desire, attraction, self-fulfillment, receiving—we are describing a love which is both impoverished and impoverishing. But the other elements of love without agape are ultimately self-destructive. Agape present with sexual desire, erotic aspiration, and mutuality releases these from self-centeredness and possessiveness into a relationship that is humanly enriching and creative. It does not annihilate or replace the other modes of our loving. It undergirds and transforms. And faith knows that agape is gift, and not of our own making.

Another Look at Self-Love

Closely linked with the question of love's dimensions is the recurring question of the place of self-love in the Christian life—and, in particular, in the Christian's life as a sexual being. In the previous chapter I have suggested that self-acceptance is an important mark of sexual sanctification. It is possible because of God's accepting grace. And it is necessary if we are to have the capacity for intimacy, if our bodies are to be fully personalized, and if we are to be genuinely open to other body-selves and to the material universe. The accent in that previous discussion was upon the psychodynamics of self-acceptance as an expression of grace. Now we return to the question—essentially the same issue—but now with a slightly different accent as we look at self-love in the context of sexual love, and in the larger Christian vision of love itself.

Gene Outka has argued that there are four typical ways in which the relation of agape and self-love is seen in Christian ethics.[19] First, some give self-love a totally negative evaluation. It is incompatible with the Christian life. It is "wholly nefarious." Self-love is acquisitive, individualistic, concerned with one's private satisfactions, and prone to use others as tools for one's own desires. (Nygren's position on eros relentlessly leads him to this conclusion.)

A second possibility is that self-love is "normal, reasonable, prudent: it is not especially praiseworthy but not necessarily blameworthy."[20] We do not need to be urged toward concern about our own welfare. That comes naturally, and it becomes a problem only when there is a clash of legitimate interests with the neighbor. But, on the positive side, self-love does serve as a paradigm or index of love for the neighbor. We naturally seek our own good quite apart from our worth, and that is also our index for loving others.

Self-love, in the third view, is "justified derivatively." Agape, self-giving love of the other, is basic to Christian faith. But some kind of concern for the self is justified *if and when* it legitimately stems from concern for others. For example, if I don't take care of myself physically, I likely will become a burden to others; thus, basically out of concern for *them* I will care for myself.

The fourth possibility sees self-love and other-love as all of one piece. They are indivisible. Neither is a means to the end of the other. I can love the other only when I love myself, and myself only when I love the other. Both loves are a moral obligation for Christians. Indeed, they are not "loves" so much as facets of one love.

Outka's interpretation has little to say about sexuality; in fact, this basic dimension of selfhood and loving is virtually ignored in an otherwise fine book. But, committed to the two-directional street of sexual theology, I believe it important to see how our experience as sexual beings sheds light upon this ethical issue (as well, of course, as how an ethics of the gospel gives shape to our sexual lives). Already my conviction that the fourth position is most adequate is obvious, but a further exploration of a few of its sexual facets may be useful.

The basic truth is that love is indivisible and non-quantifiable. It is not true that the more we save for ourselves the less we have for others. These are not alternatives, but rather an interdependent unity. Authentic self-love is not a matter of being curved inward upon the self. It is not narcissism, nor is it a grasping selfishness. It is self-acceptance and affirmation of one's own graciously-given worth and creaturely fineness (in spite of all distortions and flaws). As we have seen, the basic indivisibility of love is strikingly evident in our sexuality. Those who have rejected their bodies, who have denied the goodness of their sexuality, encounter immense difficulty in sexual responsiveness to another. "If we cannot say yes to ourselves we cannot offer ourselves unselfishly to anyone else; we can surrender to them, but we will have lost the gift that we were asked to bring." [21]

Self-love is basic to personal fulfillment. We are attracted to persons who radiate a sense of fulfillment. They seem to give out a certain unreflective and vital energy, and that vitality also appears to have a sexual base. Perhaps it is a combination of epithymia and eros. It is pervasive and contributes to the "timbre" of all love relationships.[22] It is a quality of openness to the giving and receiving of pleasure. One psychiatrist comments, "In general, we are repelled by an attitude of self-denial and drawn to people who enjoy living. I have heard many patients say, 'I wish my mother had given herself more pleasure.'" [23]

The psychiatrist is right about the unattractiveness of certain forms of self-denial. There is a type of masochism which undermines love and erodes intimacy. But there is another kind of selflessness which is possible only through a certain level of self-awareness. It is the selflessness which emerges from the person who has discovered his or her own identity in a fulfilling way. Dorothee Sölle characterizes it this way: "It is not a masochistic lust for punishment, but a partial renunciation freely given for the sake of another's fulfillment. . . . The stronger a person's self-identity . . . the easier partial renunciation becomes. . . . And so one could formulate the thesis: The greater one's realization of selfhood the greater . . . [the] ability for true renunciation. The more successful one is at living the easier it is . . . to let go of life." [24]

True sexual intimacy depends on the solid sense of identity of each of the partners. The entanglements in which identity is confused and diminished do not necessarily reflect the loss of love, but they do reflect the loss of love's dialectic. They become symbiotic relationships in which one person is reduced to being an extension of the other, and such relationships easily lead to resentment and rupture. Perhaps that is inevitable in the long run, for true intimacy is always communion—and not union without separation. [25]

Sexual intimacy is the communion of love, not unification. But such intimacy rests in some large measure upon each partner's own sense of worth as a person, each one's ability to be self-affirming. Without this, we elevate the other into the center of our lives, hoping that the other's affirmation will assure us of our own reality. But this is too large an order for the partner. The beloved has been idolatrized and confused with the divine. As David Harned fittingly comments, this confusion "is the source of the daimons that roam our world and whose shadows obstruct our vision. They are born whenever we turn to anything in the world and say, 'All I want is you.' When we mean what we say, we end up with neither you nor I." [26]

In point of fact, intimacy is always threatening to the person who lacks self-affirmation. Without it, we tend to understand ourselves in terms of social roles. Without self-love we see ourselves only as we are mirrored in others' expectations for us. And in the sexual relationship, the playing of such roles is disintegrating, for it means that instead of being the unique and beloved partner one is rather a male or a female, a husband or a wife, in bed.[27]

The literary artists best capture this quality of intimacy without absorption, of communion which rests upon each one's self-affirming identity. Rainer Marie Rilke puts it this way: "Once the realization is accepted that, even between the closest human beings, infinite distances continue to exist, a wonderful living side by side can grow up, if they succeed in loving the distance between them which makes it possible for each to see the other whole and against a wide sky." [28]

And, in the poetry of the French writer Anne Philipe: "I swim by your side in the warm, clear water, I wait for you to appear in the doorway under the wisteria. You say 'Good morning' to me, and I know your dreams, your first thoughts on the fringes of sleep—and yet you are a mystery. We talk: your voice, your thoughts, and the words you use to express them are the most familiar in the world to me. Each of us can end a sentence begun by the other. And you are—and we are—a mystery." [29]

Communion's dialectic of self-love and other-love thus depends in no small measure upon the self's growth toward androgyny. When we can affirm both types of needs within us, which Carl Jung called *animus* and *anima*—the self-asserting and the other-embracing, the initiating and the receptive—then we can embrace intimacy and respect mystery.

The Characteristics of Love

Love, then, involves commitment to the other, the willingness to risk and entrust oneself to the other. It is the desire to give and to open the self in personal nakedness to the beloved. Along with this agapeic quality, there is also the erotic desire to receive whatever the other will give to the self. Love is expectant. It recognizes the inexhaustible possibilities in the beloved, expecting that enriching novelty and surprise will emerge from the relationship. Love is the respect of individual identity. As such it is communion, the intimate relationship of life with life which can become a sacramental channel to communion with God.[30]

Another way of looking at sexual love is to observe the values which emerge from it.[31] Such love is self-liberating; it expresses one's own authentic selfhood and thus releases further potential for growth. It is other-enriching; it has a genuine concern for the well-being of the partner. Sexual love is honest; it expresses as truthfully and as candidly as possible the meaning of the relationship which actually exists between the partners. It is faithful; such love expresses the uniqueness of the relationship, yet without crippling possessiveness. Sexual love is socially responsible, nurturing the fabric of the larger community to which the lovers belong. It is life-serving. Always this means the transmission of the power of newness of life from one lover to the other; sometimes it also means the procreation of children. Sexual love is joyous; it is exhuberant in its appreciation of love's mystery and life's gift.

These are important characteristics and qualities of love which serve as ethical criteria of specific sexual acts. Beyond them all, Christian faith affirms that such love is essentially gift. Because we are loved into being, we are able to love—and in so doing, however imperfectly, continue the incarnation, the enfleshment of Word and meaning.

Components of Our Decisions About Sex-Related Issues [32]

When we come to concrete decisions, however, we discover that it is not simply a matter of having a perceptive vision of love and then having the appropriate decisions automatically appear. A variety of additional factors impinge upon us. Awareness of them can augment our own ethical self-knowledge and can also illuminate why sincere Christians often differ from each other in sex-related judgments. Consider these several factors:

First, ourselves as the decision-makers. We bring our unique personalities into decisional situations. We bring our family backgrounds, our formative sexual experiences, our sex education, the influences of peer groups, church and culture. We bring our self-images as women and men, our affectional orientations, our psychic and relational needs. We bring whatever is our consciousness of God in the midst of our relationships with others. In short, we bring ourselves—character, conscience, personal identity—and "who I am" at a given moment will profoundly affect what I do.

Second, our basic religious beliefs. Intimately linked with our identities is what we most deeply believe and in what or in whom we most deeply trust. Even though our consciously-confessed Christian beliefs may not consistently reflect our actual, operating faith, in our moments of greater integrity we strive to bring them together. Even so, it is obvious that among Christians there are seemingly endless varieties of faith definitions. Two examples, both concerning God and human nature, suggest how differing basic beliefs can press sexual decisions into different directions:

One might believe that God has established eternally-valid, binding rules governing appropriate sexual acts. On the other hand, one might believe that while God's nature is always that of unchanging love, God is intimately involved in the changing processes of history. And this means that the divine will for sexually-loving acts may vary with time and circumstances.

As a second example, one might believe that the image of God in which we are created is clearly heterosexual; hence, any homosexual expression violates our God-given human nature. Or, one might believe that the image of God essentially is a divinely-given capacity for loving communion; hence, the matter of sexual orientation is not fundamentally relevant to the fulfillment of our intended human nature. These examples of varying shapes of basic beliefs could be multiplied, but the point, I am sure, is obvious: what we believe about the realities of God and of human relationships will give significant shape to our sexual decisions.

Third, our styles of decision-making. There is no one correct style for Christian decision-making. Rather, there are several typical methods (and combinations thereof) by which persons go about deciding.[33] Three major ones are these:

The life of obedience: God is experienced principally as ruler, governor, and judge of our lives—the One to whom we are called to be faithfully obedient. In this pattern, sexual acts usually are envisioned as right or wrong, depending upon whether they reflect fidelity to the commands of the faithful God.

The life of aspiration: Here the moral decision takes shape as it fits into a larger pattern of aspiration or movement toward life's great goal. God is experienced primarily as the One who sets before us the goal and empowers us to move toward it. The ultimate goal may be seen differently by different Christians, e.g. the kingdom of God, liberation from bondage, the realization of authentic humanity, Christian perfection. However the great goal of Christian life is visualized, specific sexual acts are judged good or bad, constructive or harmful, insofar as they contribute toward or detract from that final end toward which we are beckoned and destined.

The life of response: In this third typical pattern, the moral life is perceived as a dynamic interrelationship between persons and God. We are called to respond to the presence and activity of God in the midst of varied and changing contexts. We are called to a life of responsible initiative and creative action in the newness of each situation and in its continuity with the past. Sexual acts are evaluated in terms of their fittingness to what God is doing and intending in the midst of human relationships.

We might not be consistent in the method by which we make moral decisions. It is unlikely that anyone falls exclusively into one of the above types. Nevertheless, the pattern by which we typically decide sexual moral issues will suggest the amount of emphasis which we give to each of the several elements that comprise a decision:

- the *motive: why* should I (or shouldn't I) do this?

- the *intention:* at *what* am I aiming in and through this act?

- the nature of *the act itself: how* will I implement my aims? are certain acts intrinsically right or wrong, or are acts dependent upon circumstances?

- the *consequences:* in what way will I be *accountable* for *the effects and results* of this act or relationship?

Equally sincere Christians, then, might arrive at different sexual decisions not only because they are uniquely different moral agents and have differing interpretations of basic Christian beliefs, but also because their decisional methodology differs in style and emphasis.

Fourth, "the facts" and how we interpret them. Sexual decisions are made in the midst of a welter of data—about our own personal relationships, bits of medical and psychological information, perceptions of what others are doing sexually, and so on. Several things must be said about these data:

Facts are never pure. They are always filtered through our interpretive screens—colored by our personal needs and experiences, our background information, our reality convictions. There is, for instance, a general impression that male homosexuals have a greater tendency toward child molestation than do male heterosexuals. Current research, however, indicates that precisely the opposite is true. Conscious assimilation of this new information might well alter the shape of certain heterosexual attitudes about gay men. But whether or not this datum will be taken seriously and just how it might affect one's moral stance will vary considerably from person to person.

We ought, however, to let our most conscientious grasp of relevant facts affect the decisional process. Ours is an incarnational faith which confesses that God enters into the tangled webs of human circumstances: concreteness is important. Another example: some Christians believe that sexual intercourse outside marriage is always wrong, and within a marriage it is always moral. A moral generalization such as this can indeed point *in the direction* of a significant Christian sexual value. Yet, taken as it stands, such a sweeping judgment can be made only with considerable disregard of demonstrable facts. Rape *does* occur between married partners; often the weapons are psychic ones, but wife-battering cases grimly attest to physical force as well. And, outside of formal marriage, loving and humanly enriching sexual intercourse does seem to occur in *some* particular circumstances. Such evidence by itself does not determine morality, but it must be taken seriously.

Thus, facts and values are different. As important as concrete evidence is, it does not constitute *sufficient* grounds for a moral decision. It is factually verified, for example, that properly-used contraception is now highly reliable. It is also true, according to the best studies, that the majority of both sexes have pre-marital intercourse by the time of their early twenties. Yet, dependable contraception added to the fact that the majority are "doing it" does not equal an adequate moral justification for such sexual expression. These facts should be considered in our judgments, but our valuational decisions must contain more than this.

We should be open to insights from a wide variety of sources in making sex-related decisions. For example, psychologists, sociologists, anthropologists, and historians have studied family life. Christian ethics needs their wisdom. We need to understand that the nuclear family is a relatively modern development which has arisen out of the economic patterns of an industrial society. We need to know something about the psychic strains on this form of the family today. We need to know what modifications of or alternatives to the nuclear family are being explored, and with what results. God's "common grace" is manifested in many areas of human thought and research, and openness to such is important in Christian decision-making.

Fifth, our norms and how we use them. By "norm" I mean a criterion or standard of judgment which can be conceptualized, thought about, talked about, and used as a resource in decision-making. When we are reflective about our moral judgments, we almost always use one or more norms in the process. Principles and rules are the two most common types.

A *principle* is a norm which asserts certain moral qualities which ought to be present in a whole range of different categories of acts. It is general. It does not specify particular actions themselves as approved or disapproved. A useful principle might be this: "Sexual acts ought always to express responsible concern for the integrity and wholeness of the partner." While this does not explicitly identify any particular sexual act or partner, it does identify the morally-desired quality.

A *rule*, by contrast, is action-specific. It names certain types or classes of actions, specifying them as obligatory or permissible or forbidden. A sexual rule important to many Christians is this: "Genital intercourse ought to take place only between married partners." As a specific and positive rule, it also obviously "rules out" any other intercourse patterns.

At this point, I think it important to recognize that there are differences in ethical methodology regarding the understanding and use of such norms, which contribute to the diversity of sexual convictions among church people. First, and most evidently, people can and do disagree about the *content* of appropriate Christian norms. One person, for instance, might affirm the rule that masturbation is always wrong. Another might hold to the rule that masturbation is wrong for those who are married but is morally permissible for the unmarried. Still another might affirm the rule that in marriage masturbation is morally permissible if it is not used as a preferred substitute to genital intercourse with the spouse. The reasons behind the differences expressed in these three rules could be varied and multiple, depending on the particular persons who hold them. They could include differences in personal histories regarding masturbation; differing evaluations and applications of the notion of self-love; variation in conviction about the purposes of sexual expression; dissimilarity in interpretation of and commitment to Christian moral traditions about masturbation; diversity in understandings of medical and psychological theories about the subject, and so on. In short, the content of sexual norms can and does differ for a host of reasons.

Another sort of difference about moral norms involves one's convictions concerning which *types* are appropriate: do general principles alone provide sufficient guidance, or are more specific rules also necessary? The person who opts for *principles only* might argue this for several reasons. Specific rules are inevitably time-bound and culturally-relative (witness the Old Testament rules which deal with menstruating women). Nor can they take into account the variety and uniqueness of decisional situations. Patterns of rules nurture a legalistic mind-set and subvert one's responsible freedom in Christ.

A second person, agreeing in part with this line of argument, might however assert the need for *rules also*. The reasoning could sound like this: Indeed, many sexual rules are highly culturally relative and need constantly to be reexamined and revised. Thus, I am wary about making claims of eternal validity for any version of a specific moral rule, sexual or otherwise. But I do know something else. Since I am notoriously prone to rationalize in ways that suit my self-interest and my desires of the moment, I need something more definitive than principles only. Furthermore, precisely because I, too, am part of a changing culture, I need the moral wisdom which Christian and other human experiences can pass on to us through rules. I will give rules serious consideration even while I recognize that they are human definitions and not divine.

A considerably stronger affirmation of rules holds out for their *universal validity*. This, according to the hypothetical third Christian, does not oblige one to embrace every sexual rule found in our religious heritage. The cultural relativity of some of them (the menstruation rules again as an example) is quite obvious; though even such rules, while not literally applicable to us, should be valued for the broader religious convictions which they were trying to reflect. But the point is that if some rules are relative to certain historical conditions and understandings which we do not share, and if still other rules in the tradition might have been mistaken, this does not mean that there are no universally valid moral (including sexual) rules. Some sexual acts by their very nature are right; certain others are intrinsically wrong. No changing social situation or new scientific insight will ever make rape, for example, a good and right thing to do.

As is evident, for those who want to affirm sexual rules as well as sexual principles there is more than one way of understanding the status and use of those rules. Return to the earlier example: "genital intercourse ought to take place only between married partners." One possibility is to understand this rule as *universally prescriptive*. It is always obligatory. Regardless of time, place, culture, and situation, there are no legitimate exceptions to it. On the other end of the continuum is the interpretation of such a rule as a *useful guideline*. It expresses the wisdom of the church as to what is generally the appropriate relational context for intercourse. But since rules themselves cannot anticipate every situation, there may be exceptions, and in such instances the rule can rightfully be ignored. It is a guideline to be considered, but only one of many factors which constitute an appropriate moral judgment.

The third possibility lies somewhere between these two. It says *presume in the rule's favor*. This position embraces neither the absolutism of the first approach nor the great flexibility of the second. It sees some truth in both of the other approaches, but also error. Tried and tested moral rules point to matters of genuine seriousness, as does the example concerning marital intercourse. Those who are realistic about their finitude and sin, their limitations in both knowledge and virtue, will take such rules seriously. Nevertheless, given the rich complexity of human situations and given the freedom of God to will and do the new thing, no moral rule ought to be seen as exceptionless. Yet, having presumed in favor of the rule, the burden of proof is upon the exception, upon this departure from the norm. The question then becomes: given *this* particular situation, will an exception to the rule actually express greater loyalty to that higher reality upon which the rule itself must rest for its justification? Can this particular instance of non-marital intercourse be justified as a faithful action, consistent with my best understanding of God's intentions? Those who would hold to this third possibility concerning the use of rules claim the importance of a moral life lived in that delicate balance between recognition of human sin and awareness of grace, the ethical polarity of order and freedom.

Sixth, the church as a moral community. Here is one more constitutive element of Christian decision-making which deserves emphasis. Christian morality, like the faith itself, must always be personal—willingly struggled with and affirmed in one's free decisions. But personal does not mean individualistic. We are, in New Testament language, surrounded by a great cloud of witnesses, past and present. We need their give-and-take in ethical reflection and debate, the challenge of opposing viewpoints as well as the support of our own values and identities.

As a sexual community, the church lives with its own ambiguity. At its best, it knows the God who delights in the creation of human sexuality; it knows the God who summons us to unity and equality beyond gender roles and affectional orientations. Yet, the church is not always at its best, and hence participates in both doctrine and practice in dehumanizing forms of sexual oppression and exploitation, the perpetuation of stereotypes and judgmental exclusion, as do other human communities.

It is true in a broad but real sense that all human communities are moral communities. That is, to the extent that a collection of individuals is a group, there must be some sort of moral glue holding them together—shared purposes, norms, values. And it is correspondingly true that all human communities are faith communities, held together by some sort of shared trust and more-or-less common perceptions of what is real and worthwhile. But beyond the other groups to which we belong, the church has unique functions which make it vital to the Christian's moral processes. Central to its purpose as a group, the church *consciously* attempts to articulate, proclaim, reflect about, and liturgically celebrate the presence of God. And this is the One who challenges and renews us, forgives and empowers, judges our moral myopia and expands our sensitivities. Here is the One who loves us into being, and who presses us to embody love as the meaning of life—and of our sexuality.

Some Principles for Sexual Morality

Thus far I have tried to raise what I believe are important considerations about the meanings of love and about the elements of decision-making. To bring these things all together is much more of a *lived* ethical venture than simply an intellectual one.

Still, it is important to press things further than they now stand in this chapter. My attempts to wrestle with particular sexual situations will come in the next four chapters. But before turning to these particular and diverse contexts for sexual decision, I shall propose three broad principles which I believe to be appropriate Christian norms for sexual expression. By themselves principles are never sufficient, of course. Yet, together with everything else the person brings to moments of decision, principles can be useful and even, I believe, necessary.

First, love requires a single standard and not a double standard for sexual morality. All of love's elements which we have considered imply that love must always be expressed as justice. Without justice, it becomes individualistic and shallowly sentimental. And without love, justice becomes simply a struggle for power.[34] Love expressed as justice becomes the lively concern for the empowerment of all persons, so that everyone has rightful access to the means for human fulfillment. This implies that there cannot be one sexual ethic for males and another for females, nor one for the unmarried and another for the married, nor one for those heterosexually oriented and another for those oriented to their same sex, nor one for the young and another for the old, nor one for the able-bodied and another for those with physical or mental infirmity. The same basic considerations of love ought to apply to all.

Second, the physical expression of one's sexuality with another person ought to be appropriate to the level of loving commitment present in that relationship. Our relationships exist on a continuum —from the fleeting and casual to the lasting and intense, from the relatively impersonal to the deeply personal. So also, physical expressions exist on a continuum—from varied types of eye contact and casual touch, to varied forms of embrace and kiss, to bodily caresses, to petting and foreplay, to the different forms of sexual intercourse. In some way or another, we inevitably express our sexuality in every human relationship. The morality of that expression, especially of the degree and type of its physical intimacy, will depend upon its appropriateness to the shared level of commitment and the nature of the relationship itself.

Third, genital sexual expression should be evaluated in regard to motivations, intentions, the nature of the act itself, and the consequences of the act, each of these informed and shaped by love. Let us look at these elements separately:

Motive (why should I do, or not do, this?). Each genital act should be motivated by love. Obviously, this means love for one's partner. It also means love of oneself, and celebration in love for God of this gift of communion with the other and oneself. This does not mean that sexual desire and pleasure are inappropriate or unworthy motivations. It simply means that when such is abstracted from one's care for personal wholeness, genital sex can be more fragmenting than healing and liberating.

Intention (at what am I aiming in this act?). Following from the above, each genital act should aim at human fulfillment and wholeness, God's loving intention for all persons. The intent should be the engagement of the whole person—body, mind, and feelings. Sexual fulfillment requires sexual pleasure, and good genital sex is highly erotic, warm, intimate, playful—immensely pleasurable. It can also be almost mystical in its evocation of self-transcendence and its possibilities for communication and communion.

The concern for fulfillment-in-communion involves such intentions as sustaining, healing, and growth through our genital expression.[35] The intention to *sustain* the partner involves emotional security and sensitive, empathetic communication; and these imply continuity in the relationship. The concern for *healing* involves the intention that this sexual relationship be of the sort which can significantly transform the wounds of our lives, contributing greater health to the whole person. *Growth* means the realization of our potential; it means increasing access to our physical, emotional, and intellectual resources—availability to ourselves and hence to others. Good genital sex intends growth toward greater wholeness.

The act (are certain sexual acts inherently right and good, and certain others intrinsically wrong and bad?). I find it extremely difficult to label whole classes of acts as inherently right or wrong, since moral quality hinges so heavily on what is being communicated to the persons involved in the particular relationship and context. Yet, we can surely say that acts which by their nature are loveless—coercive, debasing to the other's sensitivities, utterly impersonal, obsessed solely by physical gratification—such acts of whatever sexual sort are excluded.

Consequences (what most likely will result from this genital act, and in what ways am I willingly accountable?). The willingness to assume responsibility for the results of a sexual act is also one of love's marks. It involves responsibility to the ongoing relationship and its particular commitments and promises. It involves responsiveness to the partner's continuing needs for sustaining, healing, growth—and to one's own needs for the same. If a child is conceived and born, it means responsibility for loving nurture. Accountability also means the weighing of the act in terms of its probable effects for the wider community, for sexual acts however private are never privatistic. We are social beings. Every action has wider implications, and we are called to social responsibility.

Thus, will this sexual expression enhance or diminish the love and justice by which a human community must exist?

A Concluding Word

The above principles remain on a general level, as principles must. My intent has been to word them in a way that makes them inclusive in application to the variety of sexual situations and acts of which human beings are capable. Some readers will want to lay claim to more specific sexual rules in addition to guiding principles such as these. If so, well and good. I personally find certain sexual rules important and useful. I do not view them as exceptionless absolutes, but I presume strongly in their favor, and the burden of proof is then on me to justify any exception by its greater faithfulness to the higher loyalty. Rules can protect us at the boundaries of our experience where we encounter our limitations in knowledge and wholeness. But however sexual rules are used, they should nurture our growth into greater maturity and responsible freedom, and not inhibit it.

To love is to be open to life. Nowhere is this more evident than in the directly-sexual forms of our loving. In contemporary Roman Catholic declarations on sexuality (particularly in *Humanae Vitae* and in the declaration of Vatican II) the phrase "openness to life" is used as an essential mark of each morally legitimate sexual act.[36] Yet those documents give to that phrase a narrow biological exposition. In them it means that there can be no deliberate frustration of sex's procreative potential through artificial contraception or through non-procreative acts such as masturbation and same-sex intercourse. That biological interpretation is far too narrow. But the phrase itself is a splendid one. Indeed, sexual acts which can be deemed good, right, and fitting will always be those which embody and promote "openness to life." And the definition of "life" for us is centered in that human wholeness embodied in the One who came that we might have life, and have it more abundantly.

6

The
Meanings of
Marriage and Fidelity

HE WIDESPREAD QUESTIONING of traditional understandings of marriage and fidelity today is an exercise of the privileged minority. People who can take for granted a reasonable degree of economic and political security are in a quite different place than those in two-thirds of the world where poverty and, frequently, political oppression are the grim facts of daily life. Historically, it is largely the case that marriage was an arrangement of the sexual and generational relationships designed to stabilize that part of life so that people could get on with the task of surviving. Now, however, for the fortunate minority—perhaps a third of the world and certainly the large majority in the affluent societies of the West—there is sufficient emotional and mental energy available to spend in sorting out sexual and relational feelings.[1]

Furthermore, there is little doubt that the present confusion about marriage (and sexual morality in general) is intimately linked with the changing functions and perceptions of the family in our society.[2] Typically, the family has had six basic functions: to control sexual access and relations; to provide an orderly context for reproduction; to nurture and socialize children; to furnish emotional nurture for its adult members; to provide a context for economic activity; and to ascribe social status to its members. Without exception each of these functions is now being challenged and changed under the impact of high mobility, new perceptions of sex roles, urbanization, industrialization, and rapid technological developments (importantly including reliable contraception and markedly increased life-spans).

Thus, a recent study of family types in the United States produced the following constellation: nuclear families (both parents and their children in one household), 37%; single adults without children, 19%; single parents (usually divorced or separated) with children, 12%; remarried couples with children, 11%; childless couples or couples with no children at home, 11%; experimental family forms, 6%; and three-generation households, 4%.[3] In a word, we are moving toward a variety of family types wherein no single form is statistically normative.

The changes of this "pluralistic revolution" are now reaching deeply into the perception of marriage itself.[4] Marriage is increasingly becoming a choice rather than an imperative. It is moving toward greater equalitarianism between spouses, and women, in larger numbers than ever, are exercising their freedom to postpone marriage or remain single. The trend, particularly among middle-class young adults, of living together either prior to or instead of marriage continues. The trend toward fewer children has accelerated, as has the growth in the number of deliberately child-free marriages and primary relationships. An increasing number of couples are rejecting sexual exclusiveness as essential to marriage and are seeing intimate "satellite" relationships as positively supporting both marriage and personal growth. The exploration of "complex living arrangements" and multi-adult households has increased. In short, the search for alternatives to the traditional image of monogamy as well as of the nuclear family continues.

If for no other reason than its dramatic increase, this contemporary questioning of marriage deserves to be taken seriously by the church. It would be easy—but mistaken—to write off these signs by labeling them simply as expressions of hedonism, or of wishful and unrealistic thinking, or of the fear of lasting personal commitments. Doubtless, these things are present. But also present is a genuine yearning for more deeply humanizing relationships and sexual bonds.

Nor should we automatically assume that the "correct" form of marriage and family life is eternal and unchanging in the Christian experience. A few recollections from our distant and more recent past should remind us of some of the historical relativities.

Regarding the institution of marriage itself, the early church tended to follow the prevailing Roman practice for several centuries; its strong eschatological expectations precluded any vigorous interest in producing new marital forms consonant with its faith. The first traces of distinctively Christian rites of marriage emerge only in the fourth century, and we await the ninth century to find a detailed account of Christian nuptial ceremonies (and even then the order is quite parallel to that of the ancient Romans). In fact, only at the time of the Council of Trent did the Western church first assert that the use of the Christian ceremony was essential to a valid marriage.[5]

We have already seen how Protestantism elevated marriage by rejecting the cult of virginity. Particularly in the Puritan experience, the family was raised to new status as an indispensable moral unit of society and as the church's crucial subunit for Christian nurture. As Philippe Aries has pointed out, this new ideology of the family as religious and moral educator and, increasingly, of marriage itself as a conjugal relationship, emerged hand-in-hand with a significant evolutionary change in the nature of the family as a social institution.[6] Marriage among the bourgeois middle-class was gradually doing away with the complex extended family unit characteristic of both the nobility and of the poor. By the nineteenth century, this bourgeois pattern had become the general norm for Western society. It had several new traits. The offspring heir was no longer sharply distinguished from the rest of the children. The family home had become smaller and more personal, with servants, retainers, and relatives gradually thrust out. Childhood had come to be understood as a separate era of life, a time of extended moral, sexual, and vocational innocence. Mothering had become a full-time occupation. And the family had lost most of its earlier economic and political functions. It had gradually become the private and nuclear family which, until recently at least, was taken as the norm.

But history does not stand still. Institutional change continues, and its pace accelerates. Obviously, there is no guarantee of automatic progress, and the present search for new understandings and forms of marriage and family must be evaluated carefully. But neither should change as such be feared. We *are* historical creatures, and the radical monotheism of Christian faith would remind us that no finite, historical form ought ever to be absolutized.

Some Representative Theologies of Marriage

We can begin our quest by examining some of the distinctive perspectives of several contemporary thinkers who have particularly influenced the church's current theology of marriage. While others could certainly be added to the list, I believe that of especial importance are Helmut Thielicke, Karl Barth, Derrick Sherwin Bailey, and Norman Pittenger.

According to Thielicke, marriage is preeminently "the covenant of agape." [7] Yet, it is a "worldly" and not a "sacramental" institution. It "rests upon a primeval order of creation," and a valid marriage does not depend upon the couple's awareness of their union's theological significance.[8] Nor has marriage any redemptive significance —no one is saved through it. It is established for all persons and can be observed independently of faith. It is "an order of preservation" for the whole world—one of those crucial human arrangements which prevents the world from sinking into chaos.

Yet, says Thielicke, *Christian* marriage has particular meanings. Especially, it must be seen as monogamous, and the reason for this lies not in any clear biblical laws concerning monogamy (of which there are none, he believes), but rather precisely in the revelation of agape in Jesus Christ. The manner in which agape presses ineluctably toward monogamy is linked with the different sex roles of man and woman. A man's sexual nature is "naturally polygamous." He invests far less of himself in the sex act and "is not nearly so deeply stamped and molded by his sexual experience as is the case with the woman." [9] The woman, in contrast, is "naturally" monogamous "because she is the one who receives, the one who gives herself and participates with her whole being, is profoundly stamped by the sexual encounter." [10] The woman, then, cannot live polygamously without damage to the substance of her very nature.

But if she cannot, then the man cannot either, for his masculinity is a relational term which cannot be defined apart from the woman. "Once we see that Christian *agape* regards this 'existence-for-the-other-person' as the foundation of all fellow humanity, and that it regards man as being determined by his neighbor, it becomes apparent that under the gospel there is a clear trend toward monogamy. Because the wife is a 'neighbor,' the husband cannot live out his own sex nature without existing for her sex nature and without respecting the unique importance which he himself must have for the physical and personal wholeness of the feminine sex nature." [11]

The two most pronounced features of Thielicke's theology of marriage illustrate in a rather dramatic way two serious problems in much current Christian thinking on the subject. First, there is the sharp separation between "the order of creation" (or "preservation") and "the order of salvation." Here duality borders dangerously upon dualism, the lower separated from the higher, nature from grace. The disjunction undercuts a radically incarnationalist theology in which the whole creation is seen as the potential medium of divine salvation. But if the process of salvation occurs through the enfleshed encounter with love, surely marriage at its best is a crucial occasion for that process to take place.

The second problem, quite obviously, is the sexist dualism which underlies Thielicke's interpretation of monogamy. Certain stereotypes of masculinity and femininity are not recognized for what they are—historically relative and sinful distortions of authentic human personhood; rather, they are located in the created natures of the sexes. Moreover, it is through the man's agency that Christian marriage becomes monogamous. Though by nature he is not as virtuous as the woman is, nevertheless in a curious way the man still triumphs. He becomes the crucial bearer of divine agape, which then presses him to live for her sex nature. She, the eternal feminine, is forever the passive recipient, the one who is acted upon. In fairness to Thielicke, he is surely struggling with a central question: how does agape enter into and transform eros? But his answer is dualistically marred beyond helpfulness.

Karl Barth finds a theology of marriage emerging from the doctrine of the Trinity. God is self-related as three persons in a triunity of being, three persons-in-community. If God is thus communal in being, the human being created in the divine image cannot be complete as a solitary self. In fact, says Barth, the sexual constitution of the person as either male or female is intrinsic to the image of God. For, there is no abstract masculinity or femininity. Rather, "man is directed to woman and woman to man, each being for the other a horizon and focus . . . , man proceeds from woman and woman from man, each being for the other a center and source. . . . It is always in relationship to their opposite that man and woman are what they are in themselves." [12]

What Barth has done is to make a radical interpretation of Genesis 2:18-25. The deficiency of the solitary individual (Adam) is a basic deficiency. What we need, argues Barth, is more than a companion for life. We need a *complement*—one of the opposite sex with whom to share the meaning of history, and in relation to whom we form a marriage which is always greater than the sum of its parts. The *primal* form of humanity is co-humanity, meaning the covenanted relationship of a man and a woman.

Happily, Barth avoids the sharp nature-grace disjunction and the more obvious gender stereotypes which plague Thielicke's interpretation. And the twofold strengths of Barth's approach are indeed of central importance: that we are created not as solitary selves but as beings-in-relationship, destined for communion; and that sexuality is intrinsic to and not accidental to our capacity for such co-humanity.

There is, however, a major problem. At times Barth admits that marriage is a calling which not everyone receives, but at other times he speaks of marriage as a necessity if we are to realize our humanity. In short, he has failed to keep the distinction between a Christian view of sexuality and a Christian view of marriage. The two are closely related, but they are not one and the same. And Barth's failure at this point implicitly casts a long and unwarranted shadow over the single person and over the one who is homosexually-oriented. Is it possible for them to realize their intended humanity? I believe that it most certainly is and that Barth's direction errs badly in this respect. If the sex role issue is not as obvious in Barth as in Thielicke, it still seems to underlie this problem. Either his interpretation of the image of God makes a woman's humanity crucially dependent upon her husband's masculinity and the husband's upon his wife's femininity, or it makes their humanity dependent upon heterosexual genital intercourse, or both. In so doing, Barth's interpretation subtly but surely rests on either sex role stereotypes or on the genitalization of sexuality, and probably on both. And in so doing it unfortunately has squarely linked the doctrine of the image of God with the *alienated* dimensions of our sexuality.

Derrick Sherwin Bailey, who follows Barth in many respects, also makes the same error when he illustrates the meaning of the Genesis account. He appeals to rabbinic pronouncements to the effect that a person who remains unmarried is "no proper person" since this "diminishes the likeness of God." [13] Nevertheless, this is not Bailey's major emphasis. His approach to marriage is essentially focused on the centrality of the love relationship: "Ethically it is of the utmost importance never to lose sight of the fact that marriage, whatever else it may be, is essentially a personal union of man and woman founded upon love, and sustained and governed by love." [14] Marriage comes into full existence when love is expressed through the public exchange of consent and when the psycho-physical seal of sexual intercourse has been experienced. Its essential nature is love and its one fundamental purpose is unity—that the man and the woman shall become one, creating a common life in which the human sexual duality can find its fullest expression.

Of distinctive importance in Bailey's understanding of marriage is his interpretation of the "one-flesh" union of which the Bible speaks. One-flesh or *henosis*, he maintains, is not identical with marriage but is essential to it. It is the irrevocability of the union of persons established by their sexual intercourse with each other. Ideally, one-flesh occurs in marriage wherein it depends upon the consent of both partners, is based upon responsible love (for each other and for any child which may result), and in which it has the approval of the community. But even when one-flesh is experienced "falsely," as in non-marital sex or rape, it is always irrevocable. "Sexual intercourse is an act of the whole self which affects the whole self; it is a personal encounter between man and woman in which each does something to the other, for good or for ill, which can never be obliterated. This remains true even when they are ignorant of the radical character of their act." [15]

When intercourse takes place in a loving marriage it has several qualities and results: it expresses gratitude to God for creation; it is a means of communication more adequate than speech; through it the couple come to understand the meaning of their masculinity and femininity; and intercourse is always an accurate reflection of the whole relationship which the couple has. But when people have intercourse as merely pleasurable, sensual indulgence apart from permanent commitment, "they merely enact a hollow, ephemeral, diabolical parody of marriage which works distintegration in the personality and leaves behind a deeply-seated sense of frustration and dissatisfaction—though this may never be brought to the surface of consciousness and realized." [16] Once done, it can never be undone. "If they are husband and wife, their act is an act and a promise of love . . . a distillation and concentration of the meaning of their common life—or so it should be if they are growing in knowledge of what marriage really is. But in prostitution or casual fornication man and woman equally declare their true nature, and become united in common irresponsibility and mutual exploitation . . . [and] continual treatment of human beings as a means of self-gratification eventually impairs the capacity for true relation of any kind." [17]

I find Bailey's strong emphasis upon love as the central meaning of marriage well taken. Marriage is not centrally a union of two "natures" but of two *persons;* it is a personal relationship whose meaning is love. And, in spite of his occasional slip, Bailey's treatment gives considerable weight to the egalitarian character of the relationship between woman and man. Furthermore, his interpersonal approach opens him to the possibility of marriage as a context for salvation—it is a significant arena in which God's life-giving, renewing and healing work goes on. It is not simply an order of preservation against the chaos of the world.

In his understanding of intercourse, Bailey is obviously concerned about the dangers of trivializing sex. Yet his exposition of the meaning of one-flesh is not without its difficulties. That intercourse is intended to involve and affect the whole self, I fully agree. That persistent misuse of intercourse in casual and selfish ways damages one's capacities for authentic personal relationships, I have no doubt. But whether each act of intercourse actually does something *irrevocable* to the self and the partner quite apart from the meanings they attach to it is another matter. To press this as far as Bailey seems to do is, curiously enough, to endanger the distinctly *human* nature of sexuality, which he profoundly wishes to protect.

Human sexuality is a primary mode of expressing personal meaning. Body and spirit are essentially one. If it is a dualistic error to think that my bodily actions are merely incidental and that only my consciously-intended meanings count (a form of spiritualism, I should think), it is also a dualism to locate meaning in the physical act quite independently of intentions and feelings (a subtle form of biologism toward which I fear Bailey tends on this issue). Moreover, when one begins to speak of "irrevocability," the implication is strong that the mistakes we have made in the use of our sexual powers are effectively beyond God's healing power. This is an implication foreign to a theology of incarnate grace.

Norman Pittenger's interpretation of marriage, like that of Bailey, rests strongly upon the centrality of love—now, however, interpreted from the stance of process theology. Persons are dynamic and not static entities, human becomings more than human beings. The image of God in the self is the capacity for love, the capacity to become more fully shaped into the love which is God's own essence. As embodied selves our sexuality cannot be divorced from our capacity to love, and in the marriage of a man and a woman we have the usual way in which the relationship of embodied love is known and expressed most completely. "The uniting of man and woman in marriage has made possible an approved way to develop those qualities of love upon which we have insisted, the giving-and-receiving relationship, the mutuality, etc., are all given a setting which makes it much easier to grow in them towards fulfillment. . . . Sexuality so conceived has been raised by Christian instinct to the level of a sacrament of the church. This was not by accident. By some deep insight the Christian church saw how such a sexual relationship could be, and was, a token of God's presence as Love." [18]

The conception and birth of another human being, Pittenger claims, discloses the depths of meaning in human sexuality. It is *pro*-creation, creation on behalf of another, God. It is the fecundity of love and a manifestation of divine Charity. Though a great blessing, the procreation of children is not essential to marriage's validity. But sexual intercourse is, because the church has recognized "that a full union, a giving of oneself entirely to another self who gives in return, must of necessity include the body as well as the mind." [19] Thus, marriage is the intimate and faithful communion of two covenanted and embodied persons. What is distinctive about this relationship compared to other types of human relationships, is that through its promises and through the radical and intimate self-giving and receiving a sacramental quality emerges—a distinctive participation in the divine Love.

Pittenger's approach to marriage is helpful both in what it affirms and in what is left open. Love is utterly central. Its sexual expression is necessary, and love's fidelity is intrinsic to the union. As an Anglican he speaks with conviction of the sacramental quality of marriage. It is a decisive human arena in which the healing and humanizing love of God is encountered. Yet, it is not the only sort of human relationship in which this is possible. Nor are gender role and sex identity as such intrinsic to the covenant of grace. It is the person-in-communion, the self-as-lover who is in the image of God, not the male-female relationship as such. This has important implications for an androgynous heterosexual marriage, I believe, and it is clearly essential if single persons and same-sex covenantal unions are to be woven into the same theological fabric which includes a theology of marriage.

The Voices of Change

Theologies of marriage such as those depicted above have had a considerable impact upon the mind of the church. Thus, one representative Protestant denominational statement adopted in recent years makes these affirmations: "Christian faith affirms marriage as a covenant of fidelity—a dynamic, life-long commitment of one man and one woman in a personal and sexual union. . . . Marriage is not simply a legal transaction which can be broken when the conditions under which it was entered no longer exist. It is an unconditional relationship, a total commitment based on faithful trust. This union embodies God's loving purpose to create and enrich life. . . . Marriage is ordained by God as a structure of the created order. Thus the sanction of civil law and public recognition are important and beneficial in marriage, as checks against social injustice and personal sin. . . . The relationship between husband and wife is likened in Ephesians 5:21-23 to the relationship between Christ and the church. This depicts a communion of total persons, each of them living for the other. As with the covenant between Christ and the church, the promise of fidelity is fundamental. Therefore, Christians regard marriage as a primary setting in which to live out their calling from the Lord." [20]

While this statement undoubtedly reflects much current Christian conviction, it is clear that the mind of the church is far from unanimous. In recent years Christians as well as humanists have begun to indict "traditional monogamy" on a variety of counts: its wedding to the nuclear family form; its failure to meet the growth needs of partners through its inherent possessiveness; its propensity toward continuing sexual inequality; its cultivation of a vivid sense of failure when one partner cannot meet all of the other's needs or when the relationship itself must be terminated.

A brief look at four representative "voices" (in two instances the writings are by couples) will give a fuller picture of these arguments. In each case the writer identifies with the church.

Ronald Mazur charges that many of the assumptions underlying traditional monogamy are unproven. "For too long, traditional moralists have been passively allowed to preempt other conscientious life-styles by propagating the unproven assumptions that we cannot love more than one person (of the opposite sex) concurrently; that co-marital or extramarital sex always destroys a marriage; that 'good' marriages are totally self-contained and self-restrictive and sufficient; that only emotionally unstable people seek and need intimate relationships outside the husband-wife bond." [21] Mazur affirms the value of life-long commitment to one other person in a primary marriage relationship, but also affirms the possibility and often the desirability of enriching secondary relationships. The latter will have varying degrees of emotional and sexual intimacy, and will be engaged in openly and honestly with care that the primary relationship is not jeopardized. This is "open-ended marriage."

Anna K. and Robert T. Francoeur advocate essentially the same thing, but place their analysis of traditional and new marital forms in the framework of a cultural interpretation—the movement from "hot sex" to "cool sex." [22] Their labels (vivid if somewhat misleading) parallel some of the distinctions which I have made between alienated and reconciled sexuality. Hot sex attitudes (still dominant in our society) are patriarchal, genitally-focused, possessive, and performance-obsessed. The cool sex orientation (now making its inroads) affirms the equality of the partners, integration rather than competition and conquest, sexuality experienced as diffused sensuality, an emphasis upon unique personalities and needs, and a tolerance for a pluralism of marital forms. "We are convinced," they write, "that the one-to-one male-to-female marriage is here to stay. We are also firmly convinced of the distinct value of long-term commitments and relationships. . . . But the common American myth of romantic exclusive monogamy, which originally developed as an adaptation to an environment that no longer exists, has to yield to a more functional pattern." [23] Marriages in the new pattern will create their own intentionally-extended "family" of supporting intimate relationships, built upon commitment to open communication, open companionship, and trust.

Rustum and Della Roy argue very similarly: "our theory demands that we seek to maximize the number of deep relationships and to develop marriages to fit in with a framework of community." [24] Like the others, they seek to expand marriage's intimate and erotic community. They go beyond the others, however, in advocating several institutional changes. Premarital intercourse and cohabitation should be publicly and ecclesiastically accepted for engaged couples, with the provision that no children are to be conceived. An aggressive attempt to incorporate single persons within the total life of a family should be encouraged. The divorce system should be overhauled to make marital termination much less destructive for the two parties. Given the disparity in the sex ratio, polygamy and polyandry should be legalized. And the marriage service should be changed, not to water down the couple's commitments, but to expand them.[25]

John Snow makes a useful distinction between "passive-adaptive" and "counter-culture" patterns in the changing marital scene.[26] The passive-adaptive pattern is oriented around individual fulfillment and, possibly, hedonism. Such marriages frequently do not really become part of one's identity. They are active in regard to the concern for self-improvement, but passive in relationship to the culture which is regarded as corrupt but essentially unchangeable. The counter-culture marriages, in their diverse forms, have in common an ideological revolt against the current economic-political system of the society. If the intentionality or commitment in the passive-adaptive marriage is to personal growth, in the counter-cultural marriage it is more typically to an ideology.

Snow argues for a third and more Christian alternative: marriages which "are open in the sense of being hospitable, generous, and socially concerned. They do not regard themselves as little islands of intimacy in competition with the world for survival, but as part of a community concerned with the redemption and renewal of that world for whom Christ became incarnate, suffered, died, and rose again." [27] Such marriages are not to be found in the typical model of the nuclear family, the famous "togetherness" family. "But the church must give much more thought to what should take its place, and perhaps less attention to the futile task of trying to hold it together." [28]

These, then, are some of the voices of change, in varying ways all advocating expansion of the emotional and intimacy bonds of the traditional marriage and family model. Before engaging in some theological-ethical reflection on such possibilities, it will be helpful to review the conclusions of one of the leading sociologists of marriage. Jessie Bernard, in her thorough and balanced study, *The Future of Marriage,* maintains that marriage, indeed, has a future in our society, for men and women will continue to want and need the lasting bonds of intimacy and mutual support; they will desire children, and a supportive, stable environment for their nurture. "Still," she adds, "I do not see the traditional form of marriage retaining its monopolistic sway. I see, rather, a future of marital options." [29] Traditional marriage will remain one of the options for many people, but there will be others, options that permit different types of relationships for different stages of life, and different living arrangements according to the nature of the relationships.

Are there intrinsic limits to the forms of marriage, limits imposed by human nature or by the nature of society? If these exist, claims Bernard, they are difficult to find. Will future marriages be any happier? Bernard disclaims any sanguine optimism, yet maintains that marital behavior, generally, is improving. We have a revolution of rising expectations. "We do not tolerate today forms of marital behavior that were matter-of-fact in the past. . . ." [30] She concludes that there is no final solution. "There will never be an ultimate or last in the sense of final form of marriage. It will go on changing as the times and the people change and as the demands on it change. There is no Ideal Marriage fixed in the nature of things . . . . We are only now getting used to the idea that any form of marriage is always transitional between an old one and a new one." [31] Now, however, things are changing much more rapidly than before.

Sociological estimates of what is or what will be should not be confused with moral judgments concerning what ought to be. While the ethical process, as I have argued, should always give serious attention to all relevant data, there still is a basic difference between facts and values. Thus, no sociologist's prognosis, however carefully researched, equals a Christian (or any other sort of) ethical conclusion. In the face of considerable anxiety about change, however, I believe it needs reiteration that no single form of institutional life on earth, marital or otherwise, ought to be considered final. The sabbath was made for people and not vice versa. The form or forms which marriage takes ought always to be congruent with the authentic needs of persons—not with their shortsighted or superficial desires, but surely with their needs as persons in the process of becoming that which God intends for humanity.

What Is Fidelity?

This is not the place for analysis of the many and complex issues suggested above. But one particular question claims attention. It threads its way through each of the position statements on marriage, both those of a more traditional nature and those urging change: what is fidelity?

We have already seen how the usual definition of marital fidelity in now being challenged. To summarize, it is argued that possessiveness of an emotional and possibly a genital sort is a major detriment to the marital relationship. Thus, a distinction must be made between "infidelity" and "adultery." Adultery has a straightforward meaning: sexual intercourse with someone other than one's spouse. Infidelity, on the other hand, is the rupture of the bonds of faithfulness, honesty, trust, and commitment between spouses. On the positive side, the argument goes, fidelity is the enduring commitment to the spouse's well-being and growth. It is commitment to the primacy of the marital relationship over any other. Compatible with marital fidelity and supportive of it can be certain secondary relationships of some emotional and sensual depth, possibly including genital intercourse. Perhaps a useful approach toward clarifying the meaning of fidelity is to examine the arguments pro and con regarding sexual exclusiveness in marriage. We begin with its defense.

First, there are biblical and traditional warrants against adultery. It is condemned in the Decalogue (Exodus 20:14), elsewhere in the Old Testament (for example, Deuteronomy 22:22), and Jesus repeats that condemnation (Mark 10:19). While in the moving account of the woman taken in adultery, Jesus showed deep compassion and forgiveness, he also instructed her to "sin no more" (John 8:1-11). To be sure, the Old Testament suggests at numerous points a double standard: the wife is regarded as her husband's property, and only *her* adultery is a violation of property rights. Nevertheless, this cannot be attributed to Jesus' teaching on the issue. Indeed, the manner in which he radicalized the condemnation of adultery to include lust is evidence that he was without ambiguity on this matter. And the weight of Christian tradition sustains this position.

The radical nature of sexual intercourse would seem to justify its exclusive confinement within marriage. This argument usually rests on an interpretation of Paul's concept of one-flesh, as in Bailey's understanding of the irrevocable bond established between any sex partners. Others argue similarly. Dwight Hervey Small contends, "In becoming one-flesh a couple participates in that unity which cannot be reversed ontologically. . . . There is no reversing the knowledge of the shared secret. . . . Two human beings who have shared the sex act can no longer act toward one another as if they had not done so. The unity achieved transcends the biological domain." [32] Because the sex act is radical it in some way involves the whole person, for good or ill. Psychological opinion can buttress this judgment as Karl Menninger's statement does: "It is an axiom in psychiatry that a plurality of direct sexual outlets indicates the very opposite of what it is popularly assumed to indicate. Dividing the sexual interest into several objectives diminishes the total sexual gratification." [33]

Further, it can be argued that marital sexual exclusiveness in Christian understanding recapitulates the symbol of God's faithfulness, the bond between Christ and the church. To break the former constitutes an unfaithful denial of the latter.

While the argument for the intrinsic unity of the two functions of intercourse, the unitive and the procreative, is not a typically Protestant argument, some make that case as does Paul Ramsey.[34] Even if we believe in birth control and hope for the completely safe contraceptive, he contends, the procreative dimension ought never be sundered from the inherent meaning of coition. If such separation is made in the minds and hearts of the parties concerned, no respect is paid and no honor is given to the fact that God has joined these two functions together in our being. When one person engages in sex with another with whom he or she would not want to have a child (if such were ever to happen), the two engage in a new form of body-mind dualism, denying the sexual body as procreative. "To put radically asunder what God joined together in making love procreative, to procreate without love or to attempt to establish a relation of sexual love beyond the sphere of marriage, means a refusal of the image of God's creation in our own." [35]

In addition to those arguments for sexual exclusiveness because of something inherent in the nature of the act itself, there are arguments based upon probable consequences. Adultery hurts people. When it is deceptive, it is "bound to corrode all of the honest and fragile personal responses of the married partners; behind everything the partners say and do with each other in intimacy lurks the charade carried on outside," contends Lewis Smedes.[36] Even if it happens in an open marriage where there is no deception, the spouse left out of this relationship is bound to feel rejection. One of the sexual relationships is bound to be neglected, and it will probably be the marriage. And, because of the corrosive effect upon the marital relationship there will be harmful consequences for any children in the family and for society itself which depends upon marital strength for the soundness of the communal life.

The argument concerning consequences moves from the negative to the positive in Daniel Day Williams: "It is the protection, guidance, and release of the power to love in all the human ways, and the power to give love to God and the neighbor, which justifies the restraints, disciplines and prohibitions in the Christian ideal of the union of man and woman . . . [The person] bears the image of God as . . . power to enter an enduring, mutually supportive community which incorporates suffering constructively since self-giving always involves suffering. Love disciplines itself for love's sake." [37]

Let us turn to the other case—the possibility of non-exclusive sexual fidelity. One of the arguments, we have seen, is that unrealistic and impossible demands are placed on monogamy in today's society. The nuclear family model has carried with it an image of marriage as an encapsulated sphere, hermetically sealed from relationships of emotional depth with those outside it. But it is both unrealistic and unfair to expect that one person can always meet the partner's companionate needs—needs which are legitimate and not merely individualistic, hedonistic, or egocentric. If the gospel truly invites us to the greatest possible realization of human capacity in interdependence with others, then marriage ought to be open to precisely that.

Women, many have noted, have particularly suffered from the traditional definition of monogamy. Thus Rosemary Ruether writes, "Monogamy has especially atrophied the personal development of women who were expected to get their entire emotional feedback through a relationship to a single man while he in turn developed his personality through a multiplicity of friendships, business relationships, and even sex relationships." [38]

Personal growth for either wife or husband may well require intimate friendships beside that with the partner. This does not necessarily mean transmarital sexual intimacy. The important thing is interpersonal emotional intimacy, but intercourse cannot be arbitrarily excluded. James Ramey argues that "intimate friendship is built on the philosophy of open acceptance of *potential* sexual intimacy rather than on sexual involvement, per se." [39] On the basis of his study of open marriages he states, "Respondents often report that sex is unimportant in their relationships, relatively speaking, but that they couldn't have had such deep and meaningful friendships without the potential of sexual intimacy." [40]

That such secondary relationships can serve not only personal growth but also and at the same time serve the marriage itself is an insistence of many. Raymond J. Lawrence, an Episcopal chaplain and marriage counselor, observes that the transmarital sexual relationship will be an unfaithful act when done for inappropriate motives and intentions such as revenge upon one's spouse or reassurance of one's own attractiveness. In such instances, the person does not become involved with the other for the sake of communicating and relating intimately, but rather is using the other for ulterior purposes. But, he claims, the refusal to open oneself to a secondary sexual relationship can also be based upon inappropriate reasons. An emotionally immature, religiously self-proving desire for purity and innocence might be one. Another might be the resistance to sufficient autonomy and the persistence in a clinging dependency upon the spouse—which is different from mature interdependency. Indeed, he argues, the high degree of intimacy possible in a good marriage seems to depend in no small measure upon the relative absence of possessiveness and clinging dependency.[41]

Given current pressures on marriages, it is argued that the choice for many couples might well be between sexual exclusivity and marital permanence—and the latter is the greater value. Jessie Bernard comments, "If we insist on permanence, exclusivity is harder to enforce; if we insist on exclusivity, permanence may be endangered. The trend . . . seems to be in the direction of exclusivity at the expense of permanence in the younger years but permanence at the expense of exclusivity in the later years." [42]

Rosemary Ruether presses this further. Historically, she notes, monogamy has been closely linked with the private property relationship of man over woman in the patriarchal society. And while the church preached a single standard of exclusive sexual fidelity, in many ways it acceded to the double standard. In the modern period, however, the notion of romantic marriage has demanded not only sexual exclusivity but also lifelong companionship and sexual satisfaction. Ruether wonders if we have not lifted up the wrong priority by apparently prizing sexual exclusivity over enduring, intimate companionship and personal fidelity. We might have more of the latter if we were not so insistent as a church upon the former. "What really is the value that society wishes to preserve most? Is it sexual exclusivity, especially when divorce and remar-

riage turn this into a serial exclusivity? Or is it not long-term commitment, both for personal support and friendship and for secure
child-raising that can provide stable parental figures for the
new generation?" [43]

Both explicit and implicit in these arguments then is an understanding of fidelity which contains several elements: it is a commitment of emotional and physical intimacy with the partner; it means
caring for the growth and fulfillment of each as a person; it is commitment to the growth of the marital relationship itself; it requires
honesty, openness, and trust; it involves willingness to explore ways
of opening the self to the partner at the deepest possible level, risk-
ing the pains that may come; it includes openness to secondary
relationships of emotional intimacy and potential genital expression,
but with commitment to the primacy of the marriage.[44]

We have heard the arguments on both sides. Where are we left?
First, I believe that the case of those who would reinterpret the
traditional meanings of fidelity and monogamy ought not be too
quickly dismissed. Some will be inclined to reject it out of hand as
mere faddish self-indulgence. Some will claim that it simply reflects
fear of genuine commitment—as in Oscar Wilde's words: "the only
difference between a caprice and a lifelong passion is that the
caprice lasts a little longer." [45] But given the gospel's bias toward
judging both acts and institutional forms by their capacity to further human wholeness, the case deserves serious consideration.
There are simply too many couples today who are sincerely struggling to find more meaningful kinds of marriages.

It is true that sincerity alone is not sufficient grounds, however.
Thus another look at the main arguments raised against the rein-
terpretation of fidelity is warranted.

It will be countered that any understanding of fidelity which
does not insist upon genital exclusiveness flies in the face of Jesus'
words about adultery and lust. However (and this is seldom
noticed or emphasized), his teaching about lust in the Sermon on
the Mount applies to any and every potential object of that emotion
—*one's own spouse included.* Lust is not simply erotic attraction. It
has elements of the idolatrous, for it is overwhelming and inordinate
sexual craving. It is incompatible with the greatest of all commandments, that we love God alone with the whole heart. And because

of that it is incompatible with the authentic love of any other person and is rightly seen as an adultery of the heart.[46]

What of the one-flesh arguments? Their insistence upon the seriousness of sexual intercourse is well taken, as I have already indicated. Genital sex has great potential power for affecting personhood and the capacity for interpersonal communion. And if it is used simply for physical sensations, then we do have a new body-spirit dualism—this time a "physicalism" rather than the spiritualistic heresy. But to warn against the trivialization of sex and to insist on its seriousness is quite different from the questionable insistence that any act of intercourse creates an irrevocable ontological bond.

The more serious concern is whether *persons* are trivialized. Those on both sides of the present issue are concerned about this. The human symbol of God's faithfulness to us is our faithfulness to other people. Enduring marital fidelity is surely a key—perhaps *the* key—enactment of that symbol on the part of any who are called to marriage. If under the present strains upon marriages in the nuclear family pattern, the choice does become that between genital exclusivity and enduring lifelong commitment, I think a case can be made for the latter.

But need this be the choice? For many, surely not. Yet it is grossly unfair simply to dismiss those who find themselves facing this choice as individualistic and immature. To face and to make that choice in favor of permanence can also express substantial concern for parental stability, an appropriate family environment for child nurture, and the place of marital and family stability in a viable society. (The argument in favor of permanence, however, should never become a rigidity about divorce. Some marriages do become unbearably destructive, and of all persons Christians should be able to admit mistakes, to seek forgiveness, and undertake new beginnings in such painful circumstances.)

Does a sexually non-exclusive interpretation of fidelity break God's intended union of the "unitive" and "procreative" dimensions of intercourse? The argument has been made that even when contraception is used one must be able to say, "If something happens, you are the one with whom I would want to have the resultant child." While there is a certain persuasiveness to this argument, it becomes misleading. The real issue, I believe, is whether the unitive function of intercourse is primary and the procreative secondary, or whether they are essentially co-equal (even when the procreative is deliberately frustrated). I have argued that the primary purpose is communion, the unitive function. When people deliberately intend to prevent conception (which is the case in most Protestant *and* Catholic marriages in well over ninety-nine percent of their times of intercourse), it appears that they also are affirming communion's primacy. Indeed, if the two functions were co-equal in God's design, it would appear that the use of contraceptive methods would have an invidious, detrimental effect upon the unitive impact of intercourse (whether or not conception actually occurred). But for the great majority this does not seem experientially true; in fact, it is precisely the opposite. It is the fear of an unwanted pregnancy which can inhibit the mutual enrichment and spontaneous self-giving of sexual communion.

In light of these considerations, then, I believe that the case for the redefinition of marital fidelity cannot be summarily dismissed. Openness to the *possibility* that this might reflect a viable Christian marriage for some, then, I think is appropriate.

My second concern, however, is one of caution, and for several reasons. Sexuality, indeed, is an inevitable component of all interpersonal relations. And it is not the case that genital exclusivity in marriage necessarily means that other friendships must, for that reason, be devoid of sensual warmth and emotional depth. Nor must genital exclusivity mean the possessive "ownership" of the partner. It can be—and frequently is—reflective of the kind of commitment from which emerges a genuine sense of freedom.

Further, the empirical evidence concerning the effects (especially the long-range effects) of sexually non-exclusive fidelity is very limited at present. While a surprising number of persons now write positive testimonies from their own experience, the wider picture has many unknowns.[47]

Again, the possibilities of "sexual sanctification" are relevant to this issue. Growth in sensuousness, for instance, can mean greater diffusion of sexual feeling throughout the body and throughout the self's relationships. With the diminishing genital focus for one's sexuality, it is conceivable that the desire for genital expression outside of marriage might be lessened. Growth in androgyny, too, might coincide with sexual exclusiveness, since many instances of extramarital sex seem linked with the desire to reinforce one's sexual self-esteem as either "masculine" or "feminine." [48]

In spite of reconciliation and growth, alienated dimensions of our lives do persist. As Luther frequently reminded us, we are *simul justus et peccator.* If law can be a servant of the gospel, and rules a servant of wholeness, for most of us the better rule is marital genital exclusivity. But, I would argue, this rule (as is any other) is a "presumptive" rule which can admit exceptions. If the exception is admitted, the burden of proof must be borne—that this sexual sharing realistically promises to enhance and not damage the capacity for interpersonal fidelity and personal wholeness.

Marriage indeed has a future. And its forms will change. What is frequently called "traditional Christian marriage" itself is a product of historical development, and it is not as old as is often believed. Yet it has served many well and doubtless will continue to do so. But the future will likely be marked by plurality more than uniformity in marital forms.

Nevertheless, I believe that as marital forms take their shape from the reality of God's incarnate love there will be certain characteristics and distinctive qualities about them. They will be covenants—and not simply contracts. They will be enduring covenants —pledges of ongoing faithfulness to the well-being and growth of each partner. They will be covenants of intimacy—in which eros is undergirded, infused, and transformed by agape. They will be sacramental covenants—whether or not officially sacraments of the church, they will yet be those unique arenas in which the healing and humanizing love of God is vividly experienced. And they will be covenants which, in one way or another, genuinely enlarge the partners' capacity for communion with others and expand their willingness to be part of God's work of giving new life and renewal to the world.

7

The Morality of Sexual Variations

Sex and the Unmarried

SINCE THE AGE-OLD CONSTRAINTS against premarital intercourse—fear of pregnancy, disease, and religious disapproval—have eroded for many people, and because the eroticized patina of our society seems to nurture permissive attitudes, the assumption is widespread that we are now in the midst of a radically new era marked by "liberated" sexual expression among the unmarried. That assumption is not quite correct. True, there has been some increase in intercourse among single persons in recent decades, but the notion of a dramatic behavioral change is somewhat misleading.

Historical records reveal, for example, that in a well-known Massachusetts congregation in the late eighteenth century one out of every three women about to be married confessed fornication to her minister. In those instances, the woman was usually pregnant, for without such confession at the time of marriage the "premature" baby could not be baptized. It is likely that many other nonvirginal but nonpregnant young women made no such confession and hence were not counted in the church records.[1]

The historical picture of male nonvirginity in America is even more extreme. The western frontier, for example, was not typically a place of continence in the unmarried young man. Beyond our own society, the scene seems no different. A leading family sociologist draws this conclusion: "I have examined the historical and cross-cultural record rather closely and have found no society, at any time in history, in which the majority of even one generation of its males remained virginal on reaching maturity—say age twenty or so. The reason is very likely that since males are in power in almost all societies, it is unlikely that they would structure the societal system so as to deny themselves access to sexual pleasures before marriage." [2]

If behavior has not changed as dramatically as sometimes assumed, there has been a noticeable *attitudinal* change. The double standard between the sexes is waning among the unmarried, and "permissiveness with affection" is an increasingly accepted norm. Yet, the issues of premarital sex are not simple ones.

Scriptural direction itself has some ambiguity. The commandment "Thou shalt not commit adultery" was not largely interpreted by the Israelites as applying to intercourse between the unmarried. When that practice was condemned, the disfavor fell upon the fact that the woman's virginity was lost—a violation of her prospective husband's property rights. We have no record of specific words from Jesus on the matter, though the basic value of human dignity in sexual relations is utterly clear in his thought. Paul's vigorous condemnation of prostitution seems to represent for him every form of depersonalized sexual activity, but the *porneia* he censured was not clearly directed at premarital intercourse as such. Yet there is no question but that Paul, in his one-flesh interpretation, understood that the created intention of the sex act is to join inseparably the ones who participate in it together. In short, the Bible assists us with general perspectives but not with specific injunctions. If the Old Testament is specific about the sexual violation of property rights and about idolatrous and cultic intercourse, and if the New Testament is specific about prostitution, adultery, and incest, neither gives highly concrete guidance on premarital sex—even though their basic theological perspectives are perennially relevant.

There is little question but that traditional Christian teaching has very largely insisted that intercourse be reserved for marriage. Two of the basic reasons claimed are ones which we have looked at in some detail in the previous chapter. First is the insistence that God has joined the two major purposes of intercourse together, the unitive and the procreative, and any sundering of these violates the sex act and dishonors the Creator. "It is not (even in Catholic thought) necessary that every act of intercourse be directed towards conception, but the act is only justified within the context of a relationship which can, if necessary, provide the resources for the nurture and education of a child." [3]

The second reason centers upon the radical nature of the unitive dimension itself: the one-flesh perspective. As this applies to premarital intercourse, these are representative statements: "If it is true that sexual intercourse mediates a unique kind of personal knowledge, it is clear that a very special status must be given to the first experience of the sexual act. . . . The first sexual experience is so overwhelming and so different from any other experience that it is better reserved as a means of symbolizing and giving meaning to marriage." [4] "Before marriage, even in the most sincere and honest engagement, neither is fully and objectively responsible for the other: after it they are legally, socially and personally committed. They are no longer independent centers of action but 'one flesh,' sharing all their possessions and potentialities, all their trials and tribulations. Should not the ultimate intimacy of the body be the expression of this ultimate commitment of the person?" [5]

Linked with these central arguments about the nature and created intention of intercourse, additional considerations of consequences can be raised—consequences which are possible, probable, or even inevitable in nonmarital sex. Unwanted pregnancies regularly occur in spite of the availability of reliable contraception. Venereal disease still occurs and is of epidemic proportions among some sectors of the population. And because of the profound nature of the act, it changes the relationship of a couple—disrupting them emotionally and perhaps pushing them prematurely toward responsibilities for which they are not ready. And if the clear intent of the act is only pleasure and release, it hardens the sensitivities and contributes to the split in the body-self—the body becomes the pleasure machine.

While these are representative considerations from the more traditional orientation on premarital sex, one additional point must be made. Intercourse for the engaged couple constitutes a special theological-ethical issue. The distinction can be made between the internal, existential bond of marriage and its external manifestations before society. Before the modern bourgeois notion of marital respectability arrived on the scene, Christian tradition was clear that the ceremony of marriage itself never "married" anyone. Only the couple themselves—in their clearly-intended permanent covenant— have the power to do this. If so, it can be argued that the engaged couple who have intercourse are already married (though without ceremony) since covenant plus physical consummation equals marriage. Presumably this would satisfy the major concerns which locate intercourse appropriately only in marriage, for since marriage is a process there may well come a time prior to the public wedding when intercourse fittingly seals the couple's commitment to each other.

Yet, most theologians who defend the traditional position are uneasy about this conclusion. It devalues the importance of the church and the wider society as supportive communities for the marriage. It can place too much importance on sexual intimacy for the engaged couple and lead to wider concessions by the non-engaged. In short, if they *are* essentially married, why don't they say so? As Paul Ramsey argues, "It is hard to imagine why in this case they should not proclaim to all the world, or at least to their parents, what they mean to mean from now on to one another; or why they do not (as we err in saying) 'get married' according to ceremony, the legalities, and in accord with the respectabilities." [6]

These arguments upholding the reservation of intercourse to marriage represent serious concerns and important values which ought not to be lightly dismissed. Yet, the case is overstated when it is absolutized. I believe that Richard Hettlinger is right when he raises several pertinent questions: Does at least some of the concern about premarital virginity mask the feeling that sex is inherently suspect? Is "technical virginity" more responsible, more moral? And does the restriction of intercourse to marriage actually make happier, more durable, more fulfilling marriages? [7]

If we wrestle with questions such as these, we are once again expanding the criteria for ethical evaluation far beyond the primary emphasis upon the nature of the act itself. We are asking questions of meaning and context, questions about motives, intentions, and consequences. And these must be asked.

For example, how do we compare technical virginity with "every-thing-else-except" types of sexual expression? Petting to orgasm provides sexual release and can be a deeply intimate experience, emotionally as well as physically. Is it radically different from full intercourse? If so (and it may be so), why? If it is argued that the procreative dimension is present in full intercourse but not in pet-ting to climax, that is not fully accurate—conception *can* occur without actual penile entrance. Or is it orgasm (and regarding pos-sible procreative results, particularly male ejaculation) that is the dividing line? And if that is so, is non-orgasmic genital caressing permissible? Such questions as these are not beside the point. They press us to take seriously the meanings and the emotional and inter-personal significance of various forms of circumstances of sexual behavior.

Or, does premarital virginity promote better marriages? It is an important empirical question for sexual ethics. And the present evidence is quite unclear. On one side claims are made that pre-marital sex jeopardizes subsequent marital trust and thus hinders emotional adjustment in marriage. On the other side there is some evidence that premarital coitus is favorable to better marital sexual adjustment and to that extent frees the couple for more effective coping with the myriad other adjustments which they must make to each other.

We are driven back, I believe, to the concept of diffused sexual-ity or, perhaps, "total body sexuality." An extreme focus upon geni-tality more frequently marks sexual alienation than it signifies sexual wholeness. If intercourse is seen in the context of total body sexual-ity, then different types of intimacy are appropriate for different types of relationships and for different levels of communication. Surely, even a gentle kiss can be inappropriate and false. It is not a negative issue of eroticism which is at stake, but the positive issue of human integrity and growth toward wholeness. Christianly speaking, then, it becomes imperative to ask: given the potentially profound meaning of genital intercourse and the divine intention that it be used for human fulfillment most richly defined, in *this* relationship and context is this a faithful act consonant with God's presence and purposes?

To put the matter this way and thus leave open the possibility that there *may* be morally-justifiable acts of intercourse before marriage is vastly different from an endorsement of "recreational sex" or "fun-sex" (whose advocates are not difficult to find). The latter perpetuates the self's alienation. Body is instrument. Sex is divorced from the love which is central to its meaning. Psychologically speaking, there appears to be a direct connection between emotional maturity, on the one hand, and the wedding of sexual expression to love, tenderness, and relational depth, on the other. Sometimes sexual promiscuity is rationalized on the grounds of the need for change, for excitement, and for the freedom to enjoy uninhibited pleasure. On closer examination, however, the promiscuous person frequently turns out to be lonely, anxious, unable to form close relationships, and unable to feel safe on a truly personal, intimate level with others.[8] But again, I would contend, the image of God is never utterly defaced in any of us—sexually or otherwise. In their strange way, the actions of even the most wildly promiscuous individual are remnants of a residual health: they are the restless cries for embodied love, needing more than the church's condemnation— needing healing of the wounds of emotional and spiritual deprivation and release from the tyrannies of exploitive behavior.

Likewise, the nonpromiscuous but sexually-experimenting youth need the church's understanding. In late adolescence and not yet in adulthood, they are in a period of needing to loosen the emotional bonds with parents and to make their way in a world which is often an alienating environment. It is not surprising that some who keenly feel the isolation of this time of passage will frequently seek comfort in temporary sexual liaisons.[9]

The focus in the above paragraphs for the most part has been on premarital intercourse. But what of the single adult who does not intend marriage (or remarriage)? Some will choose a life of voluntary celibacy. If this is chosen in sexual self-affirmation and not sexual self-rejection, if this is chosen for the sake of faithful integrity and not in an anxious quest for personal virtue, then such celibacy is to be affirmed and celebrated. This is indeed the case for many religious celibates.

But for those who do not see marriage or remarriage as an expression of their vocation, and yet do not intend the life of complete celibacy, has the church any guidelines to offer? If it does not, and if the church sees that choice only worthy of condemnation, quite predictably some of these people will leave the church behind them. Others will stay, but in the face of churchly condemnation or silence regarding their sexual expression, they may turn to the popular maxims in the culture for guidance, e.g. anything is permissible for "mutually consenting adults."

Rather than this, I believe the church can recognize that a single adult's choice for complete sexual sharing with another will involve risks and responsibilities. And the church can insist that love's evaluative standards ought to apply. The relationship ought to involve genuine commitment to the other. It should have profound respect for the other as a person, a deep caring for the partner's well-being. The relationship should be marked by honesty and the concern for social responsibility. In a word, it should embody openness to life.

Variations in Sexual Expression

In addition to heterosexual genital intercourse, we human beings seem to express ourselves sexually in a rather astounding variety of ways. Homosexuality is one, and its consideration deserves an entire chapter, which will follow this. There are a number of other sexual orientations and expressions less common, which are outside the scope of this book.[10] In the remainder of this chapter, however, we will do well to look at some of the variations more commonly experienced: sexual fantasy, masturbation, oral-genital and anal intercourse, sado-masochism, and the use of deliberately arousing sexual literature. What possible Christian meanings have these?

But first, a word about a word: "variations." It is chosen deliberately. "Deviations" is frequently used in the sexuality literature, but this immediately suggests a prior moral judgment about the act (a deviation from nature or the moral norm) and the actor (a deviant). Granted, this term would be more frequently connected to something like bestiality than to, say, masturbation. Nevertheless, the term has been used at times to brand as inherently evil or at least deficient every form of sexual expression save that of married genital intercourse.

The church itself has not had an enviable record in addressing itself with sensitivity and understanding to sexual variations. Even when variations become destructive and compulsive, we ought to remember how often this is linked to the erotic suppression for which the church must assume its fair share of responsibility. And, for Christians, the sobering fact of the matter is that it was largely people who had repudiated God and the church—Sigmund Freud, Havelock Ellis, and others—who did not repudiate the anxieties of those struggling with such sexual matters.

Even among those students of personal and social behavior who have taken sexual variations seriously there has been a strong tendency to label certain acts as deviant, in either one of two ways.[11] The strong awareness of cultural relativity in anthropologists and sociologists has led them to define sexual deviance within the confines and by the norms of particular societies: deviant sexual behavior is that which offends that particular society. Clinicians, on the other hand, have generally assumed that sexual deviance is intrinsically and universally unorthodox, quite apart from what a given society thinks about it. It is assumed to be a sickness or, at least, a form of immaturity. It is defined as a deflection from "the normal sexual aim," and is assumed to be pathological, guilt-ridden behavior.

While many useful insights have come from such endeavors in personality and social sciences, I believe that we cannot understand sexual variations simply by examining the acts themselves or even the attributes of the one who expresses sexuality in such a way. Nor can we be content simply with what our society (or any other) defines as normal. We need also—and even primarily—to inquire about *meanings*. What meanings is this person attempting to communicate with this behavior, and what theological reflection can we bring to bear on those meanings? And instead of focusing primarily on the question, Why is this individual a "deviant"?, we need to ask just as importantly, What meanings is the group trying to express when it defines this person in this way?

Sexual expression is highly symbolic. Even such "normal" things as variations in positions in heterosexual coitus can be highly symbolic. Some husbands, for example, might find psychic threat in the "woman above" position, so deep is their fear of equality and temporary "subordination." Some men might find rear-entry penile-vaginal intercourse "animalistic" and hence inappropriate for their loved one, particularly when she is viewed as pure in sexual matters.[12]

So, I think we should inquire about the communicative meanings of sexual acts, and that perspective will inform this inquiry into variations. And, I continue to assume that all persons fundamentally desire wholeness and fulfillment, and that they express themselves sexually in ways that they believe will lead to this.

Sexual Fantasy

In general, dreaming and fantasizing are a common part of our lives. Specifically, this is true of sexual fantasy as well, though such is cause for confusion, embarrassment, and suppression in many people. Sexual fantasies delight us. They also can disturb and trouble us.

Such ambivalence seems dramatically illustrated by St. Jerome in the fourth century. Though consciously he had severe anti-sexual convictions and an alarming suspicion about bodily matters, and though he wrote polemical tracts against coitus, this was not the whole story. As his interpretation of the Song of Songs suggests, Jerome was engrossed with sex on a fantasy level. He interpreted the Song as a poem in praise of those virgins who mortify the flesh. Yet, his commentary also promises female virgins that if they detest physical relationships with other men, Jesus will give them sexual stimulation and satisfaction: "Ever let the Bridegroom fondle you. . . . He will put his hand through the opening and will touch your body. And you will arise trembling and cry, 'I am lovesick.' " [13]

As with Jerome, so with us, sexual fantasies stem at least in part from unmet sexual desires. In adolescence this is particularly true, where fantasy is commonly substituted for actual sexual satisfaction. This can be true in the adult, also, and in its more extreme instances sexual fantasies can become linked to whatever else is felt as deprivation. They then become symbolic of the satisfaction of all needs and desires. When this happens, the role of sex becomes exaggerated and an illusion of perfect sexual harmony emerges, a harmony which will usher in happiness to all other areas of life. Regarding this a psychiatrist writes, "Such an enormous burden on the role of sex can make for much anxiety about sexual function. If sexual activity must resolve all of life's problems, then that activity may be approached with trepidation at least equal to that incurred by any other unreal demand for perfect performance." [14]

Fantasy life of any kind, and surely that of the sexual variety, can be escapist. Real life is often difficult, sometimes dull, and frequently provides us with ample frustrations. The sexual dimensions of real life share those same problems. But in fantasy, demands, risks, and disappointments dissolve; satisfactions abound. In their extreme, sexual fantasies can become substitutes for our encounter with real people. When this happens, they turn us increasingly inward upon ourselves and deprive us of genuine interpersonal communion. [15]

But if sexual fantasy has its risks, it also has its very positive functions. Fantasy of any kind is the capacity to suspend reality and to allow the imagination free play. Children are usually adept at this, and the little child can lead us in this way as in others. For children who are of reasonable emotional health, fantasies do not mean loss of touch with the real world. Whatever their make-believe, they remain in touch with their feelings and their bodies. They do not succumb to self-deception. They seem instinctively to know that the fun of fantasy depends on keeping the inner sense of reality intact, regardless of its temporary suspension. [16]

In the adult, sexual fantasy can follow this general pattern. Without damaging escapism it can reawaken our capacities for playfulness—an important ingredient in sexual expression. It can enrich times of intercourse with the beloved not only by enhancing one's own sexual excitement, but also, in shared fantasies, it can create moods of sheer delight together. Fantasy can also allow outlet of a compensatory kind for sexual feelings and desires which our value commitments do not permit us to act out. Paradoxically, it can bring freeing and enriching qualities to the covenanted relationship by refusing to insist that the partner be the sole source of satisfaction for the varied sexual desires one might have.

But this raises the issues of intentionality and responsibility. In the Sermon on the Mount when Jesus pointed to the adultery of the heart, he created a quandary for us about sexual fantasy: "But I say to you that every one who looks at a woman lustfully has already committed adultery with her in his heart" (Matt. 5:28). I assume this applies as well to heterosexual women and to persons of same-sex orientation. But, as I have argued earlier, this teaching condemns *lust*—even when it is directed toward one's covenanted partner. And if lust is untamed, inordinate sexual desire which is not only the passion for *possession* of another but which also becomes, by its very centrality in the self, an expression of *idolatry,* then we are dealing here with something different from the usual erotic awareness expressed in sexual fantasy. I do not believe that this constitutes a watering down or explaining away of this teaching. For, on the other hand, Jesus' words remind us that sexual fantasy points up certain unhealed and alienated dimensions of our own sexuality. At times many of us do fantasize about sex with someone other than the one to whom we have pledged our lasting covenant.

But the dynamics of both sexuality and of grace are such that greater wholeness does not come through the denial of such feelings. In denial the feelings do not dissolve but rather disappear from consciousness into the turbulent emotional underworld, only to be expressed in less salutary ways. Greater wholeness comes through our acceptance of such feelings as part of the reality of who we are, even though we may well choose not to act upon them. Once again, quite paradoxically, the recognition and affirmation of the feelings expressed in such fantasies can contribute to our awareness that sexuality indeed does permeate all of our relationships—and in awareness of this diffusion, the genital tyranny of sex recedes.

The interplay of grace, self-acceptance, and responsibility thus surround a creative response to sexual fantasy. To the extent that we can accept ourselves as accepted, we will not generate self-hate about our sexual desires. Being human entails a vast array of possible feelings, urges, and thoughts, many of which are not largely under our conscious control. Yet, we can also recognize the difference between a desire and an authentic need, and the difference between a thought and an action. We can know that we are responsible for our actions. They should be evaluated in regard to their contribution to genuine human needs and to our promised wholeness. We can also know that the capacity to face even that destructive lust which can arise within is a gift of grace. In facing it rather than denying and suppressing it, the demon is named and disarmed of its harmful powers. But this same grace also permits those more benign sexual fantasies (even when they arise out of our incompleteness and our distortions) to become, strangely enough, instruments of our healing through delight and play.

Erotic and Pornographic Literature

Closely linked with fantasy is the issue of sexually-explicit literature (including graphic portrayals in art and photography). I will not attempt here to deal with the very important public policy questions. Rather, I want to raise the more limited question of the use of such literature in regard to sexual fantasy and excitement.

Definitions are important, and sharp definitions in this area are difficult to make. Nevertheless, a general distinction between *erotically realistic art*, on the one hand, and *pornography*, on the other, is a useful one (even though there may be numerous borderline cases). The distinction does not rest upon the explicitness of sexual portrayal, but rather upon whether sex is portrayed as a distinctly human activity with the full range of human feelings or whether sex is depicted in a much more truncated manner as an activity of lust, of a dehumanizing exercise of power over others, or of simple biological relief. Serious erotic realism can be vivid and explicit in its treatment of sexual themes, but it presents the figures as human beings with their complexities and capacities as persons. Pornography typically views the person as a "sexual animal." [17]

We need to look more closely at the meanings conveyed by pornography. The word itself comes from the Greek: "whore-writing" or descriptions of the activities of whores. Pornography, in both word and picture, is typically geared to male sex fantasies. Usually it is degrading of women, showing them in situations of being used by men for male sexual pleasure.

The psychological and psychiatric interpretations of pornography are illuminating even if they are not always in full agreement with one another. George Frankl attributes such literature's attraction to the numerous fixations and regressions in people. An enormous variety of transformations and displacements of the libido occur during the maturation process, particularly in a libido-negating culture. "The cult of pornography satisfies to a degree the perverse or infantile needs of repressed people, but also keeps intact the taboos upon mature sexual relationships . . . . [it] merely perpetuates the denial of love; it reinforces the sick and distorted sexuality of the man or woman who does not feel accepted." [18]

Charles May makes a similar interpretation, but (given pornography's dominance as a male phenomenon) with an emphasis on the psychodynamics peculiar to men. A man can never be sexually sure of a real woman. He can never really know if she has been sexually aroused by him, nor ever positive that he has given her an orgasm. But he needs this assurance for his own sexual security. So, "he creates one he can be sure of, he creates the fantasy woman, who always is sexually ready and eager—for *him*. Pornography offers a kind of elaborate compensation for male insecurity." [19]

According to John Gagnon and William Simon, pornography is arousing not simply because of sexual explicitness but particularly because it deals with illicit sex. When the desire to depart from one's behavioral values or from a conventional moral posture is strong, pornography offers a useful solution. It represents the illicit and desired acts, but it is easier and safer than acting out the desires. The handling of guilt is much easier and the potential complications much less severe if such sexual variations are experienced vicariously rather than overtly. Further, pornography frequently is used to deal with personal needs which are not specifically sexual in the more limited sense of that word. Thus, the management of dominance and aggression needs which are difficult to express in one's everyday relationships, or coping with attacks upon one's self-esteem and threats to one's sense of power and worth—these seem to be met in some way, at least temporarily, in pornography.[20]

If pornography has dangers, they do not appear to come from its direct excitation to sexual violence, though claims of this sort are frequently heard. One of the most thorough studies of its effects has been made by Michael J. Goldstein and Harold S. Kant. They conclude that sex criminals (rapists and child molesters) actually tend to see less pornography during adolescence than does the average person, and the particularly violent among the sex criminals tend to come from very sexually repressive families.[21] These researchers contend that pornography and erotically realistic art both serve multiple functions. For adolescents such media stimulate the emerging sexual curiosity and provide visual models of the actual "mechanics" of sexual relations—indeed, this is often the only way in which such information is gained. Exposure to such material can serve a cathartic function, providing sexual stimulation and then reduction of sexual tension through subsequent masturbation. For adults the purposes served are somewhat different. "In most heterosexual males, an exciting erotic stimulus (this varies with sexual attitudes and values, well established in adulthood) will provide a momentary boost to the sexual drive, increasing the likelihood of sexual activity if a regular sex partner is available." [22]

In their psychological studies of sex offenders, Goldstein and Kant found that these men were exceptionally ambivalent about sex. Arousal was followed by feelings of disgust and revulsion, the latter usually linked to the anti-sex attitudes found in their earlier home life. Because of this strong ambivalence, pornographic arousal typically did not spur them to express themselves sexually to other persons, but rather to seek relief through masturbation. They conclude, "Erotica, then, does not seem to be a major stimulus for antisocial sexual behavior in the potential sex offender. In fact, there is some evidence . . . that for rapists, exposure to erotica portraying 'normal' heterosexual relations can serve to ward off antisocial sexual impulses." [23]

These conclusions regarding pornography and violence were supported a few years earlier than the above study by the work of the U. S. Commission on Obscenity and Pornography, who also contended that the availability of open, direct, and appropriate sex information provided through legitimate channels would greatly diminish the use of pornography.[24] But psychologist Ernest van Den Haag contends that pornography, especially that material which includes an element of violence, still has a damaging effect: "By de-individualizing and dehumanizing sexual acts, where this becomes impersonal, pornography reduces or removes the empathy and the mutual identity which restrains us from treating each other merely as objects or means." [25] And, one could add, when children are used as subjects in pornographic media, the dangers to them as well as to the users of the material are particularly severe.

A theological evaluation of the use of pornography must begin with the question, What does it appear to communicate to the user? For men, to whom it still makes its major appeal, pornography *seems* to speak to the human needs which arise from sexual alienation. Both forms of dualism are evident and interwoven in this phenomenon. Linguistically speaking, pornography is a description of the activities of whores. And whores by definition are sexual commodities to be purchased by men whose sexual satisfaction is somehow restricted. In a society of patriarchal dualism, "ordinary" women represent sexual inhibition, and whores represent sexual fulfillment. The latter are neither the "virgin" nor the "mother." The man, feeling his sexual urges and also perceiving the definitions and requirements of society, is tempted to split himself in two. He is body (the immoral, non-respectable animal) and he is spirit (the moral and respectable citizen). Through the use of pornography he can at once uphold the purity of "his" woman and vent his animal desires onto the "others." And in a curious yet understandable way, pornography seems to afford relief to men who sense their wholeness dualistically threatened. Alienated from his body, the man finds sexual excitement and arousal reassuring. His body tells him that he is alive. And alienated from true intimacy with women and from "the woman within," he discovers temporary relief by breaking through the stereotypes of virgin and mother, and in breaking these he seems to establish relatedness, at least temporarily.

While pornography still has largely a male orientation and appeal, there now is ample evidence of increasing interest among women. As they stake their claim to being sexual persons in their own right, they become more conscious that they also have split themselves—under male pressure—in two: the good woman (feminine, wife, mother, the one protected from feeling her sexual powers) and the unconscious libertine (who finds her symbol in the pornographic representation of those women who act out what the respectable woman does not).

Pornography has its appeal, I believe, because it promises to relieve, even if momentarily, the dualistic alienation felt within. If its use is not a positive sign of health, which it is obviously not, still the attraction to pornography may be considered a *negative* sign of health. It signifies that even in the midst of the self's alienation the image of God presses the quest for those means which seem to promise reunification. But insofar as the material in question is truly pornographic in the manner earlier defined, its promise is hollow. It cannot heal, for it is an exaggerated representation of the very dualisms which require cure.

Yet it is difficult to make a blanket judgment about the morality of all erotica. Surely there is much in erotically realistic art, both literary and visual, which is immensely valuable. Some of it aids us in celebrating the goodness of our created sexuality. Some of it helps us better to understand human sexual pain—and that which we ourselves know.

Even when the dividing line between this and pornography itself is thin, the motives, intentions, and consequences for the user are surely morally relevant. Indeed, there are risks, but for the single person who occasionally uses such material as part of fantasy, or for the married one who finds occasional need of sexual stimulation not met by the spouse, clearly there are moral as well as psychological differences here compared with compulsive and escapist use. Furthermore, though Jesus drove morality inward, there yet remains a significant moral difference between lust and actual sexual aggression; though both are evils, one is the lesser of them.

And a matter of overall perspective is in order. During the Vietnam War, Herbert Marcuse was prompted to write, "This society is obscene in producing and indecently exposing a stifling abundance of wares while depriving its victims abroad of the necessities of life; obscene in stuffing itself and its garbage cans while poisoning and burning the scarce foodstuffs in the fields of its aggression; obscene in the words and smiles of its politicians and entertainers; in its prayers, in its ignorance, and in the wisdom of its kept intellectuals. . . . Obscene is not the picture of a naked woman who exposes her pubic hair, but that of a fully clad general who exposes his medals rewarded in a war of aggression." [26] If there is some oversimplification here, still Marcuse's major point is utterly important for our perspective.

Beyond easy moralisms about erotica, then, we need to ask why people desire it and what meanings it conveys. If it is non-exploitive and if it adequately portrays human sexual expression in both its goodness and its human complexity, that is one thing. But if its promises are false, if it is exploitive of persons and if it rests on the very dualisms from which we seek healing, that is quite another.

Masturbation

Masturbation is one of the most widely-practiced genital expressions of all ages and groups of persons. It is still one of the least understood and most guilt-ridden. As Morton Hunt aptly comments, "It is far easier to admit that one does not believe in God, or was once a Communist, or was born illegitimately, than that one sometimes fondles a part of . . . [one's] own body to the point of orgastic release." [27]

The Bible does not at any point address the subject of masturbation directly. A text sometimes associated with this issue is the story of Onan (Gen. 38:6-10), though the appplication is a misinterpretation of that biblical episode, a point to which I will return in the next chapter. Yet, certain biblical emphases have conditioned the historic Christian negativity toward masturbation, particularly when it is done by males. One such theme has been the procreative emphasis: when it is believed that procreative possibility is essential to a valid sex act, masturbation is by definition intrinsically wrong. Equally important has been the historic combination of sexist dualism with biological misinformation. If the male seed was the only active element in the transmission of new life (the woman providing only the ground for planting), then masturbation was tantamount to the deliberate destruction of human life—there were, after all, "pre-formed people" present in the semen. Strict Orthodox Jewish view at times even held that the death penalty could be administered to a male masturbator.

If religious condemnation softened somewhat in succeeding centuries, the medical profession took up the slack. The Swiss physician Tissot published a book in 1760, a book which was to become one of the more influential treatises in the West insofar as its impact upon human attitudes is concerned: *L'onanisme: Dissertation sur les Maladies Produites par la Masturbation.* He asserted that the practice produced convulsions, paralysis, epilepsy, feeblemindedness, impotence, and bladder disorders. Later physicians added to the list so that by the mid-nineteenth century the catalog went all the way from pimples to suicide, with falling hair, weak eyes, stooped shoulders, gonorrhea, uterine hemorrhage, tuberculosis, and schizophrenia in between.[28] One constructive result did emerge, however. Dr. Sylvester Graham, a New York physician of the last century, was so concerned about the consequences of orgasm, especially in masturbation, that he recommended a bland diet to eliminate those foods which excited the genital organs. And for a staple in the bland diet he invented the Graham cracker.[29]

Modern medical opinion is clear about the judgment that no physical harm comes from masturbation, and that the act has no invidious mental or emotional results apart from attitudes which are brought to it. A variety of studies of sexual behavior in our society have demonstrated that virtually all males have masturbated and most continue to do so throughout adulthood. Similarly, the studies indicate that the majority of females masturbate (though beginning later and with less frequency than males), and that the acceptability of masturbation by women is increasing.[30] Nevertheless, an immense amount of guilt seems to persist.

We need to return then to the influence of religious attitudes. Condemnation of masturbation has been most consistent within the Roman Catholic church. In medieval times (as we have seen earlier), masturbation was regarded as a more serious sin than fornication, adultery, or rape because the former contravened the natural order while the latter sexual sins did not. While contemporary Catholic theologians have taken psychological considerations more seriously than did their predecessors, the most recent Vatican statement on the subject is still adamant: "the moral sense of the faithful have declared without hesitation that masturbation is an intrinsically and seriously disordered act. The main reason is that, whatever the motive for acting in this way, the deliberate use of the sexual faculty outside normal conjugal relations essentially contradicts the finality of the faculty. For it lacks the sexual relationship called for by the moral order, namely, the relationship which realizes 'the full sense of mutual self-giving and human procreation in the context of true love.' " [31]

Nevertheless, more liberal statements from other Catholic sources have increasingly recognized that masturbation is an act susceptible to numerous meanings. It can mean something different in the self-exploration of the adolescent—or as a compensatory practice which signals resistance to parental control—or in the adult as sexual release in the absence or illness of the spouse—or as an act engaged in simply for the pleasure of the moment without a sense of relational responsibility—or as a sign of pathological distortion wherein it is preferred to intercourse.

Contemporary Protestant treatments of the subject likewise recognize the various meanings masturbation might have. Some suggest that it is not a cause for concern unless it becomes a persisting, self-centered choice or is a sign of pathological disturbance. Other Protestants still find it an intrinsically disordered act or at least a sign of emotional immaturity, though it is perhaps excusable for adolescents and it may be the lesser of evils for single adults or for the married in absence of the spouse.

Current psychological literature goes further in exploring the possible meanings of masturbation. It can be an outlet for forbidden or suppressed desires which arise even in persons who have regular sexual partners and who are beyond the age wherein the biological drive is urgent and imperious. It can give psychological consolation to the lonely person and feelings of reassurance to the weak ego. It can express the desire for occasional sexual variety. In marriage it can help to even out differing patterns of sexual desire between the mates; it can be used mutually as a source of sexual play; or it can be used in solitude to fend the spouse off psychically in a time of emotional conflict. In short, it can be pleasurable, comforting, vicariously adventuresome, and entertaining—or it can be a neurotic escape from a relationship and a frustrating solution to inner problems. Any theological evaluation adequate to the subject would have to assess the particular meanings and circumstances.

While the above represents typical psychological assessments of masturbation today, we can press the issue further than this with the assistance of two particular psychologists who go beyond the usual interpretations: David Cole Gordon and June Singer.

Gordon begins with the assumption that our basic human drive is for unification: "to be one in mind and body, to be one with the world, to be one with others and to resolve the subject-object bifurcation. . . ." [32] In a variety of types of "peak experiences" in life we experience a common element which is similar to that experienced in orgasm. It is the feeling of utter unification within the self and with the environment. It is a moment wherein rational thought is transcended, "simply a moment that is pure being and is timeless." [33] This unification of mind, body, and environment is so deeply satisfying that we constantly seek to renew the experience.

Among life's unifying experiences, Gordon contends, orgasm is particularly powerful—whether it comes as a result of heterosexual intercourse, homosexual activity, or masturbation. While in a committed love relationship it is likely to be a superior unification event, the positive capacity of masturbation in this respect ought not to be minimized. The physiological intensity typical in masturbatory orgasm frequently surpasses that of intercourse, and relational fantasies usually accompany the act in compensation for the absence of the partner.

Thus Gordon's interpretation is unusual not only because of the positive goodness he attributes to masturbation (albeit less than intercourse), but also because he has placed the act within a framework of philosophical (and quasi-theological) assumptions about human nature and direction.

In her theory of androgynous personality, June Singer presses the analysis further: "the physical pleasure and the release from tension that masturbation can bring about is only a minor part of what is involved. The fact that masturbation is so prevalent and that it is able to bring about an unfailing sensation of delight, or at least relief, proves that some important human need is being met by it. . . . From earliest childhood on into youth and maturity, masturbation is an act of self-assertion, the object of which is a movement in the direction of independence." [34]

Singer wonders if in their relationships to their children parents do not frequently treat masturbation as the forbidden fruit. If it is eaten, the child will learn secrets of the carnal life which are allied with the secrets of creativity and self-fulfillment—secrets for which the parents themselves often long but do not have. That knowledge is that the self can be lover and beloved at the same time. "There is great freedom in knowing that one can be whole in one's inner life, and that this wholeness need not depend absolutely upon a relationship with another person. This is not to say that we should all prefer masturbation to sexual relations. What is most important is that if one is open to . . . the value of masturbation, then a sexual relationship with another person becomes a matter of choice rather than a matter of necessity. When the sexual relationship with another person does occur, it has the character of strength coming from the union of two independently potent individuals." [35]

For the androgynous person, Singer argues, masturbation is an inner resource which may be used only rarely. Compared to the individual who is tied tightly to a sex-role stereotype in identity, however, the androgynous person is conscious of and accepts the positive meanings that masturbation can have. There is no compulsive quality about it, which so frequently accompanies the act in others. Rather, there is the knowledge that the soul can participate in the experience of the body without guilt or shame. Further, there is the self-affirming knowledge that with the capacity for "being one's own person" one can relate gladly and intimately to another in strength, not in some kind of necessary or required dependence.

While each of their cases carries some danger of overstatement, I find considerable truth in the arguments of both Gordon and Singer. This is not to minimize the possibilities that masturbation can be used in escapist, neurotic, and even self-hating ways (as can intercourse, for that matter). It is to say, however, that for those of us who do not perceive the act as "intrinsically disordered," there is reason to move beyond the common "lesser of the evils" approach and affirm the potentiality of its positive goodness.

In the midst of dualistic alienation, we do seek unification or, more accurately, communion. Orgasm is a gift of God's grace toward this end. In and of itself, however (and here Gordon's argument needs amendment), physiological orgasm has no more power to produce communion than does, for example, a drug-induced state in which there are the sensations of timelessness and transcended cognition. But when acute physiological pleasure in orgasm is a medium for the affirmation of the goodness and unity of the body-self, there can be a communion within which is not unrelated to the communion of self with others, world, and God.

At this point, Singer's insights deserve emphasis. Not only from her experience as a psychotherapist but also as a woman, she points quite appropriately toward the self-other relationship as that which needs the strength of two secure individuals if its promised intimacy is to be realized. In a patriarchal patterning of relationships, quite typically women have been taught that they must be utterly dependent upon a man for their own sexual pleasure, just as for their own identity. It should be no surprise that in breaking through forced identity-dependency, many women have laid claim to "liberating masturbation." It is both the experience and the affirmation that their wholeness does not depend absolutely upon a male.

Theologically speaking, there is the idolatrous in both extremes of independence (or autonomy) and dependence. In the former I deny my essential relatedness through a myth of completeness as self-contained-lover. In the latter I attribute to another mortal that which belongs only to God: my radical dependence for identity and worth. If we are created in and for communion, the issue is one of *interdependence*—significantly different from both independence and dependence, though drawing on each. Ethically speaking, the question is not whether masturbation is to be equalled in value to intercourse with the beloved. By comparison, it is deficient. But this does not necessarily mean "disordered" nor "the lesser-of-the-evils" evaluation. It can mean simply "the lesser of the goods."

For those without partners it is more the case, but even for those in bonds of love's covenant, masturbation then *can* be that occasional gift through which we are graced to break through the sexual dualisms that beset and alienate us. We need to pass beyond a preoccupation with the physical act itself and to inquire with greater sensitivity about its meanings.

Oral-Genital Sexual Expression

Oral-genital sex is clearly increasing in our society. A generation ago Kinsey found that cunnilingus and fellatio were avoided by the great majority of couples who had no more than high school education, but that these sexual expressions were used at least occasionally by almost half of the couples who had college education. By the decade of the 1970s these practices were being used by a majority of the former group and by a large majority of the latter.[36]

Some of the attraction of oral-genital sex may come from its association with the notion of "the forbidden." Indeed, it is still defined as a crime on the lawbooks of the majority of American states, even when done in marriage. And it is condemned by certain religious positions which interpret it as deliberately non-procreative in intent. In some other current Christian treatments of sexuality there seems to be a growing toleration for oral-genital sex, on the condition that it is used as a variety of foreplay and not as a substitute for intercourse. However, in light of the commonness of the practice, the failure of many religious documents on sexuality even to mention the subject suggests that considerable discomfort is still present.

What might some of the meanings of oral-genital sex be? There seems little unanimity among researchers in sexuality on this question, other than that the meanings seem complex.[37] In regard to heterosexual fellatio, there is apparently nothing intrinsically more physiologically stimulating about the penis in the mouth as opposed to the penis in the vagina, and usually the physical stimulation is somewhat less. Further, there are complications, given the definitions which the genitals have in regard to odor, cleanliness, and excretion. So it is likely that the symbolic meanings of the act account in no small measure for its considerable enjoyment. For some it may at times be a symbol of male domination. For others it may be an acceptable (if often unconscious) expression of a homosexual dimension of the self, given the act's common association with homosexual expression. For many men it may be a symbolic contact with the "feminine" within, for in heterosexual fellation they are the passive receivers.

The meanings of cunnilingus would seem to overlap to some extent. The taboo violation here, too, seems to enhance the act, and the homosexual association may be either consciously or unconsciously meaningful. Simon and Gagnon attribute the male pleasure in cunnilingus largely to "masculine striving for the enhancement of the capacity to produce sexual pleasure in the female." [38]

In both cunnilingus and fellatio there is an obvious focus upon the genitals—a focus more intense in its psychic dimensions perhaps than in ordinary intercourse. There may be a ritual being played out here—a celebration of the imagined authority and power of the genitals. And this can be a healing ritual, I believe. Earlier I have argued that the genitalization of sexuality typically is a mark of alienation, whereas the bodily and relational diffusion of sexuality is a mark of reconciliation. But this deserves a further word of interpretation in the present context. Alienated genitalization means the narrowing of sexuality to "sex." It means the psychic reduction of our sexuality's potential richness to a singular focus on genital expression—"having sex." Now, however, in the context of the sex act itself, the oral-genital focus upon the genitals as part of a couple's sexual repertoire may well be both sign and medium of reconciliation. There may be health in this erotic ritual in simply acknowledging that the forbidden, "dirty" genitals need to be reclaimed and celebrated as important parts of the body-self. And in the attraction of oral-genital sex there may well be a healthy reaction against the poverty of that moralism which has labeled certain activities which can contribute to human richness as forbidden and to be repressed.

The meanings, then, can be varied and mixed. If meanings of male domination or sexual performance strongly adhere to oral-genital sex, then this practice may symbolize and further entrench an alienated sexuality. But if the meanings which give these acts their psychic power stem largely from their capacity to help us reclaim psycho-sexual and physical dimensions of ourselves, then such acts can be both exquisite pleasures of sexual loving and moments of healing.

Anal Intercourse

Heterosexual anal intercourse is a much less frequent practice, according to every major sex behavior study. From a biological and medical viewpoint, "it involves tissues, nerve structures and microorganisms that are far from ideal for the purpose of coitus, to say nothing of its potential aesthetic hazards," according to one source.[39] The taboos on the practice (and even on the discussion) of anal intercourse have been considerably stronger than even those regarding oral-genital sex. And, surely, the breaking of a taboo might be one impetus, possibly a strong one, to couples who experiment with this. Such couples are still in the statistical minority, but the numbers are increasing. Current studies indicate that in the middle and older age groups, few married couples ever engage in anal intercourse. But for partners between twenty-five and thirty-five years of age, nearly a quarter occasionally express themselves sexually in this way.

One interpretation of heterosexual anal intercourse accents the meaning of male dominance and female submission. But this may well be a compensatory submission on the part of the woman: "among those females with higher levels of dominance needs, such symbolic investment of specific sexual acts with submissiveness may serve as reaffirmations of femininity which is not available to them in occupational or other spheres of life." [40] If this is true, for such persons the appeal of anal intercourse rests on the unredeemed sex role situations in the society and in the self—and it may be a physically helpful method occasionally used to counteract or cope with such, at least on the part of the woman. If the act is not compensatory in this way, if it simply means abject male dominance, then it only reinforces psychic and relational alienation. But a recent study suggests that this may not be a prominent meaning: "Whether one personally finds this practice appealing, neutral or repellent, the increase in its use does not, as some may think, represent the brutalization and abuse of wives by sadistic husbands, but generally a more or less free choice by both partners of something they want to do together." [41]

Another possible interpretation is that there may be here a symbolic focus on the excretory rather than the generative dimensions of sexuality, suggesting that the access of one person to another is through waste and chaos. [42] If this is the case, one can appreciate why married couples who do occasionally use anal intercourse find it a minor element in their sexual lives. Yet, there may even be something of Christian significance here—a psychosexual symbol of grace. One meets the beloved in intimate embrace not only in order, cleanliness, and virtue, but also in the willing and mutual exposure of the chaos of our lives, now symbolized bodily.

Sado-masochism

The practice of sado-masochism, the giving and receiving of physical pain as a means to sexual pleasure, is much more problematical. As a minor note in a couple's love play—the pinch, the love bite, even the prolonged sexual teasing—it seems to have an appropriate place for many people. But the more developed expressions of sado-masochism—the use of bondage and flagellation—are, I believe, highly suspect as sexual paths to fulfillment, even when both partners are willing and both are receiving pleasure, as apparently is usually the case.

Most psychologists of sexuality deem "S & M" as pathological, even though (and perhaps because of the fact) it seems to be the only route to intense pleasure for certain individuals. It is dramatically oriented around the symbols of control. Dominance and submission of physically extreme sorts are its trademarks. Exaggerated sex-role stereotypes seem to be played out in its rituals. All of this suggests the reinforcement of patterns of psychic body-self alienation. Furthermore, sado-masochism—whether it appears in direct sexual ways in the bedroom or in the *apparently* nonsexual violence of the television and movie screen—seems to arise out of feelings of inner deadness. It seems to reflect the struggling attempt to stimulate the self into feelings of life once again. One psychiatrist, in fact, describes the masochist as one whose "body is so contracted and the muscles of . . . [the] buttocks and pelvis are so tense that the sexual excitation does not get through to the genitals strongly enough. The beating, apart from its psychological meanings, breaks the tension and relaxes the muscles, allowing the sexual excitation to flow." [43]

Sado-masochistic practices thus appear to be much more the fruit of the alienating sexual dualisms than possible means for their transformation. The felt need for such sexual expressions should stir reflection about the causes and compassion for those who seek these painful ways to pleasure. A salutary part of such reflection might be the recognition of ways—not narrowly sexual but surely rooted in some significant sense in our sexuality—in which most of us on some occasions take pleasure in the giving and receiving of pain.

Even in Christian history and symbolism there are ample evidences. The masochistic self-flagellation common in certain Christian groups of earlier centuries and the sadistic pleasures received through the torturing of "witches" in late medieval years are surely understandable only if the sexual dynamics are understood alongside the professed convictions. But the line also becomes very thin between sexual health and distortion in our ordinary religious symbolism. So it is in a traditional hymn of adoration to the risen Christ, penned by one no less than Charles Wesley:

> Those dear tokens of his passion
> Still his dazzling body bears,
> Cause of endless exultation
> To his ransomed worshipers:
> With what rapture, with what rapture
> Gaze we on those glorious scars! [44]

The line here does seem thin: between the believer's humble gratitude for the divine suffering—and the suggestion of possible enjoyment of that suffering.

Sexual Variations and Moral Judgments

In the fairly common sexual variations discussed in this chapter, and in others less common, sexual human beings continue to seek their healing and wholeness. Certain meanings found in certain variations do in fact promise something of the needed healing and wholeness. Other meanings seem only to underscore the problem.

In making moral evaluations of various sexual possibilities both for ourselves and in regard to others, neither moralism nor sentimentalism are helpful. When a sexual variation becomes compulsive, when a person organizes his or her life around a partial principle, that person pays a heavy cost and the hungered-for communion and integration do not appear. But then moralistic exclusion from the community of support and understanding only compounds the problem. Nor does utter relativism help, for this attitude simply disregards the directions, meanings, and controls of love in sexuality.

But, in a general perspective on sex variations, it is also important to speak of Christian liberty. Nothing, says Paul, is unclean in itself (Romans 14:14), and I assume that this is applicable to sexual variety within the love relationship. Some societal sex taboos can be defended as sound wisdom regarding predictable threats to our genuine human becoming. Many other sex taboos can well be challenged. We are body-people by God's design, and distinctly human bodies are made for play and exploration—"an adventure of tenderness and an exploration into the potential of pleasure hidden in our need for love." [45]

8

Gayness
and Homosexuality:
Issues for the Church

THE GAY CAUCUSES now active in virtually every major American denomination no longer will let any of us forget that the church must face this issue more openly, honestly, and sensitively than it has yet done.[1] Beyond the legitimate pressure which the caucuses are exerting, there are numerous compelling reasons for the church to reexamine its theology and practice.[2] Among them are these:

● Gay Christians are sisters and brothers of every other Christian, and a great many are earnestly seeking the church's full acceptance of them—without prejudgment on the basis of sexual orientation.

● While antihomosexual bias has long existed in Western culture generally, the church must take responsibility for its significant share in shaping, supporting, and transmitting negative (and often hostile) attitudes toward gay people.

● The Christian mandate to seek social justice will not let us forget that discrimination continues against millions of gay people in employment, housing, public accommodations, education, basic civil liberties—and in church structures.[3]

• The church must do its ongoing theological and ethical work with a high sense of responsibility. Fresh insights from gay Christians, from feminist theologians, and from those secular scholars who frequently manifest God's "common grace" in the world remind us of the numerous ways our particular sexual conditionings have colored our perceptions of God's nature and presence among us. If the Protestant Principle warns us against absolutizing historically relative theological and ethical judgments, so also an openness to continuing revelation should convince us (as it did some of our ancestors-in-faith) that "the Lord has yet more light and truth to break forth."

• Finally, the heterosexually-oriented majority in the church has an immense amount to gain from a deeper grappling with this issue and a deeper encounter with gay Christians: an enriched capacity to love other human beings more fully and less fearfully, and a more faithful response to God's will for social justice.

The Bible and Homosexuality

It is a curious but unmistakable phenomenon that a great many Christians treat so literally the references to homosexual practice in the Bible, while at the same time they interpret biblical texts on almost every other topic with considerable flexibility and non-literalness. Why this may be so is an important question, and we shall return to it later. But at this point the major texts which mention the subject engage our attention.

A brief survey of these passages needs to be prefaced with a word about interpretive principles.[4] Let me suggest four. First and most fundamental, Jesus Christ is the bearer of God's invitation to human wholeness and communion. Jesus Christ is the focal point of God's humanizing action, and hence he is the central norm through which and by which everything else in Scripture should be judged. Second, the interpreter must take seriously both the historical context of the biblical writers and our present cultural situation. Third, we should study and interpret the Bible with awareness of the cultural relativity in which we ourselves are immersed, and through which we perceive and experience what Christian faith means. Finally, our scriptural interpretation should be informed by the revelations of God's truth in other disciplines of human inquiry.

Nowhere does the Bible say anything about homosexuality as a *sexual orientation.* Its references to the subject are—without exception—statements about certain kinds of homosexual *acts.* Our understanding of homosexuality as a psychosexual orientation is a relatively recent development. It is crucial to remember this, for in all probability the biblical writers in each instance were speaking of homosexual acts undertaken by persons whom the authors presumed to be heterosexually constituted.[5]

Even though it does not deal with homosexual activity, it is well to begin with the Onan story (Genesis 38:1-11), for it has significantly influenced attitudes toward this subject. Onan's refusal to impregnate his widowed sister-in-law—a refusal expressed through his deliberate withdrawal before ejaculation *(coitus interruptus)*—was seen by the writer as so serious a violation of divine decree that Onan was killed by Yahweh.

Three interpretive observations are particularly relevant to the subject of homosexuality. First, the Onan story clearly points up the strong emphasis upon procreation which is characteristic of the Hebrew interpretation of sexuality. The historical context is one in which a small tribe was struggling for its very survival, and thus the reproduction of children was of exceptional importance. Any sexual activity that "wasted the seed" was a threat to the tribe. Our own situation on an overcrowded planet is markedly different.

The second observation is linked to this, and I repeat this point made in earlier chapters. The Onan story illustrates a biological misunderstanding which is present throughout the Bible. The prescientific mind (particularly the prescientific *male* mind) assumed that the man's semen contained the whole of nascent life. With no knowledge of eggs and ovulation, it was assumed that the woman provided only the incubating space. Hence, the deliberate and nonprocreative spilling of semen was equivalent to the deliberate destruction of human life. Whether it occurred in *coitus interruptus* (as with Onan), or in male homosexual acts, or for that matter in male masturbation, the deserved judgment was as severe as that for abortion or even murder.

The third observation follows: male homosexual and masturbatory acts have been condemned far more vigorously than have similar female acts throughout the whole sweep of the Judeo-Christian tradition. The sexism endemic to a patriarchal society ironically bore with its logic a heavier burden upon the "deviants" of the "superior" gender. But the central irony of the Onan story interpretation through the centuries is this: its major point does not concern sexual sin as such but rather has to do with human greed (over property inheritance) and with the disobedience of God's commands.

However, it is another Genesis account which has emerged as the chief text in Christian history for the summary condemnation of homosexuality: Sodom and Gomorrah (Genesis 19:1-29). Traditional explanation has held that the destruction of the two cities is the positive sign of God's utter disapproval of homosexuality. Yet, there are compelling reasons to doubt the accuracy of this interpretation. Current Old Testament scholarship generally holds that the story's *major* themes are the affront to God's will in the breach of ancient Hebrew hospitality norms and persistent violations of rudimentary social justice.[6]

There are multiple reasons for preferring the latter interpetation. For one, some scholars doubt that the verb "to know" *(yādáh)* in this story refers to sexual intercourse. More probably it means the crowd's rude insistence upon *knowing who* these two strangers were. Lot, in their eyes, was not properly qualified to offer hospitality to strangers inasmuch as he himself was an outsider, a resident alien in Sodom.

That inhospitality and injustice coming from the mob and generally characterizing the community were "the sin of Sodom" is plausible when one examines parallel scriptural accounts (e.g., the crime of Gibeah, Judges 19:1-21:25). Even weightier evidence comes from subsequent Old Testament references to Sodom, none of which identifies homosexuality with that city. Ezekiel is typical: "Behold, this was the sin of your sister Sodom: she and her daughters lived in pride, plenty, and thoughtless ease; they supported not the poor and needy; they grew haughty, and committed abomination before me; so I swept them away; as you have seen" (Ezekiel 16:49-50). The other Old Testament references to Sodom's sin are similar (cf. Isaiah 13:19; Jeremiah 49:18, 50:40), and the identification of Sodom with inhospitality is made by Jesus as well (Luke 10:10-13). It was not until several centuries after it was written that the Sodom story was given a dominantly sexual interpretation—in the intertestamental Book of Jubilees and then in two late New Testament texts (2 Peter 2:4-10 and Jude 6-7). But if Sodom had consistently been understood as the major symbol of divine judgment on homosexual acts, we would expect that the other biblical references to such acts would also mention Sodom and its fate. None does.

Though there is considerable agreement among scholars that the basic ethical theme of the Sodom account is that of justice and its basic theological theme is God's righteousness in the face of social guilt, we can still acknowledge the possibility that homosexual acts did play some role in the story.[7] If the verb "to know" does signify homosexual intercourse, it is also patently clear that what is being threatened here is homosexual *rape*. Moreover, the men of Sodom have threatened to rape the two visiting *angels*, and since the angels represent Yahweh's presence there is a direct sin against God here portrayed. In all fairness to the text, it is extremely difficult to construe this account as a judgment against *all* homosexual activity.

Fr. John McNeill writes a fitting conclusion to our brief look at the Sodom story. Observing that its dominant use in Christianity may well be one of the supreme ironies of history, he says: "For thousands of years in the Christian West the homosexual has been the victim of inhospitable treatment. Condemned by the Church, he has been the victim of persecution, torture, and even death. In the name of a mistaken understanding of Sodom and Gomorrah, the true crime of Sodom and Gomorrah has been and continues to be repeated every day."[8]

If the dominant homosexual interpretation traditionally given to the Sodom account fails to stand up to critical examination, there are, nevertheless, several other Old Testament passages which unmistakably condemn homosexual acts. It is crucial to see in these, however, that the pervasive theme is that of cultic defilement and idolatry. There is no general condemnation of same-sex *orientation* (a notion foreign to the writers), nor is there any reference to genital *love* between gay persons who are committed to each other. What is clear is that sacral male prostitution is anathematized, for it involves the cultic worship of foreign gods and denies Yahweh's exclusive claim (see Deuteronomy 23:17; 1 Kings 14:24, 15:12, 22:46).

Cultic defilement is also the context for the Holiness Code in Leviticus (see 18:22 and 20:13).[9] Canaanite fertility worship involved sacral prostitution and sexual orgies, and this constituted a direct threat to Yahweh's exclusive claim. For Yahweh was the One who worked through the freedom of human history and not, primarily, through the cycles of biological life. If so, sexuality was not to be seen as a mysterious sacred power, but rather as part of human life to be used responsibly in gratitude to the Creator—a basic perspective of continuing relevance.

For those who do not accept this as the more appropriate interpretation of the Leviticus references, some exceedingly difficult issues of biblical interpretation emerge.[10] What is the principle of selection by which cultic injunctions against homosexual acts are held valid today but at the same time most other parts of the Holiness Code are deemed irrelevant? Should the death penalty be used against male homosexuals as the law stipulates? Why are female same-sex acts unmentioned? What is the link between female subordination and the fear of male homosexuality, both evident in these laws? And how shall a church which grounds its life in the grace of Jesus Christ deal with the law codes of ancient Israel?

Part of the Old Testament context for this issue, worthy of note, was a common Middle East practice in that day: the submission of captured male foes to anal rape. It was an expression of domination and contempt, a powerful symbol of scorn in societies where the dignity of the male was held in such high esteem. Here a man was using another *man* as he might use a woman. As long as homosexual activity of any sort had this connection, it is not difficult to understand some of these texts.

Nevertheless, at a number of points in the Old Testament there are beautiful affirmations of same-sex *love*. Two notable examples come to mind. David's love for Jonathan was said to exceed his love for women. And the relationship of Ruth and Naomi can only be described as a bond of deep love. There is no indication that there was genital expression in either of these. The point is simply that in these instances, deeply and emotionally expressed love between two persons of the same sex is affirmed. Indeed, the accounts suggest that it is something of a cause for celebration.

In the New Testament we have no record of any words of Jesus about homosexuality either as an orientation or as a genital expression. The major New Testament references are found in two Pauline letters and in 1 Timothy.

Paul's statement in Romans 1:18-32 traditionally has been taken as the strongest New Testament rejection of homosexuality, yet this passage deserves more careful examination that is often accorded to it. The writer is clearly concerned about the influence of paganism on the Roman Christians, and he had good reason to be. The moral climate of Hellenistic Rome was marred by various forms of sexual commerce and exploitation. Yet, in this passage while Paul sees homosexual acts as a *result* of idolatry, he does not claim that they are the *cause* of divine wrath. Idolatry clearly is the major issue at stake. Further, when Paul uses the word "nature" he "apparently refers only to homosexual acts indulged in by those he considered to be otherwise heterosexually inclined; acts which represent a voluntary choice to act contrary to their ordinary sexual appetite."[11] Thus, he speaks of homosexual acts as those in which people are "leaving," "giving up," or "exchanging" their regular sexual orientations. It is difficult to read into Paul's words at this point the modern psychosexual understanding of the gay person as one whose orientation is fixed very early in life and for whom "natural" (heterosexual) relations would be felt as basically contrary to his or her own sexual constitution, and might well be impossible at that. In addition, in this passage we are given a description of homosexual *lust* ("consumed with passion for one another"), but hardly an account of interpersonal same-sex love—about which Paul does not speak.

Thus, it is difficult to construe Paul's statement as applicable to acts of committed love engaged in by persons for whom same-sex attraction is part of the givenness of *their* "nature." In point of fact, Paul uses the word "nature" in his writings as a flexible concept, expressing varying concerns in different contexts. An ethical position which condemns homosexuality as a violation of natural law will have to turn to non-biblical philosophical materials for its justification—the Pauline material will not sustain it.[12]

Finally it is worth noting that in this entire section of the letter to the Romans the author's concern is to demonstrate that all persons are under the power of sin. They cannot extricate themselves from it through meritorious works of the law. In spite of his own moral judgments, Paul reveals this basic point in Romans 2:1. There he declares that those who pass judgment on others (for the various acts which he has earlier mentioned) are no better off. They condemn themselves because they stand under the same power of sin. And in Romans 3:21-25 comes the central premise of these first chapters of the letter: all have sinned and fallen short of God's glory, and all who open themselves in faith are justified by God's grace in Jesus Christ.

The point of all this is not that Paul sees homosexual acts as neutral or, much less, that he looks upon any such acts with favor. Clearly, he does not. He understands homosexual practices to be the result of idolatry. But, as David L. Bartlett has observed, Paul's argument here is not "purely" theological. It is partly based on his interpretation of Old Testament concepts of idolatry, partly based on the common wisdom of his day, and partly based on his own empirical understanding of homosexuality's nature and consequences. In regard to the latter, he looked at the Gentile world and saw idolatry but also saw homosexual practices and the prevalence of venereal disease—and he linked them firmly together. As Bartlett comments, to be genuinely "Pauline" in our understanding of homosexual practices today, we would have to demonstrate that there does indeed exist a clear connection between idolatry and homosexual acts—and then one would wonder, given the widespread idolatry of our times, why more people had not been so "punished." In addition, a Pauline methodology would have us discuss homosexuality today with our best biblical interpretation, our best common wisdom of the contemporary day, and the best empirical understandings we can find. "If our understanding of homosexuality and our empirical perception of its nature and consequences have changed, then we will not be able to understand the issue precisely as Paul did, even if we share Paul's reverence for the Old Testament, his abhorrence of idolatry, and his conviction that we are all sinners saved by grace through faith." [13]

Paul's other reference to homosexual acts (1 Corinthians 6:9-10) is similar to that of the writer of 1 Timothy (1:8-11). Both passages contain lists of practices which will exclude people from the kingdom. They are acts which dishonor God and harm the neighbor, including such things as thievery, drunkenness, kidnapping, and lying. Homosexual acts are not singled out for special censure, but they are unmistakably part of the list. What then should we make of Paul's moral judgment in this case? Perhaps we should just accept him for what he was: a faithful apostle and a profound interpreter of the central message of the gospel, yet one who was also a fallible and historically-conditioned human being. Paul's central message is clear: we do not earn righteousness by anything we do nor are we justified by anything we are—we are justified by the grace of God in Jesus Christ, and the gifts of the Spirit are equally available to all persons. If the norm of the new humanity in Jesus Christ together with our best current moral wisdom and empirical knowledge would cause us to question some of Paul's moral convictions about the status of women and about the institution of human slavery, surely his moral judgments about homosexual acts ought not be exempt.

The central biblical message regarding sexuality seems clear enough. Like every other good gift, it can be misused. The idolatrous dishonoring of God inevitably results in the dishonoring of persons, and faithfulness to God will result in sexual expression which honors the personhood of the other. Our sexuality is not a mysterious and alien force of nature but part of what it means to be human. It is a power to be integrated fully into one's selfhood and to be used in the service of love. That message, I am convinced, applies regardless of one's affectional orientation.

The Range of Contemporary Theological Opinion

Four theological stances toward homosexuality represent the range of current conviction.[14] The first can be called a *rejecting-punitive* orientation. The person who holds this unconditionally rejects homosexuality as Christianly legitimate and, at the same time, bears a punitive attitude toward gay persons.

The rejecting-punitive motif, tragically enough, is a strong one in Christian history. If we have been ignorant of the persecutions, it is not without reason. Unlike the recognized histories of other minority groups, there has been no "gay history." Heterosexual historians usually have considered the subject unmentionable, and gay historians have been constrained by the fear of ceasing to be invisible. A conspiracy of silence has resulted. Yet, the facts are there. For many centuries stoning, burning, sexual mutilation, and the death penalty were fairly common treatments for discovered homosexuals. While the church frequently gave its blessings to the civil persecutions, official ecclesiastical practice tended to be less physically violent. Nevertheless, spiritually it was even more severe, for it usually meant refusal of the sacraments and ostracism from the common life.[15]

Today no major contemporary theologian holds the rejecting-punitive position and most church bodies in their formal statements have moved away from it. Yet in practice it may still be by far the most common orientation throughout the length and breadth of the church in our society. Its theology rests on a selective biblical literalism—selective, again, because other moral issues are not treated with the same kind of literalism at all. Its punitive attitudes might be expressed less violently than was typical in the past, but they are still highly punitive and ostracizing.[16] The attitudes are rooted in familiar stereotypes: all lesbians are tough and all male gays effeminate; homosexuals are compulsive and sex-hungry; they are by nature promiscuous; male gays have an inherent tendency toward child molestation. Each of these stereotypes has been thoroughly discounted by reliable research, and yet they persist in the minds of countless Christians. And the key criticism of this whole orientation—beyond its untenable biblical interpretations—must be the incongruity of a vindictive stance with the gospel.

The *rejecting-nonpunitive* position must be considered more fully. No less a theologian than Karl Barth represents this view. Since humanity is always "fellow-humanity," Barth argues, men and women come into its fullness only in relation to persons of the opposite sex. To seek one's humanity in a person of the same sex is to seek "a substitute for the despised partner," and this is "physical, psychological and social sickness, the phenomenon of perversion, decadence and decay." [17] Moreover, this is idolatry. One who seeks same-sex union is simply seeking oneself in a quest for self-satisfaction and self-sufficiency. Hence, homosexuality is unnatural and violates the command of the Creator. But, Barth hastens to add, the central theme of the gospel is God's overwhelming grace in Jesus Christ. *Homosexuality* must be condemned, but in light of grace the homosexual *person* must not.

If Barth's arguments emphasize that there is something inherently wrong with the homosexual condition as such (it is idolatrous, a sickness and a perversion), the rejecting-nonpunitive position can also be argued on more consequentialist grounds. William Muehl does this.[18] Muehl clearly recognizes the cruelty, injustice, and hypocrisy all present in the persecution and prosecution of gay persons. He fully supports the church's obligation toward their civil liberties. Theirs, he believes, is not the only form of sexual irresponsibility, but it *is* irresponsibility which cannot be approved by Christian conscience. Human dignity is threatened by gay relationships. Homosexuality is an illness comparable to alcoholism, and sheer acceptance of it would have "implications for our view of marriage, the limitations appropriate to sexual activity, the raising of children, and the structure of the family." Since we are relatively ignorant concerning such potentially grave social results, Muehl argues, we should respect the historic position of the church, which rejects homosexuality.

The rejecting-nonpunitive stance appears to rest upon two major arguments and upon two major unspoken assumptions, each of which is open to serious question. The first argument is that of natural law and idolatry. At this point we return to Barth. Barth seems to forget our human historicity, apparently assuming that human nature is an unchangeable, once-and-for-all essence given by the Creator. Actually, our human nature is shaped in some significant part by the interaction of people in specific periods of time with specific cultural symbols and historic environments. In fact, the notion of a fixed human nature is highly questionable from a biblical point of view. "Where we read 'created' in our Bibles, the tense in the Hebrew is often in fact the continuous present, i.e. God is 'creating.' And from this understanding comes a statement that may be held to give us our vocation as 'being created in the image of God'. . . ." [19]

Committed to human historicity, Gregory Baum fittingly declares, "In other words, human nature as it is at present is not normative for theologians. . . . What is normative for normal life is the human nature to which we are divinely summoned, which is defined in terms of mutuality. This, at least, is the promise of biblical religion." After examining the evidence of mutual fulfillment in committed gay couples, Fr. Baum concludes, "Homosexual love, then, is not contrary to human nature, defined in terms of mutuality toward which mankind is summoned." [20]

In addition, Barth's claim that homosexuality is idolatrous rests on questionable assumptions which I have earlier touched upon—the norm of procreative sex and the notion of essential gender complementarity. Regarding the first, Barth (like Paul Ramsey) affirms responsible family planning, but contends that even if every sex act is not procreative, all sexual relations must be oriented to that possibility. On one level it can be countered that while responsible *love* and sexual expression ought not to be sundered, procreation (even the procreative possibility) and sex ought not to be irrevocably joined. "Be fruitful and multiply" has now overfilled the earth. On another level it can also be argued that the possibility of procreation has not consistently been insisted upon by Christian orthodoxy, as witness the validity of the marriage between a man and a woman, one of whom is known to be irreversibly sterile.

What of the notion of essential gender complementarity? Barth claims that there is no "fellow humanity" apart from the covenanted relationship with one of the opposite sex. But it is more theologically defensible to affirm that there is no genuine humanity apart from *relationship* and *community*. To insist that the relationship which constitutes the image of God must be heterosexual assumes that the psychic natures of women and men are somehow biologically-given and ontologically unchangeable. Rosemary Ruether speaks vigorously to this point: "Such a concept of complementarity depends on a sadomasochistic concept of male and female relations. It covertly demands the continued dependency and underdevelopment of woman in order to validate the thesis that two kinds of personalities exist by nature in males and females and which are each partial expressions of some larger whole. Such a view can allow neither men nor women to be whole persons who can develop both their active and their affective sides." [21]

Still another contention of Barth's position is that homosexuality means a "despising" of the other sex. But this lacks both logical and factual foundation. It equates an aversion to intercourse with an aversion to persons. Actually, many gay people exhibit the ability to establish particularly meaningful and loving relationships with members of the opposite sex precisely because sexual "conquest" in whatever form is excluded from the situation. Moreover, current research indicates the widespread amount of antipathy between persons of the *opposite* sex because of the dominance-submission patterns engrained in our sex-role stereotyping.[22] Indeed, the logic of Barth's argument would seem to be that *heterosexuals* by *their* very nature should despise members of their own sex—an unsupportable assumption.

And finally, Barth maintains that homosexuality is idolatrous because it is basically self-worship and narcissism: the gay person is just loving in the other the reflection of the self. But this claim does grave injustice to both the uniqueness of persons and the capacities which gay people amply demonstrate for self-giving love. When a person in a committed relationship deeply loves another of the same sex, it is difficult to understand how this can be construed as self-love—except if one adopts an untenable "biologism" about human relatedness and ignores the unity of the body-self.

We return to Muehl to examine the second major argument of the rejecting-nonpunitive position; that undesirable social consequences most likely would result from homosexuality's acceptance. Underneath Muehl's fears for the future of the family seems to lie the unspoken conviction that the church's approval of same-sex orientation would bring in its wake a significant increase in numbers of those choosing to be gay. But this is highly unlikely. Research shows no demonstrable increase in homosexual behavior in the quarter century since Kinsey's study in spite of some lessening of punitive attitudes in recent years.[23] Indeed, if one's dominant sexual orientation is, for the great majority, not a matter of conscious choice, this is quite understandable. It may be the case that some heterosexual people, perhaps quite unconsciously, assume that there is something so attractive in the gay experience that if it were not stringently forbidden many others would choose this orientation.

The great majority of gay persons do not appear to have any more choice about their affectional orientation than do the great majority of heterosexuals. There is no general agreement about the causes of homosexuality. Major theories cluster around two different approaches, the psychogenic and the genetic, but both remain in dispute.[24] Some researchers are now admitting that when we know more about the causes of heterosexuality (about which we know precious little at present) then we shall also know more about the causes of homosexuality. At least one thing is increasingly clear, however: sexual orientation is relatively fixed by early childhood through processes about which the individual makes no conscious choice.

If sexual orientation for the great majority of heterosexuals and gay persons is not freely chosen, neither is it easily reversed. Positive therapeutic results in that minority of gay people who have sought treatment to reverse their orientation have been minimal. One study contends that there are actually no validated instances of successful sexual preference reorientation through therapy.[25] Behavioral modification programs using "aversive therapy" have been able to condition some gays against attraction to their own sex but have been notably unable to replace that with similar attraction to the opposite sex. In 1975 the therapist who had developed and popularized the orgasmic reorientation technique disavowed his own treatment and called upon other behavioral therapists to cease, because such attempts were proving harmful to the subjects' whole personality structures—a particularly dehumanizing result.[26]

The adverse social consequences argument also hinges upon the assumption that gay people are inherently less capable of interpersonal and social functioning than are heterosexuals. It is significant, however, that in 1974 the American Psychiatric Association removed homosexuality from its list of mental disorders, saying "homosexuality *per se* implies no impairment in judgment, stability, reliability, or general social or vocational capabilities." Those clinicians who have attributed personality problems to gays *because* of their sexual orientation usually have drawn their observations from their own patients without recognizing or admitting that their heterosexual patients *also* have personality problems—and that is why they have come for therapy. The best comparative study to date remains that of Evelyn Hooker who found that when batteries of personality tests were administered to samples of male heterosexuals and male gays, neither group of which was in therapy, the clinical psychologists evaluating the test results could neither distinguish sexual orientation nor find "demonstrable pathology" among those later identified as homosexually-oriented.[27] "Neurotic" traits typically ascribed to gay persons are essentially the same for members of any oppressed minority group, and in cultures where homosexual behavior has been fully accepted such traits do not discernibly appear.[28]

Harmful consequences for the institution of family life is another fear expressed in this position. Even if gay persons were no less prone to emotional instability because of their sexual orientation, if society endorses same-sex coupling what will happen to the concept of the Christian family? Thus, Muehl asks, "Can the battered institution of Christian marriage stand the sight of gay unions being solemnized at the altar?"[29]

It is likely, however, that gay acceptance would actually bring constructive family consequences. There are several reasons for this. At present a fair number of marital difficulties and divorces stem from the fact that one of the spouses is primarily homosexual in orientation and has been pushed into marriage by social expectations and by the desire to escape detection. One priest who serves as a canon lawyer in a Catholic marriage tribunal contends that in over a third of the divorces with which he has dealt, one of the partners was homosexually inclined, a fact of major disruption for the marriage.[30] It seems highly probable in this regard that marital stability would be well served if heterosexual union were not viewed as the only avenue to respectability.

Other beneficial results for family life can be foreseen as well. Greater acceptance of homosexuality is likely to ease the current pressures toward the heterosexual's living up to rigid sex-role stereotypes. The acting out of such stereotypes when they are not authentic to one's unique personality is predictably a major factor in marital difficulties. Moreover, emotional intimacy between heterosexual family members of the same gender is likely to be enhanced. Such intimacy—between father and son, for example—too often is still inhibited by unrecognized homosexual fears. And, of no minor importance, the syndromes of alienation and rejection within families when a child is discovered to be gay would be ameliorated. Speaking to this point, Peggy Way writes out of an extensive counseling experience with gay people and their families: "I feel terrible sadness and pathos over the beautiful 'children' many parents are missing because sexuality gets in the way. All the rich humanness, spirituality, commitment, kindness I get to enjoy and share is lost to parents who cannot deal with the homosexuality of their own children, regardless of their other fine qualities." [31] In short, the picture of invidious consequences to family life from gay acceptance is highly overdrawn. In fact, the greater likelihood is quite the other way around: there are positive benefits to be foreseen.

Positive benefits more than negative consequences can also be foreseen for society as a whole. Societal health is always integrally related to social justice, and justice is served when discrimination against minority groups on the basis of unfair stereotypes is mitigated. Justice is also served when violence and the more destructive forms of competition are mitigated, and our attempt to understand the exaggerated aggressiveness of many male heterosexuals must take seriously the presence of conscious and unconscious fears of homosexuality. In a difficult-to-measure but predictable way, society would also benefit from the creative energies released in countless gay people, were they to be fully accepted. At present, closeted gays time and again report the daily energy drain inevitable for one forced to live a double life. If of a different sort, the drain on the personal resources of publicly-avowed gays is surely no less. Society presses them to make their homosexual orientation central to their identities, coerces them into spending time and energy defending their acceptability, and then through its various door-closing discriminations deprives itself of their best talents. Once again, not only is the case for harmful social consequences difficult to demonstrate, but the more persuasive arguments lie on the side of social benefit.

There is a basic flaw which underlies the entire rejecting-nonpunitive position: the assumption that it is possible to reject the homosexual orientation as such and still be nonpunitive toward gays as persons. Further comment on this is warranted, but I shall do so in the context of the next position.

Qualified acceptance might be the term for a third theological option regarding homosexuality. Helmut Thielicke is its best example, and his argument follows several steps. Similar to Barth, Thielicke first argues, "The fundamental order of creation and the created determination of the two sexes make it appear justifiable to speak of homosexuality as a 'perversion' . . . [which] is in every case *not* in accord with the order of creation." [32] But Thielicke is more open to contemporary psychological and medical research on the subject. Hence, he takes a second step: "But now experience shows that constitutional homosexuality at any rate is largely unsusceptible to medical or psychotherapeutic treatment, at least so far as achieving the desired goal of a fundamental conversion to normality is concerned." [33] Further, he says, homosexuality as a *predisposition* ought not to be depreciated any more than the varied distortions of the created order in which all fallen people share.

But what about genital expression? If a gay person can change in sexual orientation, such change should actively be sought. Admittedly, however, most cannot. Then, Thielicke contends, such persons should seek to sublimate their homosexual desires and not act on them. But some constitutional homosexuals "because of their vitality" are not able to practice abstinence. If that is the case, they should structure their sexual relationships "in an ethically responsible way" (in adult, fully-committed relationships). They should make the best of their painful situations without idealizing them or pretending that they are normal.

Thielicke's argument is important. For one thing, it is more empirically informed than the rejecting-nonpunitive position. Further, this argument now represents the position of a number of church leaders and several recent denominational statements on the issue. But the argument still is unacceptable, in my judgment. This position, like Barth's, is grounded in an essentially nonhistoricist, rigid version of natural law. And, in spite of its greater humanness, the position becomes self-contradictory. In effect, the gay person is told, "We heterosexual Christians sympathize with your plight, and if you *must* give genital expression to your orientation you must do it in a morally responsible way—but do not forget that you are a sinner *because of your sexual orientation* and do not deny that you are a sexual pervert."

An ethics of the gospel ought never forget that the capacity for moral responsibility is intrinsically related to self-acceptance which, in turn, depends on one's acceptance by others and, ultimately, by God. Gay persons frequently have been told by their families that they do not belong to them, by the church that they are desperate sinners because of their affectional orientation, by medical doctors that they are sick, and by the law that they are criminals. In the face of this onslaught, it is amazing that so many are emotionally stable and sexually responsible. If loneliness, self-doubt, depression, and promiscuity do have a higher incidence among gays, it is fully understandable. Then we should cut through the vicious circle of self-fulfilling prophecy and strike at the root of the problem—social oppression. Thielicke fails to do this. More liberal though his position might be, by continuing to label same-sex orientation as a perversion of God's natural law, he encourages the continuation of punitive attitudes toward gays. If it be argued that we can reject the sin without rejecting the sinner, the question must be asked, but what if the so-called "sin" is as much a part of the person as the color of the skin? The upshot of it all is that Thielicke's position effectively undermines its own hopes for responsible and faithful sexual relationships.

The fourth major theological possibility is *full acceptance.* Those who affirm this position most often make the assumption that the homosexual orientation is more of a given than a free choice. More fundamentally, however, this position rests on the conviction that same-sex relationships can richly express and be the vehicle of God's humanizing intentions.

Though still in a minority, the advocates of full acceptance are increasing in number. In 1963 the English Friends stated in their widely-read *Towards a Quaker View of Sex,* "One should no more deplore 'homosexuality' than left-handedness. . . . Homosexual affection can be as selfless as heterosexual affection, and therefore we cannot see that it is in some way morally worse." [34] From the Catholic side, in 1976 Fr. John McNeill published his impressive case for gay acceptance, *The Church and the Homosexual.* Among other issues, emphasizing the positive contributions which homosexual acceptance can make to church and society, he contends, "The objective acceptance of the homosexual community will potentially leave both communities (homosexual and heterosexual) free from the need to conform to narrow stereotypes, and positively free to develop all the qualities that belong to the fullness of the human personality." [35]

Among theologians it has been Norman Pittenger, however, who has articulated the full acceptance position most persistently over the years.[36] God, he affirms, is the "Cosmic Lover," ceaselessly and unfailingly in action as love, and manifested supremely in Jesus Christ. God's abiding purpose for humankind is that in response to divine action we should realize our intended humanity as human lovers—in the richest, broadest, and most responsible sense of the term. Our embodied sexuality is the physiological and psychological base for our capacity to love.

For all of its continuity with animal sexuality, human sexuality is different, continues Pittenger. As persons our sexuality means the possibility of expressing and sharing a total personal relationship in love, a relationship which contributes immeasurably toward our intended destiny. Hence, abnormality or deviance should not be defined statistically, but rather in reference to the norm of humanity in Jesus Christ. Gay persons desire and need deep and lasting relationships just as do heterosexuals, and appropriate genital expression should be denied to neither.

Thus, the ethical question which Pittenger poses is this: what sexual behavior will serve and enhance, rather than inhibit, damage, or destroy the fuller realization of our divinely-intended humanity? The answer is sexual behavior in accord with an ethics of love. This means commitment and trust, tenderness, respect for the other, and the desire for ongoing and responsible communion with the other. On the negative side, an ethics of love mandates against selfish sexual expression, cruelty, impersonal sex, obsession with sex, and against actions done without willingness to take responsibility for the consequences. Such an ethics always asks about the meanings of acts in their total context—in the relationship itself, in society,

and in regard to God's intended direction for human life. Such an
ethics of sexual love is equally appropriate to heterosexual and gay
Christians. There is no double standard.

Further Reflections

Reinhold Niebuhr argued that Christians must learn to live with
the tension of "having and not having the truth." [37] "Tolerance" in
its truest sense, he maintained, comes when we can have vital convictions which lead to committed actions and, at the same time,
recognize that our own "truth" is always incomplete and subject
to distortion. Living with convictions we also then live within the
reality of divine forgiveness and with respect for the convictions
of those who sincerely differ from us. That spirit is always essential, I believe, but when we confront issues like homosexuality on
which feelings are particularly deep and divided, it is especially
crucial.

At various times I have felt the force of each of the first three
stances which I have described, beginning as a teenager with the
full complement of anti-gay stereotypes and prejudices. Having
moved somewhat later into the rejecting-non-punitive and then the
qualified acceptance positions, several personal friendships with
remarkable gay Christian people jarred me into further reflection.
I came to believe that nothing less than full Christian acceptance of
homosexuality and of its responsible genital expression adequately
represented the direction of both gospel and contemporary research.
While full acceptance means a rather sharp turning from the majority opinion in the Christian *moral* tradition about homosexuality, I
am convinced that it does not mean an *ethical* change from the central thrust of the gospel. Rather, it means its fuller implementation.

There are times when we must challenge specific moral traditions of our heritage in the light of new empirical knowledge, new
experience, and God's on-going revelation. Our ancestors-in-faith
did not know what we now know about homosexuality as a psychosexual orientation, nor can we blame them for being persons
of their own historical time. And the dependence of early Christians on certain cultural traditions prevented them (on this issue as
on some other moral matters) from seeing some of the implications

of that gospel to which they were sincerely committed. We ought neither blame them nor pretend that we have the full truth. Our judgments—whatever they may be—are conditioned and imperfect. But we do have some insights about homosexuality now that they did not have access to, and it would be unfaithful not to use the best lights that we have.[38]

We have little definitive knowledge about the causes of homosexuality, however—or of heterosexuality, for that matter.[39] We do know that homosexuality is extraordinarily difficult to define as a coherent phenomenon, simply because gay people like heterosexuals are diverse and unique. They differ in behavior and feelings, in levels of sexual interest, in roles and ways of lovemaking, in the amount of genital activity, in attitudes about their own and others' homosexuality, in the extent to which they are open or covert about their orientation. This conclusion from the Institute for Sex Research at Indiana University bears emphasis: "Our data appear to indicate that homosexuality involves a large number of widely divergent experiences—developmental, sexual, social, and psychological—and that even after a person has been labeled 'homosexual' on the basis of his or her preferred sexual object choice, there is little that can be predicted about the person on the basis of that label." [40] One thing, I would add, can be predicted, however, precisely because it is common to all human beings: gay persons desire and seek meaning and wholeness in and through their sexuality, and their sexuality is for them (as for anyone else) of intrinsic importance to their capacity for any kind of human love.

This chapter's emphasis thus far has been upon one of the two directions appropriate to sexual theology: the movement from Christian faith to sexuality. But we need also to make inquiry in the other direction as well, asking how our own experience as sexual persons tends to give shape to our perceptions of the faith and its moral values. In doing so we can understand more fully something of the persisting power of anti-gay stereotypes as well as the intensity of feeling about this whole issue.

Some of the anti-homosexual emotion might stem from the repugnance some people feel about the physical acts of gay sexual expression. It is well to recall just what they are. The chief expressions are hand-holding, kissing, mutual caressing, and mutual masturbation (for both sexes); cunnilingus (for women); and fellatio and anal intercourse (for men). The point is that all of these physical techniques are the property of heterosexuals as well, some statistically more common than others but all widely used. It is unlikely that the foreignness of the physical act to heterosexual experience explains very much.

It may be that heterosexuals feel less personally defined by their sexual orientation and that the apparent centrality of homosexuality to the gay's personal identity is disturbing. But, to the extent that this is true, it is more effect than cause of discrimination—just as racial minority people are typically more conscious of their own skin color, through countless daily reminders from the majority. It seems, on the whole, more accurate to say that heterosexuals simply tend to be preoccupied with the narrowly sexual aspect of the gay person's life, in spite of the fact that gays "vary profoundly in the degree to which their homosexual commitment and its facilitation become the organizing principle of their lives." [41]

For this reason language becomes highly significant. The term "homosexual" is clinically correct if it refers simply to the fact that an individual's primary affectional and genital orientation is toward the same sex. Thus, to speak of "homosexuality" meaning a psychosexual orientation or to speak of "homosexual acts" where the reference is specifically to genital and other physical expression is quite accurate. But unfortunately the word carries other associations for many—especially that of clinical pathology and a focus on sexual acts *per se* rather than on human beings. Thus, gays are entirely appropriate in their insistence that *persons* who have this alternative form of sexual orientation be called gay. It is a way of saying more comprehensively and more accurately that one's identity as a sexual human being is far broader than what one does in bed. It is a way of resisting the corrosive effect of having to deal with one's own self-image so constantly in genital terms, in spite of the majority's desire to keep the focus there.[42]

To press the causes of anti-gay feeling more fully, we need to reflect once more on the two alienating sexual dualisms. Consider spiritualistic dualism. By the strange twist of heterosexual emotional-logic, it would appear that gays are resented because they seem to have succumbed less to the spirit-body dualism which afflicts us all in various ways. Feeling the internally divisive affects of spiritualism, we yearn (unconsciously as well as consciously) to be whole, to reclaim the essential unity of the body-self. But since majority stereotype insists that gays are more sexually defined and simply *more sexual* than the rest, they may well become the targets of subconscious envy precisely for that reason. Thus, the stereotype bears its curious and unintended harvest, but one which roots it even more firmly in the feelings of many who hold it.

The problem of patriarchal or sexist dualism may be even more basic to anti-gay feeling. This might be experienced in several related ways. One is the heterosexual's possible anxiety about homosexual feelings within the self. While for the sake of economy I have been using "gay" and "heterosexual" in ways that might suggest two sharply distinct and mutually-exclusive groups, current research indicates that people commonly tend toward some degree of bisexuality. Most, for reasons not yet fully understood, develop a *dominant* orientation toward one side or the other. Kinsey's early hypothesis, however, has been repeatedly confirmed by subsequent research: on the scale of zero to six, relatively few persons fall near the zero end (exclusively heterosexual in *both* feelings and behavior) and relatively few near the six mark (exclusively homosexual). Most are somewhere in between, though with a clearly felt and expressed bias toward one orientation rather than the other.

A recent study draws this conclusion: "Although we *suspect* that approximately four or five percent of American males—and half of that percentage of females—are exclusively homosexual in their behaviors throughout their lives, much larger numbers are exclusively homosexual in their behaviors at any given time, and even larger numbers engage in both homosexual and heterosexual acts from time to time. For a given individual, ratings on this homosexual-heterosexual continuum may go up or down depending upon the person's age, life circumstances, and the culture in which he or she lives." [43] Further, there is not necessarily a perfect fit between one's feelings and one's behaviors regarding sexual orientation.

Even for those whose genital expression beyond puberty has been exclusively heterosexual, there may be homosexual feelings present even if relegated to the unconscious level. Freud's notion of reaction formation becomes pertinent at this point: one way of coping with unwanted impulses felt in the self is by attacking it in others.[44]

Because of patriarchalism and exaggerated images of masculinity, such anxiety is frequently felt more strongly by men—an additional reason why male gays have consistently been more the objects of negative majority feeling than have lesbians. It seems highly probable that the much more severe condemnation of male homosexual acts in the Old Testament expresses this patriarchal phenomenon: "If a man lies with a male *as with a woman,* both of them have committed an abomination; they shall be put to death, their blood is upon them" (Leviticus 20:13, italics added). If male dignity was a primary consideration, then "sodomy" could not be tolerated, because when a man acted sexually like a woman he was committing a *degradation*—literally, a loss of grade or status—not only in regard to himself but also, by implication, for every other male. But this is not true of the early Hebrews alone. Anthropologists have noted the strong tendency of patriarchal cultures, wherever they may be, to view (especially male) homosexuality as "the unspeakable sin," while matriarchal cultures have been strikingly different on this issue.[45]

A male is supposed to feel masculine in any patriarchy. A psychiatrist comments, "I believe that homosexuality is also abhorred by men because it is felt by them to represent confused, poorly defined and poorly delineated boundaries of what constitutes so-called normal male feelings. Homosexuality, the word and the symbol, threatens masculine gender identity, and identity generally, because it is felt as potential eradication of safe limits and borders within whose confines we can rest easy and sure of what and who we are supposed to be and what we are supposed to feel." [46] Pollution rituals as studied by anthropologists (see Chapter 2) provide added insight. Those rituals and punishments, in both ancient tribes and modern societies, tend to focus upon the marginal person who does not clearly represent society's patterns and symbols of order. Such persons may be doing nothing morally wrong, yet their status is indefinable. But this places them very basically "in the wrong" for they have "developed some wrong condition or simply crossed some line which should not have been crossed and this displacement unleashes danger for someone." [47]

In spite of the lack of any demonstrable connection between male homosexual orientation and "effeminate" behavior patterns, the gay male seems particularly threatening to many other men. He seems to belie the importance of super-masculinity, and his very presence seems to call into question so much that many other men have sacrificed to be "manly." But many heterosexual women likewise have difficulty coping with the lesbian. The lesbian is independent from male control in ways that other women are not, and when a heterosexual woman has deeply internalized sexist dualism such independence becomes a considerable threat. Furthermore, both men and women of heterosexual orientation can feel diminished by the presence of a gay person of the opposite sex. Consciously or unconsciously there is awareness that the gay person has no specifically sexual interest in them. To the extent that sexual attractiveness is vital to one's sense of basic self-worth, this, too, is threatening.

There are additional ways in which gay people raise the anxieties of many heterosexuals. Because of their sexual orientation, gay folk appear to disvalue commonly-held values concerning marriage, family, and children. And because we so frequently judge others using our own standards as the ultimate and unquestionable norm, those who so obviously deviate from our experience seem to be seriously deviant indeed. Curiously enough, gay people can also awaken in others a dimly-recognized fear of death. Sometimes the hope of vicarious immortality through children and grandchildren is, in fact, stronger than the resurrection faith for many Christians. If so, the presence of the gay person who (usually) does not have children can awaken the fear of death, even though consciousness of that might be only a nameless anxiety.[48]

At its root, the issue goes beyond the insights of the psychologists, anthropologists, and sociologists, valuable though those insights be. It is finally a theological matter, an issue of faith. If we must find an important part of our personal security in a status which depends upon the negative definition of those who differ from us—and if we must find the security of our social order through rigid demarcations of behaviors regardless of their causation, their motivations, their moral intent, or their actual consequences—then we are living by something other than the grace of God.

On the other hand, through that very grace we might know something of the healing possibilities for the sexual dualisms that beset us. To that extent we will not need to project our own alienation onto others but can join with them in our common liberation. It will be liberation from a hierarchical and intensely power-conscious attitude toward life. It will be liberation from the need to organize the proper membership of both church and society around a principle of sex orientation. It will be liberation from the need to blame a minority group for the erosion of all of "our" values. But more, it can be a liberation into greater equality, more sensitive abilities to care about persons, augmented justice, in short, a freedom to love more fully—others and also ourselves.[49]

Implications for the Church

The church's unequivocal support of civil rights for gay people ought not depend upon Christian agreement about the theological and moral appropriateness of homosexuality. The matter of civil rights is a matter of basic Christian commitment to social justice for all persons.[50]

The present legal situation is highly uneven. A few states and municipalities have legisled civil protection for gays, prohibiting discrimination in employment, public accommodations, housing, and licensing on the basis of "affectional or sexual preference." But the majority have not, nor has the federal government. And the passage of such legislation is no guarantee that it will not be rescinded.[51]

Most states still have punitive legislation concerning gay people on their books, though in actual practice enforcement is varied and unpredictable.[52] In any event, laws labeling "sodomy" or "unnatural sexual intercourse" as punishable offenses have a number of inherent problems. They violate the rights of privacy. They are ineffective and virtually unenforceable except through objectionable police methods such as entrapment and enticement. Yet, whether they are enforced or not, sodomy laws stigmatize as criminal the person whose only "crime" is preference for the same sex, and inevitably such laws will take their toll in the gay person's sense of self-worth. Moreover, an important principle of church-state separation may be involved. What some Christians on fairly narrow doctrinal grounds consider a *sin* ought not to be made a *crime* unless that moral judgment can be defended on broader grounds of public welfare and unless the behavior in question constitutes a provable threat to public decency and personal well-being.

What about the internal life of the churches?[53] If and when the churches were to affirm homosexuality and its responsible expression as Christianly appropriate, the implications for church life would be many. Full acceptance of gay Christians into the ongoing life of Christian congregations is basic. Because it is still so largely absent, gay movement toward congregations organized by themselves and principally for gays will undoubtedly continue. It is completely understandable, and in the present day it may be necessary. It is also regrettable, for the majority's exclusionism then continues to fragment the body of Christ. It is an irony, indeed, for while the human sciences and contemporary culture at large have been urging the church to take sexuality more seriously, the church in regard to gays and women has made sexuality primary: it has been used as the organizing principle by which these people have been excluded from full participation.[54]

Congregational affirmation of gays would involve significant attitudinal changes on the part of many other members of the church. Full acceptance of gays as persons, for example, means that all of those gestures and behaviors which are appropriate for heterosexuals are also appropriate for gay people.

Effective pastoral counseling and support for gay persons is crucial. By training, profession, and calling the clergy should be those to whom gay people might turn in complete confidence. At present it often is not so. Lack of sufficient information, lack of insight into the problems which gays confront in a hostile environment, and lack of some deep understanding and acceptance concerning their own sexuality remain formidable problems with many clergy. And this constitutes an important agenda item for theological education.

The church's ministry is to the gay community as well as to gay individuals. While full integration into the richly diverse body of Christ is the ideal, there is also need for supportive gay Christian groups now and in the foreseeable future. A study of male gays in the United States and two European countries points this out: "Perhaps our most salient finding pertains to the beneficial effects (in terms of psychological adjustment) of a supportive environment—social relations with other homosexuals, their own institutions and publications." [55] From gay coffee houses in local churches to denominationally-supported gay caucuses, these things are needed. That gay bars and baths are still virtually the only institutionalized meeting places in many urban areas should make a claim upon the church's conscience.

The ordination question continues to be difficult. Not only division over theological and ethical issues but also differing patterns of ministerial placement and job security cause reservations for otherwise sympathetic church leaders. While there are undoubtedly ordained homosexually-oriented ministers right now in every denomination, the vast majority of them quite understandably continue their secrecy. It was not until 1972 that a major American denomination, the United Church of Christ, ordained a publicly-avowed gay candidate, and the second instance took another four years, this time an Episcopalian event. There will be others, but the process is painful and painfully slow. The recommendation made by the United Church's Executive Council to its ordaining bodies is worthy of consideration by other denominations: "that in the instance of considering a stated homosexual candidacy for ordination, the issue should not be his/her homosexuality as such, but rather the candidate's total view of human sexuality and his/her understanding of the morality of its use." [56] Though presently this may be difficult to implement in some denominational situations, it is the logic of full acceptance. Church assemblies may continue to claim "prudential grounds" as their main reason for barring gay ordinations for some time to come, but one day perhaps that form of prudence will sound as thin as when it was used to bar women and racial minorities from ministry.

Most difficult of all for the church at present is the idea of "homosexual marriage." Heterosexuals of the "rejecting-punitive" and "rejecting-nonpunitive" persuasions, of course, are adamantly opposed to any such thing. But in the "qualified acceptance" position there is a curious ambivalence. On the one hand, there is an insistence that the non-celibate gay person have a genitally-exclusive permanent relationship; homosexual relationships are tolerated only insofar as they approximate heterosexual monogamy. (This insistence,

I believe, often does not represent a genuine attempt to understand
the range of meanings in homosexual relationships, nor does it do
justice to the different social circumstances under which gay women
and men must live.) [57] But when gay persons *do* want to relate their
genital expression to life commitment, as many do, "the church in
its concern for morality turns away from these moral hungers
and concerns." [58]

It is true that the issue of marriage is complicated by the nature
of symbolic traditions. As an ordinance or as a sacrament, marriage
has a long theological and ecclesiastical history, and that history
has been an exclusively heterosexual one. Deeply-rooted symbols
are organic. They grow and develop, and sudden changes are seldom successfully legislated. But when existing symbols do not meet
legitimate needs, new symbols and rites may be developed. A "Blessing of Union" rite (by whatever name), for example, might function
for gays in ways fully parallel to the marriage rites. Such an ordinance would convey the Christian community's recognition, affirmation, pledge of support, and prayer for divine blessing to the gay
couple whose intention is lasting fidelity.

Predictably, acceptance of this is a long time off. Heterosexual
Christians who want to affirm individual gays but reject all homosexual genital love will argue that since genital expression belongs
only in heterosexual marriage, gay Christians have only one legitimate and responsible choice—celibacy. "Just as we expect the
heterosexual to be continent outside of marriage, so, too, the homosexual." [59] But this demonstrates lack of sensitivity to the gay person's socially-imposed dilemma. The heterosexual's abstinence is
either freely chosen for a lifetime or it is temporary until marriage.
But the celibacy some Christians would impose upon the gay person
would be involuntary and unending.[60]

Those others who urge the non-celibate gay to seek a permanent
relationship, and yet would withhold any liturgical blessing, are
saying something different but also insensitive. By withholding full
recognition of such sexual covenants the church only, if unintention-
ally, promotes promiscuity, for it says in effect, "*Whatever* your relationship is, it is not fit for public Christian affirmation, support, and
celebration." To urge a course of action, fully-committed relation-

ships, and then to deny communal and ritual support to those very relationships is to engage in a humanly destructive contradiction.

When and if the church moves toward liturgical support of gay unions, it should also press toward civil recognition. Such legal matters as tax laws, property rights, and inheritance rights are of legitimate concern to a gay couple and, I believe, are a matter of the equity to which love's justice presses us. Moreover, the symbolic affirmation given by the civil community through legal recognition ought not to be minimized.

On the difficult question of whether previously-married gay persons should be allowed to retain custody of their children when they enter into a gay union, the courts have taken a variety of positions. Yet the main difficulty of the question is not principally the matter of whether the children themselves would be shaped into a homosexual orientation. Dr. John Money speaks to the point: "Society's apprehensions notwithstanding, it is not inevitably psychically dangerous for children, boys or girls, to live with a divorced parent who sets up a new household with a partner of the same sex. . . . It is not the sameness or difference of the sex of the adults that counts, but the quality of the relationship between them, and the quality of the relationship they establish with the child." [81] The real difficulty lies in the fragmenting pressures which the social environment can put upon a same-sex couple, to the detriment of children. For this the church itself must acknowledge its share of responsibility—but it can also respond to the opportunity with its still considerable capacity to influence public opinion on such moral issues.

The ecclesiastical implications of full gay acceptance are doubtless complex, at least in their effective implementation. Understandably, however, many gay Christians are tired of waiting for all of the complexities to be resolved to the full satisfaction of the majority group. These minority Christians have waited—and have hurt—long enough.[62] Pushed away from the Lord's Table by subtle or blatant pressures, they have been pushed to find community in the gay bars, baths, and ghettos. One gay Christian puts it in these haunting words: "Usually, for most gay women and men, coming out *in* the church has meant coming out *of* the church. . . . Coming out of the closet, a process the church should be enabling and

ennobling, is a process which must be experienced more often in
the secular world rather than the Christian community. . . . And for
most of those numerous gay persons who choose not to come out in
the church because they want to *stay* in the church—in Christian
community—the church has meant more than just a closet . . . the
church has become for them a giant tomb, smelling of death rather
than life." [63]

Surely there is much research on homosexuality (and on heterosexuality as well) that still needs to be done. But this much is clear:
our sexuality is vitally important to the dignity of each of us. The
basic issue is really not about "them," but about all of us. How can
we live less fearfully and more securely in the grace of God? What
is the nature of that loving humanity toward which the Spirit presses
us? And what does it mean to be a woman or a man in Jesus Christ?

9

The Sexually Disenfranchised

VEN THOUGH SEXUALITY is inescapably part of our being—regardless of physical or mental condition and throughout the life-span —social attitudes often tend to desex certain groups of people. Christian literature on sexual theology and ethics typically ignores this phenomenon, as does the church at large. Perhaps this says something more about our own religious and sexual self-understandings than about the amount of factual information currently available.

Our tendency to treat groups of people as nonsexual is a denigration of personhood and thus a claim on the Christian conscience. Furthermore, it is a vivid illustration of the interaction of the biological and physical with the emotional-cognitive-spiritual dimensions in human sexuality. That our sexuality is not simply a matter of biological drive and capacity but just as importantly a matter of meanings is amply illustrated by four groups of people: the physically disabled, the seriously ill, the aging, and the mentally retarded.

The Physically Disabled

One of the major social myths surrounding the physically handicapped is that they are nonsexual beings.[1] We use words such as "crippled," "deformed," "maimed," and "paralyzed" which suggest that they are both utterly incapable of any sexual expression and totally uninterested in such. Often, the very conspicuously disabled person also is socially labeled as mentally retarded, even though mental abilities are usually unaffected and the individual might have a brilliant mind. Many also fear that the physically disabled (if they are capable of intercourse at all) will produce disabled offspring. And there is the shadow side of the common mythology: while most typically they are thought of as nonsexual, occasionally the disabled are believed to have perverted and excessive sexual needs.

Beneath these myths lie two distortions common to the alienated body-self and frequently projected onto others. One is that our sexuality somehow is incidental to who we are as human beings. (Hence, it simply does not occur to us that to desex someone is profoundly to dehumanize that person.) The second distortion is that sexuality is essentially a genital matter. (Hence, those rendered incapable of certain types of genital experience are, by that fact, nonsexual.)

One problem with any social projection, of course, is the possibility of self-fulfilling prophecy. Stereotypes are internalized—but at profound personal cost. Even if such internalization is resisted by the disabled, they must still struggle for self-acceptance and legitimate sexual expression in a hostile environment.

At this point we need to identify the general types of disabilities under consideration. Dr. Theodore M. Cole, a leading researcher in physical rehabilitation and sexuality, notes that there are both nonprogressive and progressive disabilities, and in each category are types which have their onset early in life and those which typically come in postpubertal years.[2] Nonprogressive disabilities include brain injuries, spinal cord injuries or diseases, skeletal amputations and deformities, genital injuries, blindness, deafness and similar conditions. Progressive disabilities include cystic fibrosis, muscular dystrophy, heart disease, strokes, diabetes mellitus, multiple sclerosis, and end stage renal disease. But *none* of the above conditions makes the individual nonsexual. Indeed many disabled persons discover that the injury or disease does not significantly alter their desire for genital sex.

Nevertheless, any disabled individual will experience sexual problems—whether from the disability itself or from social attitudes rooted in ignorance, fear, and sexual alienation. Several types of problems are reported. One, of course, is actual physical impairment of sexual functioning. Another may be the lack of a sexual partner. Further, there is often the lack of knowledge of what is sexually possible, a factor directly related to the lack of initiative and attention which medical personnel and clergy typically give to the sexuality of the disabled. In addition, the young adult with a genetically-based progressive disease frequently experiences a particular burden: "he or she may feel an obligation not to produce children and therefore feel not entitled to sexual fulfillment." [3] And those who have experienced the onset of their disease or injury very early in life have an additional handicap. Typically they have simply missed the more usual sexual socialization, for during their formative years parents or institutional personnel have been unable to accept the fact of their sexuality.

In spite of such problems, the capacities for both physical and emotional sexual expression are surprising. Much of the current research has been directed toward spinal cord injured people, and a brief look at their possibilities is illuminating.[4] The majority of spinal cord injured men have reflex penile erections, though most are unable to ejaculate and most are infertile. Women with spinal cord injuries find their fertility virtually unaffected. In both sexes the extent of injury to pelvic nerves will of course determine the amount of physical sensation (if any) experienced in the genitals. The crucial finding, however, is this: "Persons of both sexes report *achieving orgasm in spite of complete denervation of all pelvic structures.* Fantasy apparently plays a large role. Some patients report being able to reassign sensation from a neurologically intact portion of their bodies to their genitalia and experiencing orgasm from that sensation in their fantasy. Many report this type of orgasm to be entirely satisfying and leading to a comfortable resolution of sexual tension." [5] Sexual desire does not depend upon the presence of actual physical sensation for these people. "It is not uncommon for paraplegics to experience phantom sensations of genital awareness by erotic stimulation of other erogenous zones." [6]

The physically disabled person thus gives significant testimony to human body-spirit unity. "The orgasm of the mind" is not independent of the body. Rather, this phenomenon underscores the fact that orgasmic sexual fulfillment must involve the mind and emotions as well as the body. Indeed, when the genital nerves themselves are impaired, so powerful is the quest for mind-body unity that orgasmic sensations can be experienced even in nerve-dead organs.

The sexual possibilities for the spinal cord injured, then, are more varied than most of us recognize. There is the possibility of orgasm itself, often reported in terms comparable to the sensations experienced by able-bodied people, and bringing with it profound emotional satisfaction. Still, the question of penile-vaginal intercourse is a problem for many. Paralysis of the limbs may make such intercourse extremely difficult. The man's capacity for erection induced by psychological and physical stimuli may be gone (even though spontaneous erections will still occur). Even so, many couples find the "stuffing" technique possible: the paralyzed man's flaccid penis is stuffed into his partner's vagina where by her muscular contractions she can hold it, creating pleasure for both and at times even a semi-erection. Religiously this can be of considerable importance, for some beliefs dictate the necessity of penile-vaginal intercourse if the marriage is to be valid in the sight of the church.

But when penile-vaginal intercourse is impossible or at least very time-consuming, many couples find oral-genital expression highly valuable. Once again, acceptance of oral-genital sex importantly hinges upon attitudes absorbed in one's socialization and attitudes conveyed by the religious community. If such sex expression is deemed improper, dirty, or at least suspect, then one of the major possibilities for the spinal injured person is undercut.

One of the most important capacities which remains to the paraplegic or quadriplegic is the ability to give sexually to the partner. Even if the injured partner is unable to experience orgasm, the capacity to give sexual pleasure is itself an enormous satisfaction, and it adds immeasurably to one's self-esteem. In short, loss of physical sensation does not mean loss of feelings nor does loss of fertility mean loss of ability. Most importantly, even in the most severely handicapped situations, the person is still male or female, is still "masculine" and "feminine," and has all of the sexually-based needs for giving and receiving love.

While physically-disabled persons have particular needs for information, counseling, and reassurance concerning their sexuality, few physicians, ministers, and hospital chaplains appear to be helpful in this regard. Many such professionals will simply ignore the sexual dimensions of these patients' or parishioners' lives, and the minority who do attempt to communicate often ignore the range of pleasuring techniques and the use of fantasy which are so important in the sexual expression of the disabled.

The disabled person's recovery of a positive sense of his or her sexuality, however, goes beyond direct sexual pleasure, communication, and tension-release with the partner, important though these be. On the negative side, research has found that sexually nonfunctioning paraplegics have showed a markedly diminished ability to engage in vocational training or in gainful occupations, and their sexual inabilities seem to be expressed in general feelings of insecurity and helplessness. On the positive side, disabled adults who have been assisted in the recovery of their sexual self-assurance show markedly less social withdrawal, less need for special medical and social supports, a greater interest in and capacity for gainful employment, and a general increase in self-esteem. Indeed, I have talked with a number of severely disabled persons in a sexual rehabilitation program who speak glowingly about their rediscovered sexuality as a powerful form of rebirth.

The theological implications are obvious enough. Sexuality is not incidental to who we are as persons, and when we deny it in another there is a corresponding denial of the other's full humanity. But when this dimension of life is rediscovered and reaffirmed, there is, without exaggeration, a miracle of grace. The story has been repeated time and again in lives of the disabled—from defeat, self-condemnation, withdrawal, and alienation to self-acceptance, new engagement with life, hope, and a new capacity to express care and love. And that is one expression of the mysterious and gracious power of God at work in and through human relationships.

The Seriously Ill

Persons diagnosed with a serious, possibly terminal, illness constitute another group of the sexually dispossessed. Since our society tends to define them as nonsexual, various helping professionals who work with them in their illnesses also tend to avoid the subject, further cementing the assumption in the patient's mind. Yet, there is abundant evidence to show that patients suffering from serious and even fatal diseases *do* have conscious sexual concerns and in many cases have sufficient health to enjoy some form of genital activity.

Serious illness is frequently a prelude to death. Death and sexuality are mysteriously intertwined, and this makes the picture doubly complicated. Both eros and thanatos are exceptionally powerful forces surrounded by social taboos and anxieties. Each has its own pornographies. Frank and honest communications about each is restricted. When the two are met together—as in the sexual concerns of the terminally ill person—the problems are multiplied.

Sexuality and death appear to be vastly different, and in some important ways, of course, they are. Death is an ending, while sexuality seems to represent life, new creation, vitality. But in other ways the two are intertwined. In sex as in dying, there is a letting go. In each there is both invitation and threat regarding loss of identity and absorption. In both the radical question of the meaning of our embodied existence is posed.

The various ways sexuality intertwines with serious illness is illustrated by several testimonies, the first from a medical educator. Dr. Daniel H. Labby writes, "During illness, the loss of a sense of intactness, especially as related to body image, can cause great anxiety about the capacity to function sexually; feelings of self-worth and attractiveness to others are threatened at a time when need for intimacy is greatest. Loneliness and isolation add to the psychologic stresses of illness. The result is sexual deprivation—loss of an important means of tension reduction at a time when it is most useful and necessary. Illness can so powerfully block normal expressions of feeling that sexual acting out occurs, sometimes in grotesque and socially unacceptable forms, reminding us that our sexuality is a critical component of our expressive life, necessary to general well-being, and devastating in its loss." [7]

Lois Jaffe, a professor of social work (herself suffering terminal cancer), says this: "It is a myth that once you have become terminally ill, you no longer have any sex desire. The drive and capability can still be there. . . . Sex desire may actually increase . . . but doctors, nurses or family members will not recognize or discuss this need. Sexual problems thus arouse anxiety that is added to the anxiety about dying." [8]

JoAnn Kelley Smith, in a book written shortly before her own death of cancer, speaks of her own changing sexuality during the course of her illness: "My problems are deeply rooted in who I am as a sexual being. I feel that sexuality has been taken from me. [After breast removal] I needed help in learning to accept myself. . . . But our sexual relationship has always been an important part of our marriage, and because its mutual enjoyment is gone, I now realize death has come to another area of human existence. . . ." [9]

The patient remains a sexual being until death comes. Regardless of the degree of physical incapacitation, if there is consciousness there is still self-awareness of one's masculinity and femininity, one's body image, one's desire and need for intimate human relatedness. The capacity for genital sex expression will vary. Sometimes the disease itself will be genitally incapacitating, though frequently the loss of this ability is more related to psychological than to physical reasons. [10] Indeed, the patient may often feel the desire for increased sexual activity with the spouse, as a way of clinging to life's vitalities and as a way of coping with death's anxieties.

Terminally ill patients report a variety of sexual problems directly related to their illnesses. Some of these problems stem from their physical condition. They may simply feel too ill or too tired for sexual activity and then feel personal failure because of this. They might refrain from coitus out of the fear of frustrating both the spouse and themselves. Because of the disease's marks upon the body there may be a sense of the loss of sexual attractiveness to the partner. There may be worries about bodily injury which might be sustained during sexual activity, worries unresolved because of ignorance concerning what is possible. There may be loss of erectile capacity in men and loss of lubricating and vaginal swelling capacity in women.

Nevertheless, the patient's typical sexual problems appear to be related to psychological and emotional more than directly physical factors. And it is precisely here that the conspiracy of silence surrounding both death and sexual matters with the terminally ill is most destructive. Often the patient is confronted by "double-bind" communication patterns regarding the impending death.[11] Those close by give incongruent messages in well-intentioned but misguided attempts to conceal the seriousness of the disease. The patient then responds to the gaps in knowledge with fantasies, fears, and with a sense of helplessness and frustration all of which further complicate relationships and threaten considerable estrangement from the spouse. Thus, death dishonesty compounds sexual dishonesty.

Long-hospitalized patients also report their acute need for simple physical touch. But the healthy partner frequently has fears of touching and stroking, fears which have not been alleviated by appropriate counsel and information. In such a situation, the patient's sexual fantasies may become transferred from the spouse to doctors or nurses who now are the only ones handling and soothing the body.

There are a host of other potential complications for the relationship of the patient and spouse. In a remarkable article, Lois and Arthur Jaffe report their own interpersonal adjustments during her terminal cancer.[12] The intensity of the relationship itself is increased with the knowledge of terminal illness. But the ill partner and the healthy one must also cope with movement in different directions. Both experience "anticipatory grief," with the patient needing to withdraw at times from the intense marital and family relationship to cope with the meaning of impending death. The healthy spouse may have unconscious fears of contagion—that the disease or even death itself might be contagious if too close physical contact is made. The healthy spouse must cope with anticipated loss of the partner; the relationship has only a limited future. This realization might mean that sexual interaction is avoided or even sought with someone else as an antidote to the impending loss. Thus, there can be both sexual and emotional movement away from the dying one.

Long-term hospitalization usually means sexual abstinence. In this situation the healthy one might experience guilt over continuing sexual desires and unconscious anger at the patient for having the disease, thus depriving them both of sexual fulfillment. Both guilt and anger can lead to depression which inevitably lowers the sense of one's own sexual health and further threatens self-esteem. Wives and husbands also report problems in staying synchronized to each other's needs. Cancer patients may have periods, sometimes long, of temporary remission. During such times the ill partner may look quite healthy and yet is still dependent upon the other to bear additional physical and emotional burdens. The net result may be guilt and relational strain at a time when both desire to experience their limited remaining time together most fully. Then there is the return to the hospital for additional therapy—treatment which may cause loss of hair, miserable and continued vomiting, and a renewed sense of the impending death.

For all of the difficulties incumbent upon a sexual relationship during terminal illness there are also immense possibilities. Patients and their spouses report the deepening of their bonds and the clarifying of their real values. They report a more intense orientation to the possibilities of the present moment with each other, and the graceful appreciation of just being, not always doing.

All of this raises important questions for the church as a sexual community. We must reexamine both those theologies and personal insecurities which lead the healthy to desex the ill. Part of the problem lies in traditional sexual attitudes, many of them Christianly-rooted. Part may simply be due to ignorance. But at least some of this phenomenon springs from our own sin. It is the propensity of those of us who are physically healthy to take ourselves as the norm by which all others must be judged. So doing, we assume that those significantly different from us have no right to be as sexual as we.

The persisting coupling of sex dishonesty with death dishonesty should stir the church to nurture honest and open communication about both of these areas, communication appropriate to every age level. Medical professionals can press for continuing education in such matters as well as for effective learning situations regarding sexuality and terminal illness in medical and nursing school curricula. Theological seminaries should do likewise.

Hospitals and long-term care facilities have opportunities which few yet have faced. Both individual and group counseling about sexual issues should be a regular part of patient care, especially in lengthy and terminal illnesses. Hospital policies which restrict sexual contact between long-term patients and their spouses can be changed. Before her own death JoAnn Kelley Smith spoke to the point: "One of my strongest feelings about the hospital environment is that there should be two or three rooms equipped with double beds for conjugal visits. . . . I believe it should be possible for a husband or wife to stay with his or her mate, even if it is just over-night and if the patient doesn't need a lot of nursing care, particu-larly if it's a terminal disease." [13] In the typical hospital there is much loneliness but very little privacy. A "quiet room," argues Lois Jaffe, could easily be set up in almost every hospital—furnished with couch, carpeting, music, and soft lights—to be used for times of sexual expression with the spouse as well as for family visits and counseling. Reclining lounge chairs could be available for every hospital room which terminal patients occupy so that a loved one can be comfortably near the patient who needs the reassurance of a continued caring presence.

We ought not underestimate the breadth of human sexual needs in terminal illness. Sexuality is the physical communication of em-bodied selves. If healing frequently comes in the laying on of hands, it may in these situations be the emotional-spiritual healing so cru-cial to those near life's end. Elsewhere I have written about the experience of a close friend and clergy colleague of mine—an expe-rience which deserves repeating in this context. "His mother was dying of cancer. Her body was clearly showing the ravages of the disease, and she was distressed by her altered appearance. On the one hand, she was resistant to the visits of those close to her be-cause of her disfigurement. Yet, at the same time, her need for physi-cal closeness and personal intimacy was great. Her son came to the hospital to visit, and as they talked, he rubbed her back to relieve some of the pain. After a time, sensing her need for even greater closeness, he lay down on the hospital bed beside her and held her closely in his arms. In that position they talked for a long time that afternoon, sharing thoughts and feelings more deeply than ever before. Later that night she died." [14] It was, said my friend, clearly a sexual experience of the most appropriate kind between mother and son—an experience of physical closeness which deepened love's bonds and eased the pain of impending death.

The Aging

The aging also belong to the sexually disenfranchised. Just as our society continues to have punitive attitudes toward the physically disabled because they violate our criterion of "normal health," so also we punish the elderly for violating our criterion of youth. The American zeal to knock down old buildings and replace them with the modern and new simply points to our phobic obsession with age. Growing old is viewed as an insulting and dehumanizing process. The media parade the cult of youth, and vast amounts of self-hate are nurtured in the elderly precisely because of the power of these social attitudes. Sexuality, accordingly, is seen as the appropriate province of the younger. Our language denies the elderly permission to be sexual persons: a sexually active young man might well accept as a compliment the term "stud," but if a male in older years continues to be sexually interested, he is "a dirty old man."

Mary S. Calderone trenchantly observes that society seems to inflict sexual incapacity on older persons as a type of wish-fulfillment. They are told, in effect, "You are old and finished with life, so you should be finished with sex—especially since trying to meet your sex-related needs might add to the bother of looking after you." [15] Thus, in institutions for the aging (except for the supervised lounges and planned events), women and men often are segregated, and relatives give tacit approval to this arrangement as if ashamed that their parent or grandparent might still be human enough to experience sexual loneliness. As Calderone says, "Denial of the right to feel affectively and of opportunity to fulfill affective needs is not only one of the many ways in which we dehumanize the aging, but is one of the most effective in that it strikes at that part of each one that is most personal, most meaningful, most private, most difficult to acknowledge." [16]

Professionals who work with the elderly—doctors, nurses, ministers, social workers—too frequently participate in this dehumanizing ritual, based upon unexamined stereotypes. "Many physicians," notes one of them, "do not include sexuality in their questioning of a patient. They demur." [17] Observes another physician, "The family doctor or specialist to whom the older person may turn for advice on sexual matters may himself have difficulty in handling sexual problems or guiding his older patients' sexual activities because of lack of medical data and lack of medical training in this aspect of social life." [18]

Family pressures may be put upon the elderly. A widowed parent may be urged in subtle or less-than-subtle ways to be "faithful" to the dead spouse, or at least to live in accord with the beliefs of the children, who themselves may never have been able to think of the parent as a sexual being.[19]

The result for many of the elderly is self-fulfilling prophecy. Lacking social permission to express their attraction to another person, afraid of appearing ridiculous or immature if they were to reveal their sexual needs, overwhelmed with confusing guilt feelings about sexual desires, they themselves deny their own sexuality.

Several common beliefs linking sexuality to youth and hence denying it to the aged need reexamination. The indivisibility of sexual function from procreation, nurtured by centuries of Christian tradition, suggests to many that when procreative possibility ends at the woman's menopause sex activity is suspect. This idea is waning, but for numerous of the now-elderly it still has some effect.[20]

Also common is the notion that sexual activity and passion physically can occur only in young adulthood and (to some extent) in middle age, but that sexual tension and the need for its expression decline quickly in the middle years and disappear completely in old age. The now-known facts of the matter indicate quite differently. To be sure, the major studies of sexual performance indicate a steady decline in the frequency of intercourse in the middle years and a steady rise in male impotence after the forty to fifty age period.[21] On the other hand, given the pressures upon the elderly to become nonsexual, the amount of sexual vitality still being expressed by many is surprising. A well-known Duke University research project studied two hundred sixty men and women, black and white, married and single, all over sixty years of age. It discovered that from 40 to 65 percent of the people between the ages of sixty and seventy-one were still having sexual intercourse with some frequency, and of those aged seventy-eight and older upwards of 20 percent still reported sexual activity.[22]

The work of Masters and Johnson with the sexual functioning of aging people is also instructive.[23] In the aging process, they report, sexual responsiveness gradually declines in its physiology. The male sex hormone, testosterone, is reduced and there is somewhat less ejaculation and fewer viable sperm, and yet reasonably healthy men can continue to sire children until the end of life. It takes somewhat longer to achieve an erection, but once achieved, it can be maintained for longer periods of time before orgasm. Masters and Johnson find six main reasons for loss of sexual interest and responsiveness in the aging men. Significantly, only one of them is directly physiological: debilitating diseases (arthritis, strokes, Parkinson's disease, etc.). The others tend to be psychologically induced: monotony or boredom in sexual relations, preoccupation with career and money, mental and physical fatigue, overindulgence in food and drink, and performance fears relating to these factors.

In the older woman there are corresponding physiological changes. Importantly, this research refutes the notion that postmenopausal women usually experience considerable decrease in sexual satisfaction. In fact, for many there is a gain because of the absence of conception worries and, for mothers, freedom from the demands of a family at this age. To be sure, the gradual aging of the body reduces the rapidity of physical sexual response: the sexual organs lose some elasticity, vaginal lubrication lessens, and (as with men) the duration of physiological orgasmic sensations is somewhat shorter. But significantly, the most notable reason for loss of sexual activity and responsiveness in women is the husband's loss of interest or capacity.

For both men and women an important correlation has been discovered: the maintenance of effective sexual expression in the aging years depends heavily on the regularity of sexual activity throughout adult life. Those who have established a high level of sexual activity between the ages of twenty and forty report a continuance of significantly high levels of sexual functioning both in middle age and older years. Not only, of course, do many of the physical capacities for intercourse and masturbation continue throughout the life span, but also strong sexual interest persists in many of the elderly. Studies conducted of nursing home residents indicate that considerable sexual interest and fantasy persist even though activity levels are low because of the lack of a partner and the lack of social permission.[24]

Most importantly, even when genital activity, for varying reasons, has severely diminished or even ceased in the elderly person, she or he continues to be very much a sexual being. In a recent video-taped discussion, five panelists (ranging in ages from sixty-eight to eighty-seven and all widowed) defined companionship and compassion as crucial components of sexuality, and all echoed the feeling of being starved for affection.[25] Mary Calderone says it well: "The drive built in at birth for warm, close, intimate contact with another human being never diminishes in intensity and meaningfulness, and in the older age person can have a kind of last chance quality of such strength that its frustration may quickly lead to despair and irreversible apathy. Yet satisfaction of this drive may bear little relation to sex acts." [26]

Another crippling notion strongly rooted in our culture contends that sexuality is built principally upon physical attraction between the sexes. This is part of the cult of youth and is strongly reinforced by the advertising industry, much to the detriment of the aging person. Not only sexual attraction but also romance itself is pictured as the special (often exclusive) province of the young. Such prejudicial "agism" destructively merges with sexism to the profound detriment of the older woman. Susan Sontag expresses the point in these searing words: ". . . the point of women dressing up, applying make-up, dyeing their hair, etc., is not just to be attractive. They are ways of defending themselves against a profound level of disapproval directed toward women, a disapproval that can take the form of aversion. . . . Aging is a process of becoming obscene sexually, for the flabby bosom, wrinkled neck, spotted hands, thinning hair, waistless torso and veined legs of an old woman are felt to be obscene." [27]

Thus, apart from the onset of serious physical or mental illness, what deprives older people of their ability and desire for sex expression is not primarily physiological but attitudinal. Poor sex education, shame about having sexual feelings in older years, the prudery of earlier generations, marital disabilities, and economic and social rejection by society—these are the major incapacitating factors. And the tragedy is that such attitudes, coming in from the outside, can be internalized in a vicious spiral of depression, mild or severe, which in itself further desexualizes the older person.

A further complication, of course, is the absence of a partner. Current welfare and social security laws frequently make it economically difficult if not impossible for the widowed to remarry, forcing many who have found a new love into frustration or reluctantly chosen non-married cohabitation. For some other elderly singles, remarriage is out of the question for other reasons, not the least of which is the absence of enough single males in this age group.

In the light of these complications, awareness of the range of possibilities for the elderly is important if their sexuality is not to be continually denied. The simple matter of touching should not be overlooked. The older person's physical needs are sometimes met simply inappropriate and affectionate touch. In institutions, however, this is often linked with power hierarchies. Staff persons (who have more power than residents) feel some freedom to touch the residents, but the latter, in spite of felt needs to initiate touching themselves, seldom do.[28]

Institutional policies need ongoing reassessment at a variety of levels. The policy of strict male-female segregation in nursing homes—even to the point of separating spouses who wish to be together—seems calculated to repress sexuality. Residents' displays of affection toward one another are too often met with the staff's condescending humor or outright disapproval. A director of gerontological nursing writes this: "Have you ever seen a double bed in an institution? I never have. Nor do I expect to in my lifetime, especially when I hear all the rules or reasons why something can't be done. Yet we continue to separate husbands and wives, ignoring the fact that they may have slept together for fifty years or more. And if they climb in bed with someone else, then we chart, 'Patient is confused and disoriented.'"[29] The author later adds, "We are as skillful in avoidance of sexual matters as we are in talking with the dying patient who wants to talk about his [or her] own dying."[30]

Relief from genital tension through masturbation may be a possibility for the single elderly person. When a partner is no longer present or is temporarily unavailable, continued sex activity both physiologically and psychologically is crucial for the maintenance of sexual responsiveness. Masturbation physically serves this need as well as intercourse, even though its emotional and spiritual satisfactions are clearly less. For some older folk to accept this as an appropriate and healthy outlet may require continuing sex education, particularly in light of negative attitudes internalized in childhood. Masturbation as a harmless and possibly desirable sex activity ought to produce neither guilt nor shame in the older person. Indeed, it can expand that person's sense of continuing to feel the self as a sexual being. But it requires privacy, and that necessary ingredient ought to be respected.

What of homosexual expression in the elderly? The aging gay person frequently seems to feel an increased paranoia about sexual identity. This is not difficult to understand if we acknowledge the immense amount of energy which those who have chosen to remain "in the closet" must expend in daily concealment. And this energy drain continues in the face of diminishing vigor. In spite of society's punitive attitudes about homosexuality, some widowed persons do turn to same-sex affectional behavior in their later years. In this regard Dr. Ivor Felstein states, "There is no evidence that there is a sharp rise of inversion in older years—it is more likely that bisexual individuals cheated of a heterosexual partner by divorce or demise turn to the same sex for outlet." [31] Once again, our attitudes toward the entire homosexuality issue need reappraisal if agism and homophobia are not to combine with devastating results for some older persons.

The same criteria of Christian sexual ethics ought to apply to the older person as to persons in any other age group. But particular reticence and resistance to hasty judgment is called for on the part of the younger. "At this stage of life who is competent to assume the authority to draw the fine sensitive line in deciding for others what is permissible or what is impermissible, what is moral or immoral, or whether a door must remain open despite a longing for the privacy that those in control take for granted for themselves?" [32]

The Christian vision of wholeness appears with particular poignancy in regard to the sexuality of the aged. The one who feels removed from the mainstream of life in so many ways—socially, politically, economically, physically—ought not to feel the further indignity of sexual removal. Emotional well-being nurtures mental well-being, important in overall health. It is no accident that the continuation of sexual feeling is strongly correlated with the sense of mental alertness for a great many elderly folk. Moreover, physical-emotional sexual tension which is not relieved by some appropriate expression can produce general anxiety, body tension, and irritability, conditions which frequently aggravate blood vessel illnesses, ulcers, and colitis—fairly common ailments of the aging.

If overall health includes sexual health and if the wholeness of life refuses any body-mind dualism, the so-called "golden age" of life ought never to be made dross by the sexual disenfranchising of those who live their later years with a continuing human need for affection, intimacy, touch, and even genital expression.

The Mentally Retarded

Prior to the work of Sigmund Freud, children were believed to be asexual. Some adults still believe that to be the case. In any event, mentally retarded teenagers and adults frequently are viewed as perennial children who either have no sexual needs or, more likely, who may be sexual but not to express that in the ways other people do. Perhaps our slowness in recognizing the sexuality of the retarded is not altogether surprising, given our slowness in understanding sexuality as a basic and integral part of all human personality. In another sense, our desexualization of the retarded (as with the groups previously considered) expresses a combination of lack of information, fear, stereotypical attitudes, and also legitimate concerns about sensitive and difficult matters.

At the outset it is well to remember that the mentally retarded are not a homogeneous group. They represent a wide range of capacity and incapacity, of ability and inability, of mild retardation and profound retardation, and any generalizations must be tempered by this realization. Granted this, it is fair to generalize at least in this respect: the overwhelming majority of the mentally retarded are keenly aware of their own sexuality in their need to express and receive tenderness, bodily touch, affection, and love. Further, the majority are also very much aware of their own genital needs and desires.

First, I think it important to sketch some brief pictures of the sexual behavior, sex education, genetic possibilities, and institutional life of the mentally retarded in our society. As to sexual behavior, we have only limited systematic data. One of the more thorough studies, for example, was restricted to white males. Nevertheless, even this sample is instructive.[33] Reporting for The Institute for Sex Research, Indiana University, Paul H. Gebhard notes that the studied group was composed of eighty-four males, half of them aged eleven to twenty, and half over twenty. Most of the group were not severely retarded, for the majority of I.Q.s were between 50 and 70. Out of this group, "Only one person, a 17-year-old with an I.Q. of 36, was sexless—lacking response to any of the stimuli or experience of any overt sexual behavior."[34] (It is, however, reasonable to assume that even this more profoundly retarded young man was sexual in the broader sense earlier defined.)

The study did reveal some differences between the sexual expressions of these men and youth, who had been institutionalized in a number of different facilities, compared with males of similar socioeconomic level but of the normal range of intelligence. There was a higher incidence of prepubertal homosexual play and less heterosexual play. More in every age group masturbated, but the frequency of masturbation was less than with normal males. Fewer had experienced premarital heterosexual petting or coitus, and relatively few had seen the genitalia of an adult female. As might be expected among those in sexually segregated institutions, there was a higher incidence of homosexual behavior, though about a third of those so expressing themselves confined their same-sex activity to periods of institutionalization. Regarding sex education, there were more instances of extreme ignorance, and the acquisition of sex knowledge came later than for males in the normal group. Gebhard's report concludes: "The sexual lives of these mentally retarded persons were obviously profoundly influenced by institutionalization. This finding places an enormous psychiatric and ethical responsibility upon the clinicians who determine the policies of institutions."[35]

A developmental specialist, Warren R. Johnson, makes these observations about the sex education of the mentally retarded.[36] First, and importantly, they share with the rest of us the basic human interests in closeness, affection, physical contact, and simply "being in on things." Further, in virtually every specific way, the similarities regarding *possibilities* for sex education are greater than the differences between the retarded and those of normal intelligence.

In other words, with most of the retarded there is interest, there is the capacity to understand and use contraceptive information, there are the same range of difficulties (language barriers, the discomfort of those providing the education, etc.). But with the retarded, at least two major differences occur. They have been given less adequate sex education than most normal persons (however inadequate the latter may be). Also, because the retarded are typically supervised and scrutinized more carefully and have less privacy, their sexual experimentation is more frequently observed—and "because it is visible, it is regarded *as a symptom of retardation* rather than of the goldfish-in-a-bowl circumstances in which the retarded commonly live." [37]

About the genetic picture there is little uniformity of opinion, though there is agreement that we do not yet have the ability to distinguish clearly between most genetic and environmental factors in retardation. Beyond that consensus, geneticists vary. For example, Sheldon C. Reed and V. Elving Anderson observe that the number of children produced by retarded parents is somewhat smaller than the proportionate number per individual in the non-retarded population. They estimate that presently retarded parents produce about 17 percent of all retarded children. "Consequently, if no retarded persons had any offspring, there would be a 17 percent decrease in the proportion of mentally retarded persons in the next generation." [38] Reed and Anderson believe that society should never encourage retarded people to produce children, and exceptions to this general rule should be especially rare when both members of the couple are afflicted since they are at highest risk in producing a retarded child.

A different emphasis comes from another geneticist, Edmond A. Murphy. Noting that somewhere between 95 percent and 99.9 percent of all people carry harmful genes, Murphy is suspicious of drawing lines which would deprive some people of their rights to reproduce. But he would make this qualification: "That the prospective parents must have sufficient insight into the nature of sexuality to be capable of deliberate and responsible consent." [39] If this is too difficult to determine, he suggests that retarded persons then ought not to be hindered in their rights to reproduce. Their offspring could be placed in foster care homes when a couple's parenting abilities are clearly too limited. Such, he believes, would be a less drastic step than denying a group of people the rights of parenthood altogether. As this comparison of Reed and Anderson with Murphy suggests, current genetic knowledge can be read in different ways, and different moral conclusions can be drawn, depending on the philosophical-religious-ethical assumptions brought to the data.

One further area of information is useful at this point. What are the sexual policies and practices of institutional staffs regarding the retarded who are in their care? Surely, institutions vary considerably, and attitudes and practices are changing. Yet, the available data suggest several things.[40] First, these facilities typically have one dominant fear regarding sexuality: pregnancy. In some this means rigid female-male segregation. In others it means careful supervision of any structured activities between the sexes. In a few it means the provision of contraceptive information and materials, but these latter institutions appear to be somewhat rare. A second observation is that most institutions have no clear policies regarding what types of sexual expression should be allowed, and hence staff attendants act on the basis of their own personal values. Some are fairly permissive regarding masturbation, displays of homosexual affection, and heterosexual contacts short of coitus, while others are restrictive and sometimes punitive about these things. A third generalization which seems warranted is that administrators of publicly-supported institutions are wary of establishing any policies which would allow sexual expression, for fear of public reaction which might retaliate in funding cuts.

With this survey of some elements in the current picture, what ethical comments seem warranted? Let us consider the three major genital possibilities: masturbation, homosexual and heterosexual expression.

Sex educator Sol Gordon writes of addressing aides and nurses at one institution, inviting them to submit questions before his presentation. "The majority of questions could be summed up as one: *how can we stop masturbation?*" [41] It was apparent that in this particular place, considerable staff energy was being devoted to catching or curbing those engaged in this outlet. Perhaps only two things need be said here beyond the reflections in Chapter 7. First, to those denied by their circumstances the opportunity for genital expression with a loved partner, masturbation should be viewed as an appropriate outlet. Punitive attitudes toward it in the retarded can only result in encouraging guilt, compulsiveness and internalized self-destructiveness. We then deny to those less fortunate than we perhaps their one major avenue of genital expression. The second comment regards privacy. Genital activity should take place only in privacy out of consideration for the feelings and sensitivities of others. But institutions for the retarded are notably devoid of opportunities for privacy. Hence, a liberal definition of the word is appropriate: bathrooms, one's own bed, and the bushes on the grounds might well be considered private.

What about homosexual activity? Available evidence strongly suggests that the higher homosexual activity in retarded people relates directly to sexually-segregated institutional life. For example, among the group of male retardates studied by the Indiana project, none of those between the ages of twenty-one and thirty who had little institutionalization were engaged in same-sex activity, while every man with extensive institutionalization was doing so. Furthermore, in spite of the influence of institutionalization and the relatively high degree of homosexual behavior, the retarded men in institutions remained remarkably heterosexual in orientation and interest.[42] It is noteworthy to combine this observation with that of a different study conducted on the attitudes of staff personnel in representative institutions. Asked what action they would take if they found two male residents kissing or petting, eighty-six percent of the interviewed staff said that they would stop it, and fourteen percent said they would ignore the activity.[43]

Thus, a "double-bind" situation is created. Situational homosexual activity is encouraged by institutional life, and yet institutional staff, representing prevailing cultural values, are heavily negative toward this sexual expression. The desire to relate affectively and with physical expression is strong, but, for these unfortunate people is frustrated.

One answer, of course, is for institutions to allow more heterosexual interaction by their residents which, presumably would decrease the same-sex activity among those for whom this is not their basic psychosexual orientation. In addition, however, staff people could be educated toward greater understanding and acceptance of affectional, non-coercive homosexual relationships among the residents. It is highly unlikely that significant changes in psychosexual orientation will occur among those retarded people institutionalized for a relatively short time and then returned to the community. Again, the homophobia that fears the change to gayness betrays a curious twist: the apparent belief that homosexual relationships really are so attractive and fulfilling that if heterosexuals are permitted to experience them they would be permanently changed.

When we come to heterosexual relationships among the retarded, several important issues arise: contraception, sterilization, the appropriateness of marriage, and the capacity for parenting.

Consider marriage first. What is the evidence? Here, once again, because of the enormous range of individual differences in capacity and personality among the retarded, generalizations must be made with great caution. Nevertheless, some insights from recent studies will help us. Janet Mattinson of London's Tavistock Institute reports on a small but intensive study of thirty-two marriages in which both partners had been judged retarded. All had had extensive periods in a hospital for the sub-normal. Their social and emotional deprivation had been unusually severe—many had been orphaned, had come from broken homes, or had been seriously ill-treated as children. Mattinson says, "My ultimate conclusion about these former patients of a hospital for the retarded was that, paired, many of them were able to reinforce each other's strengths and established marriages which, in the light of what had happened to them previously, were no more, no less, foolish than many others in the community, and which gave them considerable satisfaction." [44] Similarly, Robert B. Edgerton concludes, "We do not know what might result from a policy that would permit certain institutionalized retardates to marry or to cohabit, but we do know that many mildly retarded persons, whether previously institutionalized or not, are capable of maintaining stable, happy marriages with other retarded persons." [45]

The question of the capacity for parenting, however, is another matter, and it is far less clear. Some of those who discourage all marriages between mentally handicapped persons do so explicitly because of grave doubts about their parental adequacy. [46] Again, the degree of retardation is a significant factor, but most studies indicate that it is a statistical minority (perhaps a third) of retarded parents who seem able to provide adequate child-rearing for their off-spring. To concern about the children can be added legitimate concerns about genetic consequences and inflated public assistance rolls.

If many marriages between retarded persons can be mutually fulfilling and, indeed, life-giving relationships, but if among such couples only a minority could be adequate parents, we are left with the considerable issues of contraception and sterilization. Such issues, of course, apply to the unmarried as well.

The ability of the mentally handicapped to use contraception effectively hinges heavily upon the degree of retardation, but also upon attitudes and instruction conveyed by others. Representative opinions appear to be these: "Among [those] with verbal ability, receptiveness to contraceptive advice is about the same as in a normal population. . . ." And, "Even persons with very low I.Q.s could be trained to take [contraceptive] pills regularly." [47] Another states, "I have known many mentally retarded persons who were irresponsible about contraception, but I have also known others who have used contraceptives responsibly over an extended period of time. The problem, again, is to find out which [people] can use which techniques under which conditions and then to offer them an educated choice." [48]

One rather common assumption needs to be challenged: the belief that the retarded are less capable than the rest of us in controlling sexual impulses. Robert Edgerton speaks to this: "My own research indicates that the mildly retarded, at least, are capable of truly remarkable—almost puritanical—sexual self-control both in a hospital and in a community setting. In the groups studied, such self-control was a product of internal regulation—their own values, if you will—and not of external social constraint." [49] A somewhat different picture may well emerge from the more profoundly retarded, but it is important to correct unfair and gross generalizations at this point.

If contraception is feasible and workable for many retarded people, what of the issue of sterilization? Given present medical technology, sterilization procedures must be assumed to be nonreversible and permanent. While a much more extended discussion is warranted than we can undertake here, several things can be said. First, voluntary sterilization of a retarded person ought to be preceded by careful counseling to ensure that the individual genuinely understands the implications and probable irreversibility of the procedure, and is acting out of meaningfully free choice.

Compulsory sterilization of certain retarded persons who have demonstrated their incapacity for responsible contraceptive use, who are sexually active, and who are likely carriers of genetic disease ought to remain an open possibility. The opportunities for abuse of the individual's freedom are certainly present, but in some cases the obligation to prevent the multiplication of personal and social tragedy may be overriding. The question of "who decides?" is not, perhaps, susceptible of any single answer. It is unlikely that the physician alone should have the moral authority to make such decisions. Sometimes such judgments can be made through counseling sessions with the parents. Sometimes a special jury of outside advisors ("patient advocates") selected for their understanding of similar situations and for their humane sensitivities, may be appropriate. Genuine caution in these decisions is warranted.

State laws which not only permit but encourage compulsory sterilization of the mentally retarded ought to arouse our anxiety even if they are rarely applied. In 1927 Supreme Court Justice Holmes upheld one such law with the oft-quoted aphorism, "three generations of imbeciles are enough." [50] However, the court in that decision was markedly insensitive to its role in protecting vulnerable minorities.[51] Law professor Robert A. Burt believes that such laws which single out any clearly-defined and stigmatized group for special restrictions in sexual or family life violate the Constitution. Further, "The simple existence of laws that aim at vulnerable, stigmatized groups as such presents intolerable dangers of abuse and overuse." [52] New medical advances in intrauterine diagnosis of many gross genetic abnormalities are changing the context of such laws and weakening the case for their maintenance.

Ethically, what can we say about sexual activity (heterosexual or homosexual) among retarded unmarried persons? Our hopes for the interpersonal context of genital expression ought to be the same: that a relationship exist where there is genuine affection, mutual commitment, and freedom of choice. But institutional situations and degrees of retardation ought to make us reluctant to judge by too rigid a standard. When contraceptive precautions are ensured, the better question about sexual activity of the retarded is not whether it conforms to certain rules appropriate to persons of more normal situation, but whether such activity contributes to the humanization of those involved.

Again, we are led back to the importance—the Christianly gracious importance—of self-esteem in our humanization. It is difficult to study the research concerning both mildly and moderately handicapped persons without reaching the conclusion that one persistent finding is their acute loss of self-esteem through the very process of being labeled mentally retarded. Denial of access to normal dating and sexual relationships, prevalent institutional policies of sexual *apartheid*, and widely-held stereotypes that the retarded ought not to be sexual persons further damage the individual's precarious self-esteem. It is, finally, a question of justice and of compassion, a question of the relation of sexual affirmation to human affirmation—in short, the question of what, in our still fragmentary knowledge, does God intend for the greater humanization of this group of the handicapped and sexually dispossessed?

10

The Church
as Sexual Community

HE CHURCH is a sexual community. If our consciousness of this is taking a new turn, the realities of the situation are as old as the church itself. On the more obvious level, of course, the church has always been concerned about the sexual. From its beginning it has dealt in positive and negative ways, in creative and destructive ways, with the sexuality of its members—in doctrine, in moral guidance and command, in status and office. On the less obvious level, the church's doctrines and liturgies, the shape of its community and its vision of mission have also been significantly shaped by the sexual perceptions of its members. It is a two-way street, but awareness of the second direction of traffic is only beginning to emerge.

Resexualizing the Church's Theology

Resexualizing our theology does not mean putting sexuality into a theology from which it has been absent. It has always been there. It means a new level of consciousness about the ways in which our sexuality, for good and for ill, has shaped our expressions of faith.

The negative side of the task (which itself has a basically positive direction) is the elimination of sexual dualism. It means awareness of both sexism and spiritualism and the conscious effort to transcend them both. Addressing *sexist* dualism, Mary Daly contends that "the entire conceptual systems of theology and ethics, developed under the conditions of patriarchy, have been the products of males and tend to serve the interests of sexist society." [1] If this charge seems overstated, it nevertheless must be taken with great seriousness.

Language itself is highly significant, and the feminist insistence upon inclusive language is no trivial matter. Language is that symbol system by which a culture articulates its conception of things and events. Linguist Edward Sapir argues that "modern psychology has shown us how powerfully symbolism is at work in the unconscious mind. It is therefore easier to understand . . . that the most rarefied thought may be but the conscious counterpart of an unconscious linguistic symbolism." [2]

Further, as Rollo May argues, we cannot *per*ceive something until we can *con*ceive it. If our symbols are not adequate to the reality, we cannot fully "see" and experience that reality. Thus, years ago a memorable event took place when Captain Cook's ship sailed into the harbor of a primitive society, and the people of that tribe were unable to see the ship because they had no word or symbol for such a ship. Most likely they saw a cloud or an animal, something for which they did have a symbol. Language, says May, is thus "our way of *con*ceiving what we may *per*ceive," and the other use of the word "conceive"—to become pregnant—is also appropriate, "for the act of perceiving also requires the capacity to bring to birth something in one's self. [3]

What, then, of our words commonly used to refer to people? If our symbolic concept is inadequate, our perception will be distorted. Gayle Graham Yates thus fittingly observes, "If 'man' means 'male human being' and also 'human being,' there is room for the interpretation that standard humanity is male, with the female being some kind of appendage, an afterthought, an other-than-standard version of humanity." [4]

Moreover, our basic religious modes of thought have been conditioned by stereotypical masculine and feminine ways of perceiving spirituality. The masculine mode has emphasized God as structure, judgment, intellect, logic, and order, while the feminine mode has accented nature more than society, mystical oneness more than intellectual analysis, immanence more than transcendence, change more than stability. In the culturally-shaped feminine perception, "God is more like an infinite Sea or Womb within which all things rise and fall, and with which to merge is perfect peace." [5] But this makes the patriarchalist uneasy. The universe seems too fluid, no longer firmly and hierarchically structured with a definite chain of command. So sexist dualism continues to infect our theological thought forms as transcendence competes with immanence, order with change, cognition with feeling, society with nature. Yet, there are also androgynous stirrings in the experience of many which tell them that *both* sides must be claimed—in the theological vision and in the self.

Theology is also resexualized when *spiritualistic* dualism is recognized and transformed. Erotic dimensions of theology then supplement and balance the agapaic. Love as desire is affirmed as well as love as self-giving. As in Rudolf Otto's interpretation of the Holy as mystery *(tremendum* and *fascinans),* before the Holy we tremble and acknowledge our fascination, our desire, our hunger. We are drawn toward that which promises life for the whole body-self. Furthermore, we recognize that the ear alone is not the medium of salvation, as if healing came only from *hearing* the Word of God; a theology of the *incarnate* Word means that the body itself receives the divine presence and at the same time receives its new definition —as the means of human loving.[6]

God in Doctrine and Experience

Inevitably our key theological symbols are those for God. In a sense, these symbols have been both too sexual and not sexual enough. We are facing here the inescapable paradox of divine transcendence and divine immanence. Because God transcends human sexuality, the sexism which projects the image of a masculine God is inadequate. And because God is immanent, the spiritualism which essentially denies the divine presence in embodied existence is likewise inadequate. Both dualisms have left their heavy marks, but neither is beyond transformation.

While theological imagery is not simply the product of human history, it is always inextricably related to that history. Thus, the exclusive use of masculine pronouns for God and the prominence of metaphors such as King, Lord, and Judge are clearly rooted in social conditions, institutions, and experiences of particular eras, eras which had a heavily patriarchal and military cast. But the problems with this God language are manifold. Such imagery makes it difficult for women to think of themselves or to be thought of by men as fully in the divine image. It buttresses male domination: "if God is male, then male is God." [7] It hinders the development of richly androgynous humanity in people of both sexes. It lends support to the socially destructive side of exaggerated masculinity, for a purely masculine God is as intolerable as a purely masculine male.

Biblical writers were creatures of their culture's grammar and their culture's experience of sexuality. At the same time that the Bible uses sexually anthropomorphic language for God, however, it also repudiates and transcends anthropomorphism. Israel's rejection of Canaanite fertility religion was an affirmation that Yahweh is neither male nor female. The Creator of human sexuality is the One who transcends human sexuality.[8]

Yet, the Bible sharpens the paradox: the God beyond sexuality is also the God experienced through our sexuality. We are sexual beings—male, female, feminine and masculine—and we do not leave our sexuality behind us in the encounter with the divine. In this regard, one of the little recognized facts of the Old Testament is the use of feminine imagery for Yahweh: Yahweh provides food and water in the desert—traditionally a woman's work (Exodus 16 and 17), makes garments (Genesis 3:21), is described as a seamstress (Nehemiah 9), has birth pangs (Isaiah 42:14), gives birth (Isaiah 66:9), is a comforting mother (Isaiah 66:13) and a nursing mother (Isaiah 49:15), and can be compared to a midwife (Psalms 22:9-10; 71:6; Job 3:12).[9] Further, God's self-disclosure as Wisdom (Sophia) is feminine, particularly in the Hellenistic Jewish and Greek Christian traditions where Sophia was a feminine parallel of the Logos.[10]

While in Christian history the "Fatherhood" of God has been used most persistently as the ultimate hierarchical symbol of masculinity, a closer look at its biblical usage gives us a different perspective. In the Old Testament the kingship metaphor is the major image for God, and the references to God as father are rare. Israel strongly resisted the notion of a people's "physical" descent from the gods, a common notion in surrounding cultures, and the language of fatherhood might have implied this. In later Judaism the use of the term was formal and liturgical. Jesus' understanding of God as Father comes as a distinctive change from those associations conveyed by the term's use, minimal though it had been, before his time.

It is not too much to say that when Jesus speaks of God as Father there is a decidedly androgynous motif present, a motif often overlooked in subsequent Christian history. This can be seen in two related ways. First, interestingly enough, Jesus uses that term only in private conversations or in situations with the disciples alone present, and his use of the term strongly suggests the closeness, the nearness of God. It is a radical corrective to the suggestion of remoteness conveyed by the conventional language of the day which emphasized God's Kingship and Lordship. In short, Jesus' conception of God as Father brings a correction from the "feminine" side of human experience. Further, Jesus links God's fatherhood with the notion of a servant ministry. While "servant" is normally the correlative term to "king," Jesus does not hesitate to redefine servanthood in relation to the divine fatherhood. God's fatherhood now cannot be the justification for human relationships of dominance and submission, rulers and ruled, or male lordship in family and society precisely because the implication of the divine fatherhood is that the greatest shall be the servant—"the waiting on tables, the lowly role of women and servants, is to be the model for ministry." [11] Once again there is an androgynous, anti-patriarchal cast to Jesus' use of the fatherhood metaphor.

In regard to later developments in the Christian tradition, Protestants typically have had great difficulty understanding Mariology in the medieval church. Yet it is here that the feminine dimensions of God were most dramatically symbolized. Mary now was no longer just a saint. She was queen of angels and saints, a status finally to be symbolized through the doctrines of her immaculate conception and her bodily assumption. Medieval theology had found a way to represent, more dramatically than had the Scriptures, God's "feminine" dimensions. And these were crucial, for, as medieval art amply attests, Christ had become increasingly envisioned as the eternally suffering one, symbol of the enormity of human guilt, and as the stern judge of the last day. Then Mary's mediation was essential. If Christ was the way to the Father, Mary was the way to Christ. She was the symbol of divine humanness and mercy. The Protestant Reformation tended to reverse this, locating the feminine in the passivity of the church and of the individual soul waiting before the transcendent masculinity of God. But medieval thought and piety had found the feminine symbolism crucial to the Christian's experience of divine immanence and accessibility.[12]

Medieval traditions of spirituality, however, did not limit the divine femininity to Mary. St. Anselm of Canterbury repeatedly referred to Jesus as "our Mother," using the New Testament image of Christ the Mother Hen (Matthew 23:37). The thirteenth century prioress Marguerite d'Oingt identified Christ's crucifixion agony with that of a woman in labor. Dame Julian of Norwich in the fourteenth century found Christ our Mother feeding us as a mother suckles her child. Reflecting upon this medieval piety, Eleanor McLaughlin fittingly concludes, "We need to recover today, not an artificially resurrected copy of fourteenth century God-language, although liturgical reform in this area is absolutely necessary. No, we need to recover the reality which that naming reflected, an experience of God within, God our Mother, God who unconditionally accepts our and her broken world, God who takes into herself and affirms by her wholeness the full potential of man and woman to be Godbearers." [13] Indeed, the image of God nursing humanity at her full breasts is a helpful corrective to the image of God marching his armies off to war.[14]

The religious testimony that both feminine and masculine images are necessary symbols for God is a testimony of the divine androgyny. But androgyny does not mean bisexuality. As a metaphor applicable to God it bears witness to something the Israelites were attempting to say about Yahweh, though they were limited in doing so by the patriarchal assumptions of their society. They were using sexual images for communicating about God. At the same time they were testifying that God transcends as well as includes our human sexuality. And that is what the contemporary image of androgyny does. It says that those qualities traditionally labeled "masculine" and "feminine" are both essential for wholeness, and it also says that personhood must always transcend gender.[15]

In another and related way our imagery about God has not been sexual enough. Hellenistic dualism in our religious tradition has divided body from spirit, located sexuality in body, and identified God as spirit. The prevailing conclusion of both theological treatise and popular piety then has been this: to think of God as sexual or of the divine-human relationship as having a sexual quality is foreign to the Christian mind—even debasing and ignoble. But this deserves reexamination.

First, we must be clear that when we speak of "the sexuality of God" we are speaking in and through limited, finite human categories. "Anything we predicate of God—whenever we say: 'God is . . .'—necessarily carries with it the contrary assertion that God is at the same time *not* this which we predicate. For example, if I say that God is good, at the same time I need to say that God is not reducible to the goodness you or I have known in this finite world in our own limited, relative existence. The sacred is far more than this." [16] But, the *via negativa*—the theology and religious experience which approaches God by emphasizing what God is *not*—needs to be balanced by and held in tension with the *via positiva* or *via affirmativa*—the positive affirmations about what, in our received experience, God is.

Urban T. Holmes is correct in drawing the parallel between "the personhood of God" and "the sexuality of God." [17] We commonly attribute personality to God, even when we insist that God transcends personhood. God is not to be thought of literally as *a* person, one being among other beings, one person among other persons. But what we are attempting to say is that the *relationship* which we experience with God can and, indeed, must be described as a personal relationship. Analogously, the same thing can be said of the sexual.

But unfortunately Holmes then argues that it is appropriate to continue to use the masculine symbolization for the three persons of the Trinity. The three functions traditionally assigned to the Father, Son, and Holy Spirit respectively are creation, redemption, and sanctification, which "are purposeful actions in a masculine mode." Therefore, Holmes concludes, "it is utterly appropriate to refer to the particular persons of the Godhead in all cases as 'he.'" [18] The feminine dimension of the Godhead, he suggests, is the mystery of God's fullness. "This means that when we engage God in the fullness of the divine being, without differentiation, we encounter God as 'she.'" [19]

This argument, while suggestive, suffers for more than one reason. Even if we accept the cultural definition of the masculine mode as "purposeful" or "initiating," why should the divine activities of creation, redemption, and sanctification be limited to the masculine? Is not creation preeminently a feminine mode—fecundity and birth and nurture? Is not redemption, experienced as divine acceptance and mercy, just as "feminine" (if not more so) as "masculine"? Is not the growth elicited in sanctification grounded in the divine nurturing capacity, which we typically associate with the feminine side of personhood? There is, I believe, no more reason for describing the "persons" of the Godhead in masculine terms than the oneness of God as feminine. Further, the argument errs by pressing the point a bit too literalistically, even though this may not be its intent. When we ascribe sexuality to God—even in the *via positiva*— we ought to remember that we are speaking of the *relationship* which we sexual human beings experience with God. We are not attempting to make statements about God's being itself.

Biblical monotheism, it is true, rejects any direct attribution of sexuality to God. God has the power to create alone—without a sexual partner. When divine sexuality is taken literally in other religions, it has been expressed through the affirmation of at least two gods—bi-theism, the dual principles of male and female.[20]

But, if biblical monotheism resists any literal assumptions about divine sexuality, it does not resist the sexual dimensions of the human-divine relationship. The bridal metaphors are a chief case in point. According to Hosea, Yahweh says, "I will betroth you to myself forever, betroth you in lawful wedlock with unfailing devotion and love; I will betroth you to myself to have and to hold, and you shall know the Lord" (Hosea 2:19). That "to know" in this statement connotes sexual intimacy is clear inasmuch as the entire metaphor is sexual. And when Paul boldly calls the church "the bride of Christ," we should recall that he speaks out of the Jewish tradition which held that marriage without sexual consummation was no marriage at all.

It is true, there are risks in affirming the sexual qualities of our relationship with God. Luther may have had these in mind when he repeatedly expressed his preference for "faith" rather than "love" as the human response. And when his sturdy hymns are compared to the pallid individualism and romanticism of certain nineteenth and twentieth century hymns, the point is made. Yet, the passive reception of God which does not also know the active and passionate desire for God is one-sided to the human experience.

To say that the human relationship with God is sexual obviously does not mean that it is *only* that. It does mean, however, that if our sexuality *is* intrinsic to our capacity for love and trust, to our possibility for creativity and wholeness, then surely it is part of the human communion with God. It does mean that the radical bond which we know possible in sexual love with another person bears more than just a distant analogy to the bond possible with God, the wedlock of unfailing devotion and love of which the prophet speaks.

On the negative side, the sexual dimension is recognizable, too. In human marriage when one partner treats the other as a disembodied spirit certain reactions are predictable: a sense of rejection (for a vital part of oneself is not being taken seriously); confusion and self-doubt; the temptation to find fulfillment elsewhere. So also when people believe that God treats them as disembodied spirits, that their sexuality is somehow "beneath" the divine-human relationship, similar reactions are not unknown. One cannot help but wonder to what extent this affects the attitudes of many adolescents and young adults toward the church and Christian faith, those for whom their own sexuality is experienced as real and important.

The affirmation of the divine-human relationship as significantly sexual draws upon both Hebrew and Greek ancestry. For the Hebrew, the dominant context of sexuality was historical and future-oriented ("now-and-future"). This maximized their emphasis upon procreation. For the Greek the dominant context was present-oriented and eternity ("now-and-eternity"), which gave sexuality meanings quite apart from procreation. Paul Hessert puts it this way: "For the Israelite, sexuality has a horizontal significance—the family, community, and ultimately, God's kingdom. For the Greek,

sexuality has a vertical significance—the self, the cosmos, and, ultimately, the eternal itself. The Israelite view is ordered toward the
future of God's people, the Greek towards the fulfillment of human
personality as a microcosm of the whole order of things." [21]

The contrast, of course, can be overdrawn. But there was a difference in emphasis, and we can affirm that the Greek insight is an
important addition and balance to the Hebraic. Finding the erotic
life part of our life with God does not ineluctably lead to a nonhis-
torical world view, nor to individualistic fulfillment at the expense of
community, much less to temple prostitution. Such dichotomized,
either-or, Hebrew-or-Greek thinking simply fails to do justice to the
richness of Christian experience. We need the creative tension between Hebrew and Greek on this matter, and its benefits promise
to be several.

One is more vivid awareness of God's immanent presence. The
theology of transcendence, typical of both Protestant Reformers and
mid-twentieth century "theologies of the Word," was an important
corrective to particular situations, and it served well. But Eleanor
L. McLaughlin is right in claiming, "It has in the last years come
to be destructive of and unfaithful to the God experience of those
twentieth-century Christians, men and women, who feel and know
the One within, the God of boundless mercy and love, the ground
of our being who seeks us out of the fullness of creation and the
stillness of our soul. The Protestant focus on the God of transcendence has helped undermine and deny our experience of the feminine in the Ultimate and in ourselves." [22]

Reclaiming the sexuality present in the divine-human relationship
also invites a heightened awareness of God as the dynamic and
unfolding One. This perception is present in the Bible, and process
theologians have accented it in our time. But it is still largely
absent from the experience of many Christians. It is God as Verb
more than as Noun. It is recognition that God's absoluteness does
not mean divinity above and beyond all change but rather God's
absolute relatedness to creation in and through all change. God's
eternity is not timelessness but the fullest conceivable divine experience of creation's time and history. God is who God does, disclos-
ing Love's absolute meaning for the world, suffering in the life of
the world, and rejoicing in creative human growth.

But our sexuality is part and parcel of this mode of perception of God. Many people know that greater acceptance of their own sexuality brings with it new richness in their responsiveness to reality itself. It brings greater openness to life's joys and delights, but it also enhances the capacity to undergo change, to feel suffering, and to be sensitive to pain. Life somehow appears less static and more dynamic, less closed and more open. That the deep sexual love of one human being for another can do this is beyond question. That the affirmation of the sexuality present in our love for God can affect us even more grandly with the dynamism of the cosmic Love is no less real.[23]

Nor is it too much to claim that openness to the sexual qualities of the divine-human relationship also invites a greater concern for human liberation. "Liberation theology," writes Letty Russell, "is an attempt to reflect upon the experience of oppression and our actions for the new creation of a more humane society." [24] It involves consciousness of oppression. It means a new awareness of one's potential in community for participating in the reshaping of the world. It is the affirmation that change and openness are necessary, that freedom means a journey with others toward God's more human future. The experience of sexual oppression—particularly that of women and gays but also others—has opened these perceptions of God's nature and activity to numerous Christians with new vividness in recent years. God is no longer the stopgap for the incompleteness of human knowledge, nor the other-worldly divinity indifferent to patterns of oppression, nor the God of unchanging human structures. God is the One whose transcendence becomes known in immanence and whose presence is made real in the commitment to humanization. The point is that many have discovered this through their sexuality. Many have realized that, in this sense, only if their relationship with God does in fact have a sexual dimension can they be empowered for human liberation.

Human Nature and Destiny

While we have examined at length some of the meanings of sin and salvation in sexual theology (Chapters 3 and 4), two related issues deserve further comment at this point: sexuality in Christian interpretations of human nature and of human destiny.

The affirmation of human sexuality is basic to a positive doctrine of the *imago Dei*, the image of God in humankind. This becomes painfully clear when we recognize two basic distortions in Christian tradition and practice—the identification of women with evil and the association of the fullness of the image of God only with males. Of the two, as Margaret Farley has observed, the denial of the fullness of the *imago Dei* to women has been the most basic problem.[25] When the Hebrews looked for a human analogue to the wholly transcendent God of their experience, they found only masculine terms appropriate. "It was, after all, masculinity that connoted strength in relation to feminine weakness, activity in relation to passivity, fullness in relation to emptiness, autonomy in relation to dependence. The doctrine of God and the doctrine of the human person were already inextricably intertwined."[26] But now, as Farley notes, two things are happening simultaneously. Spurred by feminist theologians, the church is discovering that there can be no responsible theological justification for female subordination. Women are claiming that integrated self-transcendence belongs to them just as to males. "But it is no less important for theology that women have refused, finally, to be satisfied with a total abstraction from, disrelation to, distancing from, their bodies."[27] Women are refusing to capitulate to spiritualistic dualism in their struggle to overcome sexist dualism.

This is a positive affirmation that human sexuality is essential to a full understanding of the *imago Dei*. My body is my being-in-the-world. It is through my body that I am in the world and that I am destined for others. Indeed, the experience of our sexuality is nothing less than the experience of "trans-subjectivity" which is the basis for all interdependence.[28]

The doctrine of the *imago Dei* thus is another illustration of the organic nature of theology. The various doctrines are not like parts of a machine which can be disassembled, with one part replacing another. Rather, Christian doctrines all have a living, organic interdependence. One implies the other. Each flows into every other one. So it is in the instance at hand. The failure to find femininity in God is matched by a truncated notion of the *imago Dei*. The insistence upon human bodiliness is also an affirmation of human transcendence. And the move to find sexual identity as incarnational is a move toward radical human equality which itself is inherent in an adequate understanding of the doctrine of the *imago Dei.*

A resexualized theology can also bring fresh insights to Christian understandings of human destiny. This is particularly true with regard to death and resurrection. There is abundant evidence in literature, psychology, anthropology, and in human experience generally that sexuality and death are closely intertwined—though theologians have seldom probed this linkage.

The fear of death finds a variety of sexual expressions. It can erupt into a cult of sexual naturalism which exalts living for the moment and finds security in the passions of the body. In this way one can escape the sense of lack of control over events, the sense of powerlessness "in a mechanical world spinning into decay and death." [29] Because sex and death seem to have similarities—the loss of control, the loss of personal boundaries (thus the French call orgasm "the little death")—death-denial and sex-denial can be joined together. They are commonly feared. Or, death fears can be temporarily warded off through sexual reassurances—the maintenance of the youthful body, the sexual companionship of a younger person.

Otto Rank has described the links between sexuality, death, and the loss of religious belief—an interpretation recently affirmed and expanded by Ernest Becker. [30] "The romantic solution," argued Rank, had become the answer for the modern person who had lost belief in God. Another person as the love object became the God-substitute providing the meaning and assurance for which God had become mere abstraction. Thus, sexuality became a quest for life's meaning. When self-consciousness became too painful, one could wipe it away in emotional yielding to the partner. Yet, claimed Rank, this is no final solution. Trying to resolve the ultimate problem of life's meaning through the sexual relationship, we discover that it cannot carry this weight. The demands of being the God-substitute are too heavy. We feel diminished by our human partner's fallibility, threatened by our partner's decay and mortality. Our gods have clay feet. Thus the spiritual burdens which many couples put upon the love relationship become impossibly heavy and result in depersonalizing the relationship itself. The sexual bond cannot deliver what it seems to promise: life's final answer.

Furthermore, in the creation myth, the discovery of sex and the advent of death are intertwined. It is as sexual beings that we discover our mortality. It is as sexual beings that we become aware of our animal nature. This makes the sex-death connection all the more evident to us, for animals procreate and die, and their short life span seems somehow connected with their procreation. Moreover, the sex experience brings with it a threat to the individuated personality. It reminds me of my animal nature, and as an animal I am just a member of the species.

The sexual act, says Rank, thus represents a double negation for the human being. It makes the person conscious of mortality and death, and it threatens the loss of distinctive individuated personality. "This point is crucial because it explains why sexual taboos have been at the heart of human society since the very beginning. They affirm the triumph of human personality over animal sameness." [31] Sexual taboos were created because of the human need to triumph over the body, and the need to triumph over the body was the need to insist upon the undying uniqueness of human personality. In a word, the pleasures of the body were sacrificed in favor of the highest pleasure of all—self-perpetuation as a spiritual being throughout eternity. So inner conflict about sexual matters becomes universal because the body is a universal problem to the creature who must die.[32]

In the face of this ambiguous interweaving of sexuality and death, I believe that the Christian affirmation of resurrection of the body becomes particularly healing and life-giving. It speaks directly to the threats just described. In the first place, it affirms personhood over animal sameness. As *resurrection* rather than immortality, the symbol carries faith's recognition that the distinctiveness of personhood is more powerfully affirmed by the uniqueness of each of our body-selves than by the notion of a disembodied soul. In contrast to doctrines of the immortality of the soul, the symbol of resurrection of the body does not trade in such spiritualistic dualism. We do not have eternal souls awaiting their release from mortal bodies. The body-self lives and the body-self dies. Death is real and total. But the resurrection promise is that death is not the final word. In God's goodness we are to be "caught up into God's life, where beyond death Love abides." [33] In God's life we are remembered in all of our unique bodily individuality—and as the Hebrews knew, "to remember" is to recapitulate and to make alive once more.

In the second place, the symbol of resurrection is a *theocentric* affirmation. The focus is upon God, and not primarily upon our own survival. Human destiny is fulfilled through incorporation into Christ's resurrection, so the New Testament proclaims. And Christ is received into the fullness of God's life. This then becomes another witness that the ultimate problem of life's meaning has only a theocentric solution. We are released from placing the weight of that spiritual burden on the human sexual relationship. The partner is freed from being a God-substitute, and we are freed to live and to love one another in our delicious mortality.

Affirmation of the resurrection of the body thus frees us into fuller sexuality. I think Rank and Becker are right in saying that sexual taboos have their primary origin and power in the human quest to triumph over animal sameness—the human need to triumph over the body. But the resurrection faith carries with it the affirmation that the body need not be sacrificed through a host of sexual fears in order that self-perpetuation might be assured. The promise of our incorporation into the divine fullness is enough. Resurrection of the body as an eschatological event thus means resurrection of the present sexual body in the present day also.

But the movement can go in the other direction as well—from reclaimed sexuality *to* resurrection faith. Insofar as, by the grace of God, we can affirm our bodies now, death seems to lose some of its threat and the eschatological resurrection can be more readily and fully affirmed. A clue to this lies in current psychological evidence suggesting that women appear to be less threatened by death than do men because they are more secure about their bodies.[34] It is quite possible that the male in our society finds death more threatening because his cultural masculinity has more invested in the notion of the aggressive hero who wins out over life's odds, who wins by controlling and dominating. But death is beyond control and domination. There is passivity and submission in dying. Further, the woman through menstruation and, possibly, pregnancy is more accustomed to the experience of drastic body change than is the man—a fact which might make death's drastic corporeal change at least somewhat less overwhelming.[35] In the sexually reconciled self, the body is not foreign. Androgyny is real. The self, whether male or female, can affirm its passive and receptive side. It can affirm that controlling and winning over life are not always the self's prerogatives, and surely they will not conquer death. But in the gospel's perennial paradox, such loss is gain.

So there seems to be an interactive character in the human experience of resurrection of the sexual body now and the capacity to trust in the final resurrection. Salvation of our sexuality nurtures confidence in the face of death, and trust in God's triumphant and deathless love nurtures a more self-accepting and other-enriching sexuality.

Church: Worship and Community

Part of the church's calling is to be a community of worship, a community of sacrament and celebration. Throughout the centuries liturgy, literally "the work of the people," has been deeply marked by rites which underscore the fact that the church is also a sexual community.

Among the meanings of infant Baptism, the birth of the child is celebrated, as is the sexual relationship of its parents. When adults are baptized by immersion, the water enfolds the body not only like the grave from which new life symbolically is risen but also like the womb out of which new life is born. In confirmation young people affirm their commitment to the Body of Christ and, at the same time, the church celebrates their adolescence as a passage into the sexual maturity of adulthood. The rite of marriage witnesses to the conviction that the sexual covenant established by the couple is also a sexual covenant with God and with the community of faith. The Eucharist with its elements of body and blood is preeminently a sacrament of body theology. The funeral with its celebration of the gift of life, its expression of grief over death, and its affirmation of faith in the resurrecting power of God, is marked by the radical recognition that we are body-selves.

A moment's reflection on this liturgical and sacramental life produces startling reminders that the church is not composed of disembodied spirits nor does it, in its better moments, understand its life as such. It is Christ's body, a body community, a sexual community.

To be sure, the church has long been ill at ease with the sexual implications of its worship. Spiritualistic dualism has denigrated body meanings and made them incidental to "the life of the spirit." Sexist dualism has largely masculinized the liturgy in language and image.

Nevertheless, in one sense the church has had reason to fear the sexual implications of its worship over the centuries.[36] A sexualized liturgy might have led Christians back into the fertility cults where people were simply natural functions and not persons. And with today's rediscovery of the basic importance of human sexuality, there is a temptation, at least among a small minority of Christians, to move back in the direction of the fertility cult. The problem before us is that of finding appropriate liturgical ways of expressing our sexual beings, as individuals and as a community, without reducing the richness of personhood to a particular sexual function.

Until our sexuality is incorporated more fully and consciously into the church's liturgy, our rituals will continue to fragment life in this respect—even if it is only through their silence. Life *can* be more holistically represented in ritual, however. Anthropological studies of the manner in which certain "primitive" peoples use pollution rituals are a case in point, as we have seen. The Western scientific mind mistakes these for magic. Actually, they are complex and profoundly meaningful symbolic systems which express the group's view of the ordering of the cosmos. Mary Douglas compares the hygiene and cleaning rituals of the modern Western household with the purity rituals of the Bushman and Dinka cultures and observes, "The difference between us is not that our behaviour is grounded on science and theirs on symbolism. Our behaviour also carries symbolic meaning. The real difference is that we do not bring forward from one context to the next the same set of ever more powerful symbols: our experience is fragmented. Our rituals create a lot of little sub-worlds, unrelated. Their rituals create one single, symbolically consistent universe." [37]

How, then, can the sexual dimensions of our lives be more consciously and meaningfully incorporated into the church's worship life? That the church is inescapably sexual seems obvious. That Christian faith is inescapably incarnationalist is evident. But that vast numbers of Christians find the liturgy of little positive help with their own sexuality is also true. We, no less than the Bushman and the Dinka, need a symbolically consistent universe. One possible approach to this problem is through recognizing "the sacramentality of sex."

The Church and the Sacramentality of Sex

Various groups and people have found various ways of orienting themselves to sex. Some, to be sure, have been primarily sex-negative. Among those who have valued sex, however, some have accented its pragmatic worth (procreation and enjoyment); some have valued its escapist possibilities (release from boredom and frustration, the assertion of autonomy in the face of social restrictions); some have prized sex's romantic dimensions (its unitive possibilities and the value of desire). Still others, however, have seen sex as sacramental, bearing the power to link human and divine in cultic act.[38]

Sex has been understood as sacred mystery by different groups with various levels of sophistication. In some primitive forms it was simply a powerful magic expression, appealing to the sacred generative power which brought fertility to crops and tribe, a fairly common understanding in certain earlier and more corporate cultures. But in ancient Greece and Rome where personal self-awareness began to emerge, sex in some cultic expressions became a vehicle for *communion* with deity.

It is easy to write this off as grossly pagan and obscene. Yet, historical studies also show positive elements. In one variation, intercourse at the temple with the priest or priestess was sacramental. G. Rattray Taylor comments: "This is the temple prostitution which has so often scandalized Christian observers. But the term prostitution, with its connotations of sordid commercialism and . . . lust, wholly misrepresents the sacred and uplifting character of the experience as it was experienced by those who took part. It was nothing less than an act of communion with God. . . ."[39] True, such cultic sex always bore the danger of deteriorating into simple lust and gross distortion, and this sometimes happened. But in its more ordered forms certain values appeared which cannot be written off lightly.

In the Greek worship of Dionysus there was not only communion with the deity but also an approved cathartic medium for releasing various tensions, unrelieved in daily existence. In a subsistence economy where there was unending heavy work, little leisure, and scant economic or psychic security for most people, such a Dionysiac festival, as Rosemary Haughton comments, "however disgusting it may appear to us, was in fact a healing and peace-bringing act." [40] Further, the Greeks recognized the presence of the divine in all beauty. Their unashamedly open and delicate appreciation of the human body flowered in the superb artistic creations of that age, and it is not surprising that they found beauty in the sexual act in a religious context and hence divine meaning in that situation.

Significantly, however, the Greeks did not appear to associate "ordinary everyday sex" with divine union. Ordinary sex was pleasurable and necessary for procreation, but it was undignified and not sacramental. Even the approved and celebrated male homosexual relationship between an adult and a youth was, in its ideal form, devoid of intercourse. Sacramental sex appeared only in the cultic context.

As far as I am aware, one voice in the ancient world boldly asserted that ordinary married intercourse was sacramental—the apostle Paul.[41] If later Christians spiritualized his words, Paul's original intent seems clear. And this, perhaps, is one of the great surprises of sexual history: that this apostle, who himself was so ambivalent about sexuality in many ways, should raise the possibility that the intercourse of wife and husband could have divine meaning and could celebrate the divine mystery. This possibility was submerged for centuries of Christian history. Hints of it emerged much later in Shakespeare and John Donne, and still later in D. H. Lawrence.[42]

While I have spoken of spirit-body dualism in completely negative terms to this point, it did have a positive result at an earlier stage of human history. In some ways it nurtured the growth of the notion of a distinctly human personality. The spirit separated from the body was also the spirit released from total earth-boundedness into the possibilities of self-transcendence, future-orientation, and transformation of the environment. Thus, in an ironic way, the very dualism which saw sexuality as deeply suspect if not outright evil contributed to the personalization of the sex drive and its fusion with self-transcending love and commitment. And, in its unintended way, spiritualistic dualism has paved the road to the possibility of sexual love as sacramental.

But what, more specifically, might the sacramentality of sexual loving mean? Christian tradition has insisted in its wiser moments that a sacrament is not simply a *sign* of grace, as if grace were experienced quite apart from the sacrament itself. Rather, it is a *means* of grace. One can experience God's wholeness-creating love in the sacrament itself and through it become receptive to that same love elsewhere in life. By this functional definition, it would seem that sexual love is sacramental. Yet, should it be considered a *Christian* sacrament and identified as such by the church?

Instructive parallels can be drawn between Baptism and the Eucharist, on the one hand, and sexual love, on the other.[43] Like Baptism, a loving act of sexual intercourse is a reenactment of dying and rising. Orgasm's "little death" occurs in temporary sense of loss of self-conscious individuality, but with this comes the self's death in surrender to the other. Then the self is received back with new life, joyful and replenished from the divine plenitude itself.[44]

With the Eucharist, there are even more sacramental parallels. The Eucharist's body language is obvious. Its promised unity is not a unification which erases individuality but rather a union or communion which bonds together deeply unique individuals. The appropriate mood of participation in the Eucharist is that of joyful gratitude to God. There is in the sacrament an eschatological dimension: it is an earthly experience of the ultimate unity promised to all in the kingdom. All of these things also characterize acts of true sexual love.

Both Baptism and the Eucharist are rituals for communicating something that cannot adequately be expressed in words alone. The experience itself is intrinsic to the communication. And both sacraments can be misused. With improper understanding of their intention and significance, with distorted motivation for their use, the sacraments do not function in a sacramental way at all, but rather can harm the individuals so participating in them. And all of these things can be said of genital sexual activity.

Theologians from more sacramental traditions of the church have been quicker to recognize this potential of sex. Thus, Evgueny Lampert writes of sexual intercourse as "the mystery of the breaking down of all the limits and limitations of human life and isolated human existence . . . It is the mystery of a sudden merging and union into a single indivisible being of flesh and spirit, of heaven and earth, of human and divine love." [45] Likewise, Philip Sherrard contends: "It may be concluded therefore that this sacramental form of sexual love is not simply a human emotion or impulse or even a created cosmic or elemental force. Still less is it to be identified simply with a bodily or psychosomatic energy. It is, in its origins, a spiritual energy. . . . Hence, to be united in this love is to find oneself returned to oneself, to one's full being and primal condition. In this sense, it is not simply to be born in beauty. It is also to be regenerated in God and to have the divine Paradise revealed to one." [46] In a very real way, this mystery of sexual love is also the place where many of today's young adults find their most real sense of the sacred. Beyond society's acquisitiveness and pragmatism, here there is honesty, intimacy, tenderness, and mutual surrender. Many find here the occasion where awe and religious language are once more meaningful.[47]

If we grant the capacity of sexual love to break the self open to the true meaning of divine-human communion, still the question remains: should it be considered a Christian sacrament, and if so, how? Perhaps, as John W. Dixon, Jr., has argued, the wisest course is to affirm sexual love as sacramental or, in the tradition of some churches, "a sacramental," without attempting to identify it as a sacrament as such.[48] In the historic Christian community, sexual intercourse has not been seen as a carrier of the image of Christ in the ways that a true Christian sacrament must be. Part of this reason, undoubtedly, has been the anti-sex dualism which infected the church. But it is also due to the fact that Jesus, while blessing married sexuality, did not single out either marriage or sexual love as such for unique status in the new community.

At the same time, to consider sexual intercourse as no more than a natural good of the human life is to underestimate its power. Its power to create and to destroy, to give utter ecstasy and to produce brokenness, goes beyond many of God's other "good gifts" of the natural life which are far less central to personhood. Even the language of sex testifies to its potency—it can be used as curse, as magical incantation, or as invitation to passion.

Where then is the sacramentality of sex? It lies in its power to invite wholeness through relationship. Dixon says it splendidly: "In this is the reality of the sacramentality of sex. We are not whole persons [by ourselves] and cannot be. Our sexuality is not only a paradigm of our completion but a paradigm of our humanity as well. Nowhere in our life are we so remorselessly taught our creaturehood, the earthiness of our origin. Nowhere are we so subject to the powers of nature, to the terrible passions of our flesh. . . . Nowhere is failure so abjectly humiliating or power so personal and destructive. Nowhere is pleasure so joyful, delight so satisfying. Nowhere are the possibilities so endless: for charity and forgiveness, for patience and understanding, for an infinite range of patterns of dominations and submissions, for exorcising evil by turning it into a game, for balancing ecstasy with the sweaty realities of the flesh, for power and gentleness, for giving and receiving, for glory and patience." [49]

In this particular discussion I have drawn heavily upon insights from theologians of the Anglican and Catholic traditions wherein sacramental life is so central. Those of us from other Christian traditions can be enriched by this emphasis even if we do not give it such primacy. Nevertheless, it is a mistake to accord inherent mystical qualities to sexual intercourse *per se*, as some of the sacramental writers tend to do. As a physical act, intercourse is susceptible of many and varied meanings. What it means, what it communicates—in short, its language—is not "biologically constant" nor is there anything automatically sacramental about it. Indeed, it would seem that it is sexuality in a broader sense that is much more grace-bearing than any particular sexual act. It is physical intimacy over a period of time, in the context of loving commitment and mutual growth, and in the context of many other dimensions of shared intimacy that has the special power to create the gracious communion of persons. But in precisely *this* kind of setting an act of sexual intercourse *can* be a sacramental act. Again and again it can teach us the secret of human wholeness and be an authentic means of divine grace. And, if liturgists are imaginative, sensitive, and careful, appropriate language might be found to celebrate this in public worship. By doing so, perhaps its sacramental power could be celebrated even more fully by Christian people in the privacies of their own committed relationships.

Sexual Dimensions of the Church's Communal Life

The church has many definitions, and no single metaphor does it justice. Nevertheless, there are two major families of metaphors, both biblical and both essential. They are the images of *organism* and *covenant*.[50] Christian community is organic. Its life is more than just the sum of its parts. It has continuity and interaction with its environment. Organic metaphors also point to the church's true life as integration, harmony, and wholeness. The church is also cre-ated in and through covenant, the relationship of promise and re-sponse between God and the people, and among persons themselves. In genuine community there is always an ongoing conversation among the covenanting parties who are free as unique, distinct, and personal beings to interact with each other.

As I have written elsewhere, "The church needs both metaphors. The body of Christ and the people of the covenant are one community. The entrance covenant does not establish a relationship that was absent before, yet that organic relationship requires the conscious acts of promise and faithfulness. Without the covenant, the organic understanding leads to the imperialism of group over individual; without the organic understanding, the covenant can become little more than a contract assumed to be created by the promises and interests of its members." [51]

While the sexual dimensions of these metaphors are seldom articulated or perhaps even recognized, they are highly significant. They are most striking in the organic images, which clearly point to a body theology. Indeed, the image of *the body* is central to Paul, and salvation is corporeal—incorporation. "To be 'in Christ' (a phrase which occurs repeatedly in his letters) is incomprehensible apart from the deepest participation in the community which bears Christ's name." [52]

But the capacity for abandoning oneself to such community also appears to be linked significantly with our sexuality. This is illumi-nated by the adult-child polarity in creative personalities. "With the adult we associate all the ego qualities: self-consciousness, achievement, rationality, individuality, and culture. The child is the symbol of the qualities associated with the body: spontaneity, pleasure, feeling, community, and nature." [53] The adult who is in touch with the child within is the one who has the capacity to be truly a communal person. By no accident those primitive people who have a strong sense of communal living seem to have a child-like quality about them. It is a capacity for closeness and identification that has not been dissolved by the individualism of modern adult society. Unless, then, we become as little children we shall not know the meaning of community. But this also implies the capacity for affirming the qualities of the body—spontaneity, pleasure, feeling—which are all deeply sexual. The Body of Christ is thus antithetical to any spiritualistic dualism. It is not a community of discarnate spirits but of body-selves bound to each other in and through their incarnate Lord.

The church as body is also antithetical to sexist dualism. The image of the church as "sisterhood" in contemporary feminist theology speaks to the point.[54] Those deeply involved in the women's movement testify that sisterhood means a redemptive and revelatory cohumanity. It is a therapeutic community, enabling women to deal with their repressed alienation. It is a supportive community which counters isolation, a healing community which allows its members to find their strength in solidarity with each other. But sisterhood is also an image which transcends biological gender. It points to the body which the church as a whole is called to be.

If the church is organic and body, it is also the community of covenant—covenant which by its very nature also has significant sexual dimensions. The covenant metaphor complements the organic metaphor by pointing to that community which is composed of free and unique historical beings, never uniform, never swallowing one another up in group imperialism. If the transcending of spiritualistic dualism allows the self to be truly communal, paradoxically it is also basic to the covenantal self. Psychologists of a variety of persuasions bear this out. It is not typically the person alienated from his or her body who can relate effectively among equals. It is rather the person relatively secure in the body-self integration who has both sufficient security and sufficient freedom to enter into meaningful commitments, promises, and into ongoing dialogue with other unique persons.

Genuine covenant community must transcend sexist dualism, too. It presses against domination-subordination patterns and toward genuine mutuality. Letty Russell, reflecting on the possibilities of entering into the consciousness and experience of others, particularly those who have been oppressed, says this: "it is possible to 'think black, or Buddhist, or poor, or woman.' Possible, because we share a common humanity and can learn to move beyond *identity* toward *mutuality*. At the same time we realize that it is impossible, literally to enter into the life of another person or group completely. Mutuality means that one shares consciousness and trust, not that one becomes identical with the other person." [55]

In such ways, both the organic and the covenantal metaphors in creative tension with each other can inform the meaning of Christian community. While both point beyond sexuality as such, each has inescapably sexual dimensions. The church as *sexual* community is both organic Body of Christ and covenanted People of God. And as such a *community* the church is of prime significance in making love a reality in human life—incarnating the Incarnate Love.

Because these images affirm not only intimacy and mutuality but also inclusiveness, there are implications for a diversity of sexual patterns within the congregation. Different sexual life-styles being lived out with integrity and in Christianly humanizing ways need not simply be tolerated—they can be positively supported. The "family of God" can ill afford to make the nuclear family its sole model. Single persons and couples, heterosexual and homosexual in orientation, celibates and those covenanted together can all compose a rich fabric of Christian community.

Sex education for persons of all ages has its legitimate and important place in the church's educational program. It can be of a type which will help people to claim and to reclaim the feeling dimensions of their sexuality within a context of rigorous reflection on the theological-ethical implications of the faith. Counter to any spiritualism, such sex education can celebrate the goodness of the body and the promise of wholeness to people as body-selves. Against the pedagogy implicit in sexism, it can resist the temptation to make authoritative pronouncements, instead inviting young and old into a common quest to discover and live out genuinely Christian images of human sexuality. But the wise congregation will also recognize that (just as in a family) sex education is going on all the time. The absence of healthy carnality in worship, for example, speaks loudly in favor of a disembodied spiritualism regardless of words spoken to the contrary. And the dominance of males and conventionally masculine values in the church's leadership will drown out any spoken words about equality and mutuality.

As it has been said frequently in recent ecclesiological discussions the church is always congregation-in-mission. If it is to be truly a *koinonia*, the personalizing community of love, it is also necessarily oriented toward the kingdom, God's universal presence. And as a community conscious of life's pervasive sexuality, the church can also recognize and respond appropriately to often-overlooked sexual dimensions in the major social issues of our time.

The Church, Social Justice, and Sexuality

"In a world of mass murder and mass starvation, of unprecedented terror, odious tyrannies, and the threat of nuclear holocausts—in such a world there is something obscene about an order of priorities that starts off with bigger and better orgasms." [56] Peter Berger is certainly right, as were the great Hebrew prophets who saw that Yahweh's demand for earthly righteousness and justice was sadly deflected by the cheap grace of the fertility cults who made cakes for the Queen of Heaven (Jeremiah 7:18). But the *sacralizing* of sex is far different from recognizing its *sacramentality*. And if there is danger of trivializing sex into superficial pleasure, there is also the danger of so trivializing sexuality that we fail to see the intricate, subtle, and far-reaching ways in which it permeates current social issues—issues which demand attention to those very sexual dimensions if significant alleviation of their injustice is to come.

Most obvious, of course, are a variety of justice issues which are *clearly* sex-related.[57]

● There are issues concerning women's rights to bodily control: the availability of therapeutic abortion services without regard to income or race; the elimination of coercive medical interference (particularly reflected in the alarming increase in sterilization of low-income women and in medical experimentation on the poor and institutionalized).

• The prostitution system—infected by organized crime, violence, and the inequity of prosecuting prostitutes but not their customers—is an important area for more creative public policy.

• The issue of pornography requires a sensitive balance between, on the one hand, freedom of the press and the rights of adult access to material of their choice, and on the other hand, the rights of persons to be free from the intrusion of sexual materials deemed offensive and dehumanizing.

• Rape and wife-beating, crimes of alarming proportions, need to be seen for what they are: not primarily acts of sexual lust, but rather crimes of violence used to keep women "in their place." As such, not only vigorous prosecution of the male offenders and sensitive treatment of the victims is needed, but also public education regarding the nature and psychic sources of these crimes.

• A whole variety of issues relate to economic justice for women: not only equal pay, job access, quality child day care facilities, and Social Security benefits, but also new and creative ways of addressing the economic value of housework itself.

• The protection of minors from physical and sexual abuse, including the use of children in pornographic material, is an issue of major proportions.

• Laws which effectively prevent many single retired people from establishing new marriages for fear of difficult economic loss need to be changed.

• Gay persons are still discriminated against in a host of ways, as noted in Chapter 8.

• The sexual well-being of persons in prisons and mental institutions deserves public policy attention if these institutions are to become more rehabilitative.

● New reproductive technologies and the astounding possibilities unfolding in genetic science have vast social implications which require thorough public discussion and, quite possibly, effective monitoring.

● Government policies which preclude or curtail the development of non-traditional but stable family forms need examination.

● And, preeminently, the world's over-population calls not only for the widespread use of effective fertility controls and responsible family planning but also for a sexual philosophy and ethic which releases couples from the procreative demand.

All of these, and perhaps more, are public policy issues obviously sexual in nature. But a holistic vision of human sexuality can lead the church to see more clearly and respond more effectively to important sexual dimensions in vast social issues which, on the surface, seem to have little to do with sexuality. Three issues provide illustration: social violence, racism, and ecology.

Social violence is an immensely complex phenomenon. It assaults both individuals and groups. It destroys property and institutional life. It involves subtle forms of violence expressed in both psychic attacks upon people and the organized denial to them of resources and opportunities. Its sexual elements alone surely are not an adequate interpretation. In the words of classic philosophy, these sexual factors are a "necessary but not sufficient" cause. But they are significant in the intricate web of causation and they must be addressed. The sexual roots of social violence can be located, in somewhat differing ways, in each of the two dualisms which have been our concern.

Sexist dualism—man-over-woman—is the more evident and more potent of the two, and the story begins in the sex-role socialization process.[58] In our society males quite typically learn an adversary and dominance style of human relating. The young boy is taught the values of performance and competition. He learns that strength and being at the top are virtues. The family itself frequently becomes infected with subcurrents of hostility and manipulation

because of the resentment of its female members over their subordination. This hostility in turn begets lack of self-worth in the
developing male, which in turn can nurture compensatory aggressiveness. School and peer groups further the competitive, "machismo" image of masculinity with its fear of homosexuality, its cult of
toughness, and its demand for potency. Cultural values buttress the
process: the rewards and the images of male success in professional
football and corporate economic enterprise are obvious examples.

The political arena is particularly revealing as a manifestation of
such male socialization. The individualistic masculine ethic of the
hunter-hero-winner is there. The value of (male) power without
regard to the means of its acquisition was an obvious theme of
Watergate, and the value of winning-without-compromise an obvious theme for years in our Vietnam policy. The cult of toughness
finds its ideal arena in foreign affairs and defense policies where
there are fewer constraints and pressures for compromise than in
domestic politics. To be sure, not every male policymaker is driven
by the aggressive masculine ideal, but most are significantly influenced by it in one way or another.[59]

The masculine image conducive to violence is found not only in
the obvious cult of toughness-and-winning. It is also present in patterns of thinking which prize technical rationality above meaning
and effect. Hannah Arendt describes how this type of rationality
among "scientifically minded brain trusters in the councils of government" can promote violent solutions to problems: "They reckon
with the consequences of certain hypothetically assumed constel-
lations without, however, being able to test their hypothesis against
actual occurrences. The logical flow in these hypothetical construc-
tions of future events is always the same: what first appears as a
hypothesis . . . turns immediately, usually after a few paragraphs,
into a 'fact' which then gives birth to a whole string of similar non-
facts, with the result that the purely speculative character of the
whole enterprise is forgotten." [60]

We have already seen (Chapter 4) that there is no persuasive
scientific evidence that aggressiveness or violence *per se* are biologically more innate in the male. The causes must be sought in
those social values and in those patterns of socialization which continue to reflect the alienation of a sexist dualism. But it is precisely

in such areas as values and socialization patterns that the church can have considerable impact.

Spiritualistic, anti-sex dualism also contributes to social violence, if in less apparent ways than its sibling. Bernard of Clairvaux is a significant case study, as William Phipps has suggested.[61] This notable twelfth century monastic and church leader, often praised as one of history's most Christlike figures, gave many evidences in his life and writings of his dread of sex. For him, the Christian love of which he so persuasively and voluminously wrote was purged of any sexual component. Yet, the erotic needs of his own life, perhaps through an inverted sublimation, were expressed in a particularly virulent hatred of those alleged to be heretics and infidels. His violence against Abelard and his passionate support of holy revenge through the Second Crusade are illustrations.

Anti-sex dualism looks with suspicion upon bodily pleasure. The link between deprivation of physical pleasure and tendencies toward physical violence has now been demonstrated in a number of reliable studies.[62] One study of child abuse in three generations of families found that "parents who abused their children were invariably deprived of physical affection themselves during childhood and that their adult sex life was extremely poor." [63] A massive cross-cultural study of forty-nine different societies discerned an extremely high statistical correlation between violence, deprivation of bodily pleasure during infancy and adolescence, and punitive-repressive sexual attitudes, and it showed the reverse with other societies. "These findings overwhelmingly support the thesis that deprivation of body pleasure throughout life—but particularly during the formative periods of infancy, childhood, and adolescence—are very closely related to the amount of warfare and interpersonal violence." [64] Cross-cultural studies also show the reverse correlations: positive attitudes toward the body and sexuality correlate with a minimal orientation toward violence. One case in point: Eskimo society is known for its positive affirmation of sex, and at the same time war is something incomprehensible and repulsive—indeed the Eskimo language has no word for it.[65]

Psychologically, the phenomenon is understandable. According to Rollo May, when an anti-sex dualism is internalized within the self there occurs a distancing from one's emotions and a consequent deadening of the sense of personhood. Violence then affords "ecstasy" and fascination. It puts us back into contact with the powerful emotions which we want to feel, it takes us out of ourselves, and in an utterly primitive way makes us feel that we are alive.[66]

There is simply too much evidence here for the church to ignore. Both forms of sexual alienation nurture interpersonal and social violence. A theology concerned with the roots of human behavior will know that sexual reconciliation has direct relevance to this vast social issue.

In *racism* a similar interweaving of sexual elements can be discerned. The writer James Weldon Johnson summarizes: "In the core of the heart of the American race problem the sex factor is rooted, rooted so deeply that it is not always recognized when it shows at the surface. Other factors are obvious and are the ones we dare to deal with; but regardless of how we deal with these, the race situation will continue to be acute as long as the sex factor persists." [67]

The patterns of white racism directed toward blacks in America are particularly instructive. Historically, blacks were wrenched from their African societies in which sexual behavior was orderly and under firm family and community controls. But under slavery blacks were bred like animals, white men sexually coerced black women, families were frequently broken up, and legal marriage was often prohibited. Thus was sexual instability forced upon the black.[68] While it is widely recognized that racial differences in sexual behavior have their origin not in biology but in culture and history, the stereotypes persist.

A return to the two forms of sexual dualism is necessary for understanding these dynamics. Sexist dualism is a profound dimension of white racism in the American experience.[69] The "schizophrenic" male attitudes toward women in general—either the virgin or the whore, Mary or Eve—were organized along racial lines. The white woman was the symbol of delicacy and purity, while the black woman represented an animality which could be exploited for both sex and labor. White male society handled its sexual guilt about the use of black women by projecting its pathology onto the black male. He was fantasized as a dark sexual beast. To protect them from the white man's terrorism, black mothers tended to socialize their sons into patterns of docility. This, in turn, complicated the adult marital relationships of black men and women. And, it nurtured a compensatory black male chauvinism (as evidenced in black church patterns and black nationalism movements) to restore the "manliness" of the one who had traditionally been humiliated by being deprived (according to a patriarchal model) of being the protector and provider for his family. In such manner, here only briefly summarized, sexist dualism has been a core ingredient of the development and perpetuation of racist attitudes in our society.

The other dualism, anti-sex spiritualism, has also been at work. Eldridge Cleaver recognized this in saying, "Only when the white man comes to respect his own body, to accept it as part of himself, will he be able to accept the black man's mind and treat him as something other than the living symbol of what he has rejected in himself." [70]

There are several clues of theological relevance to the psychic dynamics at work here. Discomfort with our own bodies leads us to fear any human body which departs too much in appearance from our own. Anxiety evoked by seeing a different kind of body has been documented in psychological research. The comfortable sense of a dependable body frequently is hard-won in our society, and the one who departs markedly in body appearance from oneself can jeopardize the fairly vulnerable body image.[71] Related to this, the role of body feelings in Hitler's racism was apparently strong. He was preoccupied with images of the Jews as people with dirty, grotesque, and distorted bodies.[72]

The psychological hypothesis of bodily scapegoating also has persuasiveness, and the phenomenon is particularly evident in white-black relationships. Black has become a symbol for evil and dirt. Thus, the invitation is present for the white to project onto the black person any dirty and disgusting body feelings which he or she has. Indeed, it appears that the strength of one's hostility toward the "different" body is quite proportionate to one's own negative self-feelings.[73]

It is likely that many persons experience dualistic alienation from their bodies in particular relationship to their anal functions. The messages absorbed by the young child frequently convince him or her that feces are the most disgusting and potent form of dirt in the universe. But then the child must cope with the realization that its own body never ceases to produce this "filth," and many will feel permanently soiled. They seek ways to render themselves more bodily-acceptable, and the projection of dirty-body feelings onto someone of another race, usually of darker skin color, becomes a pathway, however perverse, to self-acceptance. Thus, studies of white subjects have demonstrated that those who are particularly concerned about dirt and about their own feelings of uncleanliness are most likely to view black people negatively.[74]

As long as we feel insecure about our own bodies we will likely be made anxious about bodies so obviously "deviant" from our own, for they suggest that in some strangely uncontrolled way we too could be changed. This appears to be true not only with persons of other races, but also with those of one's own race who are most obviously physically handicapped.[75] And our language suggests the importance of body image and body stability to us. The most dehumanizing expressions of hostility in vulgar speech are linked with depreciating the body or the body functions of someone else. But the greatest dehumanization occurs when a person of a rejected body group internalizes the judgments made by others and becomes convinced of his or her own bodily (and thus personal) inferiority.

Racism, like violence, is an immensely complex phenomenon. Its dimensions are many—historical, economic, political. But the sexual elements are also there and are important. Neither racism nor violence will be erased by dealing only with these, but neither will they be mitigated to any considerable degree without attending to them. Because the church is a sexual community, because its gospel of reconciliation means also sexual reconciliation, and because it has access (in ways that many institutions do not) to the processes of sexual socialization, there are important opportunities for making an impact on this often-hidden part of racism's dynamic.

In social attitudes toward *nature* and *ecology* the two forms of sexual dualism intertwine in a complex manner.[76] In preexilic Hebrew faith, as evidenced in the Psalms and the prophets, while patriarchal thought forms flourished they did not produce a view of nature as ontologically inferior to the spirit. The message was this: nature is not the source of disobedience and evil—human beings are; in Israel's unfaithfulness nature becomes destructive, but in human faithfulness nature becomes beneficent and a sphere of the revelation of God's power and glory.

However, spiritualistic dualism began to intrude. After the fourth century B.C. Greek philosophy began to sunder the earlier Hellenic view of the harmony of body and spirit. Now the created world, like the human body, became that from which detachment and escape must be made if one were to find salvation. Postexilic Hebraism, in a somewhat parallel development, began to accent an apocalyptic world view, and emerging Christianity became heir to these two influences. In early and classic Christianity it was a mixed picture. In some ways the goodness and sacramentality of the earth were affirmed and celebrated. But in competition with this was spiritualistic dualism, represented in forms ranging from the heretical Gnostic extreme (matter is evil—the world's creator is not true God but demon) to a highly eschatological faith (redemption comes not in and through this world, but in spite of it and beyond it). Such is the mixture in our heritage.

The rise of the modern technological society is a complex story of many strands. But one strand of very basic significance is the intrusion of sexist dualism. If the early Hebrews had resisted the extension of their patriarchal thought forms to the world of nature, later Christian generations did not. In the emerging scientific mentality, nature became not only a neutral and value-free realm to be manipulated according to human design it also represented an ontological dualism. "The woman, the body, and the world were the lower half of a dualism that must be declared posterior to, created by, subject to, and ultimately alien to the nature of (male) consciousness, in whose image man made his God." [77] Thus, the human race, notably its male component, was free to manipulate the earth's resources according to its own designs. The vision of dominion over the earth became domination. Caring for the earth gave way to subjecting the earth. Redemption of the earth was overshadowed in many Christian interpretations by the notion of destruction by the God of history in order that a "new creation" might be made.

While this is a vastly oversimplified summary, I would contend that the present ecological crisis cannot be grasped—nor creatively responded to—apart from a recognition of the twin and intertwining sexual dualisms that form its cornerstones. The sexual language so frequently used in speaking of our present dilemma is no accident. We recall, with admiration and longing, the (sexual) kinship imagery of a St. Francis—"Brother Cloud and Sister Moon"—in which blood ties bind human beings to the created earth. We use the language of sexist violence—rape—to speak of the human abuse of nature. And, almost instinctively, we know that somehow the recapturing of our sexual kinship to nature is necessary, for one does not rape a sister or a brother.

Antithetical to any spiritualistic dualism is the affirmation of the goodness of body pleasure. We have already seen some connections between social violence and the denial of bodily pleasure. In a related way, the affirmation of the body seems positively correlated with a sense of belonging to and caring for the earth. As one psychiatrist observes, "Pleasure is the feeling of harmony between an organism and its environment."[78] This is qualitatively different from the sense of alienation, combat, and control.

Antithetical to any sexist dualism is the affirmation of reciprocity. The dominant image of patriarchal religion is that of the utterly transcendent God who commands and whose subjects obey. That imagery is all to easily translated into a corollary: the people command and the earth obeys. But reciprocity marks the more androgynous experience of God as the One who is forever transcendent and forever immanent, the One who gives and the One who receives. That imagery, too, can be translated into a corollary: nature is not simply instrumental, a "thing" to be used; nature and people are part of each other in reciprocity, giving and receiving. Thus a new sexual relationship is manifested: "a change from the pornographic sensibility that has developed in the West—for which the world is a prostitute to be mounted with lust or rejected with loathing—to an erotic sensibility, for which the world is to be affectionately caressed and embraced with self-forgetting love." [79]

Some may object that this is an oversimplified and romanticized

picture of the ecological dilemma. If that objection m̄
many times and in many ways nature must be struggled
resources developed, its natural face altered to create a
healthful and feasible human existence on this overcrowde
it is true. But to prevent development from becoming expl̄   ,
to prevent dominion from becoming heedless domination, not only
new attitudes of the mind are required but also new sensibilities
of the body-self. They are erotic sensibilities.

The sexual elements of ecological crisis and future are not its
whole story. But, as with social violence and racism, unless we
recognize the sexuality that *is* involved in both problem and in
promise, we cannot meet these issues with either the depth of understanding or with the hope that are so sorely needed. The church as
sexual community, if and when it can affirm the sacramentality of
sex, might also recapture the vision of a sacramental world.

*exchanging things
with others for mutual benefit*

Epilog

OUR HUMAN SEXUALITY is God's good gift. It is a fundamental dimension of our created and our intended humanness. To explore some of the ways in which sexuality enters into our experience of Christian faith has been one major purpose of these pages. More clearly to recognize our alienation from our sexuality and to lay bold claim to the gospel's promise of reconciliation to our embodiment has been the other.

Where have we gone wrong? It is not totally fair to blame the Greeks for the spiritualistic dualism in which we participate, though that is much in fashion. Nor can we simply blame the history of sexist dualism which our Hebraic past manifested and which, too, has been embedded in the intervening centuries. Nor can we just blame modernity, though that seems also in vogue. The root cause of our problem can only be described as human sinfulness. As it pertains to sexuality, such sinful alienation indeed pervades our history and our present social structures, though each of us must claim our own responsibility as well.

Christianly perceived, the fundamental answer to sin is the gracious love of God—the Cosmic Lover who promises to make better lovers of us all, in the fullest, richest, most responsible sense of that good word.

Some may object that this answer is too simple. The familiar Freudian explanation may well surface at this point—the view that the repression of sexuality is at the service of civilization and that, without the various kinds of neurotic repressions and compromising sublimations which we have evolved, civilizations would not be born. But I do not believe that this essentially pessimistic and tragic view of Freud's can dominate the Christian story.

True, we do live between the times. But the vision of a more reconciled embodiment is not only eschatological, in the sense of a future hope that can be anticipated but not really experienced in the present time of our lives. It *is* a vision of an important dimension of the New Age, but by God's grace that vision *can* invade and transform something of our present sexual reality. Some such recovery of our embodiment as persons, as a church, as a society may well be one significant way in which God's reforming *kairos* comes in our time.

But the sexual fears are deep-seated. The amount of sexual misinformation is great. And the burden of sexual guilt is heavy. Perhaps in no other area will resistance and avoidance be quite so evident.

Nevertheless, the promise has been given. The Word became—becomes—flesh. The embodied Word dwells among us, full of grace and truth. And we can and do behold that glory.

W. H. Auden in his Christmas Oratorio *For the Time Being* describes the invasion of grace on that star-filled night into the lives of some Bethlehem shepherds. Talking among themselves about the meaning of that manger vision, this is what the shepherds say about their own lives:

> We never left the place where we were born,
> Have only lived one day, but every day,
> Have walked a thousand miles yet only worn
> The grass between our work and home away.

> Lonely we were though never left alone.
> The solitude familiar to the poor
> Is feeling that the family next door,
> The way it talks, eats, dresses, loves, and hates,
> Is indistinguishable from one's own.

[Then,]

> Tonight for the first time the prison gates
> Have opened.
> Music and sudden light
> Have interrupted our routine tonight,
> And swept the filth of habit from our hearts.
> O here and now our endless journey starts.[1]

So it is with the recovery of our embodiment. Insofar as that happens, it will be interrupted routine. And while the filth of habit will not easily be swept aside, it must be. And it will be an endless journey. But God *has* promised to make better lovers of us all.

Notes

Preface

1. André Maurois' insight is described by Rollo May, *Love and Will* (New York: Norton, 1969) 170.

1: The Church and Sexuality: A Time to Reconsider

1. Newspaper sources are *The Guardian*, September 6, 16, and 17, and October 14, 1976; *The Cambridge Evening News*, September 3, 1976; and *The Times*, September 16, 1976.
2. Rosemary Haughton, "The Theology of Marriage," in Ruth Tiffany Barnhouse and Urban T. Holmes, III (eds.), *Male and Female: Christian Approaches to Sexuality* (New York: Seabury, 1976) 216.
3. See G. Marian Kinget, *On Being Human: A Systematic View* (New York: Harcourt Brace Jovanovich, 1975) 115f.

2: Embodiment in Sexual Theology

1. D. H. Lawrence, *Lady Chatterley's Lover* (New York: Pocket Books, 1959) 83. I have quoted this passage in an earlier essay, "Bodies, Sexuality, and Personal Health," in *Rediscovering the Person in Medical Care* (Minneapolis: Augsburg, 1976). With the permission of the editor, I shall quote from and expand upon various passages in that earlier essay in this present book.
2. See John Y. Fenton, "Bodily Theology," in John Y. Fenton (ed.), *Theology and Body* (Philadelphia: Westminster, 1974) 127.
3. Ibid., 129ff.
4. Merleau-Ponty's argument here is paraphrased by Arthur A. Vogel, to whom I am indebted for this interpretation: *Body Theology: God's Presence in Man's World* (New York: Harper & Row, 1973) 15. Cf. 88.
5. See ibid., 63f. and 89.
6. See Seymour Fisher, *Body Consciousness* (Glasgow: William Collins, 1976) Chap. 1.
7. Ibid., 33
8. See Seymour Fisher and S. E. Cleveland, *Body Image and Personality* (New York: Dover, 1968).
9. John W. Dixon, Jr., "The Sacramentality of Sex," in Barnhouse and Holmes, 252.
10. Mary Douglas, *Purity and Danger: An Analysis of Concepts of Pollution and Taboo* (London: Routledge & Kegan Paul, 1966) 122.
11. Ibid., 128.
12. Ibid., 115.
13. Ibid., 3f.
14. See ibid., 35f.
15. See ibid., 130, 139.

16. Ibid., 124.
17. See Kinget, 11.
18. See ibid., 50ff. for the discussion of language. The applications to sexuality are mine.
19. As quoted in Abel Jeanniere, *The Anthropology of Sex* (with foreword by Dan Sullivan), trans. by Julie Kernan (New York: Harper & Row, 1967) 70.
20. This is the general approach of symbolic interactionist social theory. See, for example, Herbert Blumer, *Symbolic Interactionism: Perspective and Method* (Englewood Cliffs, N.J.: Prentice-Hall, 1969) 2.
21. See Kenneth Plummer, *Sexual Stigma: An Interactionist Account* (London: (Routledge & Kegan Paul, 1975) 34ff.
22. Useful interpretations of Freud from the symbolic interactionist perspective may be found in *ibid.*, 37ff., and John H. Gagnon and William Simon, *Sexual Conduct: The Social Sources of Human Sexuality* (London: Hutchinson, 1974) 5ff.
23. John H. Gagnon and William S. Simon, "Sexual Deviance in Contemporary America," *Annals of the American Academy of Political and Social Science*, Vol. 376 (1968) 121. Cf. Plummer, 6.
24. This perspective informs Plummer's useful treatment of homosexuality.
25. Quoted in Charles Davis, *Body as Spirit: The Nature of Religious Feeling* (New York: Seabury, 1976) 11.
26. Ibid., 9. I am indebted to Davis' interpretation of feelings in these paragraphs.
27. John W. Dixon, Jr., "The Erotics of Knowing," *Anglican Theological Review*, Vol. LVI, No. 1 (Jan. 1974) 3.
28. See William E. Phipps, *Recovering Biblical Sensuousness* (Philadelphia: Westminster, 1975), Chap. 2; also Davis, 126f.
29. Phipps, 49.
30. Quoted in ibid., 51.
31. Dietrich Bonhoeffer, *Prisoner for God* (New York: Macmillan, 1953) 131.
32. Davis, 126.
33. See ibid., 78ff. for a helpful discussion of this issue.
34. Harry A. Williams makes this point powerfully in *True Resurrection* (London: Mitchell Beazley, 1972) 97.
35. See Vogel, 92ff.

3: Sexual Alienation: The Dualistic Nemesis

1. Alexander Lowen, M.D., *The Betrayal of the Body* (New York: Collier-Macmillan, 1969) 2.
2. Ibid., 209.
3. Bernice Slote, et al., *Start With the Sun: Studies in the Whitman Tradition* (Lincoln, Nebraska: University of Nebraska Press, 1960) 3.
4. See Alan Bell, "Homosexuality, An Overview," in Barnhouse and Holmes, 132f.
5. For insightful descriptions of this phenomenon see Davis, Chap. 2.

6. Rollo May, *Love and Will* (New York: Norton, 1969) 40.
7. Lowen, 84.
8. Gagnon and Simon, 104.
9. See Williams, 28.
10. Ibid., 31.
11. See Davis, 117.
12. Fenton, 133.
13. See Herbert Marcuse, *Eros and Civilization*, 2nd Edition (Boston: Beacon, 1966) esp. 46ff. Cf. Paul A. Robinson, *The Sexual Radicals* (London: Paladin, 1972) 143ff.
14. William H. Masters and Virginia E. Johnson, "Contemporary Influences on Sexual Response: The Work Ethic," a paper presented at the second SIECUS Citation Dinner, October 18, 1972, as quoted by Richard Hettlinger, *Sex Isn't That Simple* (New York: Seabury, 1974) 90.
15. Don Cupitt, *Crisis of Moral Authority* (London: Lutterworth, 1972) 45.
16. See Rosemary R. Ruether, "An Unexpected Tribute to the Theologian, *Theology Today*, Vol. 27, No. 3 (October 1970), 337ff. Cf. Eric Mount, Jr., *The Feminine Factor* (Richmond, Va.: John Knox, 1973), 137f.
17. See Rosemary Haughton, *Love* (London: Watts, 1970) 32ff.
18. Plato, *The Last Days of Socrates*, trans. Hugh Tredennick (Harmondsworth, England: Penguin, 1969) 110, 112. I will typically use the term "spiritualistic dualism" to denote the experienced split between the person's capacities for self-transcendence, self-awareness, relationality, and rationality-cognition, on the one hand, and the person's physical body (including sexuality), on the other hand. In discussing the possible expressions of the self's dualistic division, a case might be made for distinguishing between the *spirit*-body split and the *mind*-body split. Thus, Reinhold Niebuhr contends that the "classical view" of human nature, comprised primarily of Platonic, Aristotelian and Stoic conceptions, is a mind-body split—understanding the human being primarily from the standpoint of the uniqueness of the rational faculties, the *nous*: "*Nous* may be translated as 'spirit' but the primary emphasis lies upon the capacity for thought and reason." *The Nature and Destiny of Man, Vol. I* (New York: Scribner's, 1941, 1943, 1949), 6. Distinguishing between spirit and mind (as Niebuhr does at this particular point) admittedly has the advantage of greater precision if one wishes to single out those dualisms which are especially rationalistic in cast. However, for our purposes the more inclusive use of "spiritualistic dualism" is generally sufficient, and "spirit" should be understood to include the rational capacities as well as those capacities for self-transcendence, etc. unless otherwise specified. Indeed, throughout much of his two-volume work, in juxtaposing "spirit" and "nature" Niebuhr himself uses "spirit" in this justifiably inclusive manner.
19. Rosemary Radford Ruether, *New Woman, New Earth: Sexist Ideologies and Human Liberation* (New York: Seabury, 1975) 3f.
20. Vern L. Bullough, *Sexual Variance in Society and History* (New York: Wiley, 1976) 75.
21. See Phyllis Trible, "Good Tidings of Great Joy: Biblical Faith Without Sexism," *Christianity and Crisis*, Vol. 34, No. 1 (Feb. 4, 1974) 12-16; "Eve and Adam: Genesis 2-3 Reread," *Andover Newton Quarterly*, Vol.

13, No. 4 (Mar. 1973) 251-258. Cf. *God and the Rhetoric of Sexuality* (Philadelphia: Fortress, 1978).

22. Useful sources in the interpretation of Greece and Rome are Bullough; Phipps; Derrick Sherwin Bailey, *The Man-Woman Relation in Christian Thought* (London: Longmans, Green, 1959); and Demosthenes Savramis, *The Satanizing of Woman: Religious Versus Sexuality*, trans. Martin Ebon (Garden City, N.Y.: Doubleday, 1974).

23. Morton Scott Enslin, *The Ethics of Paul* (New York: Harper, 1930) 180.

24. See (Derrick) Sherwin Bailey, *Common Sense About Sexual Ethics: A Christian View* (New York: Macmillan, 1962), 21f.; and Bailey, *The Man-Woman Relation in Christian Thought*, 8f.

25. John A. T. Robinson, *The Body: A Study in Pauline Theology* (London: SCM, 1952) 9.

26. See ibid., 25.

27. See Bailey, *Common Sense About Sexual Ethics*, 23f.

28. See Rudolf Bultmann, *Theology of the New Testament, Vol. I*, trans. Kendrick Grobel (London: SCM, 1952) 202, 241; cf. Cupitt, 44. It must be said in fairness to Paul that while he did appropriate not only Hellenistic language but also Hellenistic concepts, he often interpreted these differently than did native Greeks, precisely because of his own Jewish background. But when Paul's terminology was subsequently interpreted by Greek minds imbued with dualistic world views, overtones unintended by Paul were accented. See Stephen Sapp, *Sexuality, the Bible, and Science* (Philadelphia: Fortress, 1977) 58ff.

29. See 1 Cor. 11:4-10 and 14:34-35. Cf. the interpretation by Bernard P. Prusak, "Woman: Seductive Siren and Source of Sin? Pseudepigraphal Myth and Christian Origins," in Rosemary Radford Ruether (ed.), *Religion and Sexism: Images of Women in the Jewish and Christian Traditions* (New York: Simon and Schuster, 1974), 98f. Also Sapp, 73ff.

30. See Donald F. Winslow, "Sex and Anti-Sex in the Early Church Fathers," in Barnhouse and Holmes, 28. Winslow's entire essay is a careful interpretation of patristic attitudes, and I rely on it in this section.

31. Tertullian, *Adv. Marc.*, i. 29, cited in Bailey, *The Man-Woman Relation in Christian Thought*, 21.

32. Jerome, *Epist.*, xxii. 20, cited in ibid., 23.

33. Original sources for Augustine's views on these matters are *De continentia, De bono conjugali, De sancta virginitate, De bono viduitatis*, and *De nuptiis et concupiscentia*. Some interpreters accent more of the positive aspects of Augustine's views on sex in marriage. See, for example, Anthony Kosnik et al., *Human Sexuality: New Directions in American Catholic Thought* (New York: Paulist, 1977) 36f. My own interpretation is more in line with those of Philip Sherrard, *Christianity and Eros* (London: SPCK, 1976) 8ff., and Dorothea Krook, *Three Traditions of Moral Thought* (Cambridge, England: The University Press, 1959) 274ff.

34. See Bailey, *Common Sense About Sexual Ethics*, 45f.

35. Useful interpretations of sexuality in the thought of the Reformers will be found in ibid.; Bailey, *The Man-Woman Relation in Christian Thought;* William Graham Cole, *Sex in Christianity and Psychoanalysis* (New York: Oxford, 1955; and Eleanor L. McLaughlin, "Male and Female in Christian

Tradition: Was There a Reformation in the Sixteenth Century?" in Barnhouse and Holmes.

36. See Savramis, 78f.
37. See Bailey, *Common Sense About Sexual Ethics*, 54f.
38. For clarification of certain developments in Roman Catholic thought, I am indebted to Kosnick et al., Chap. II. This study was commissioned by the Catholic Theological Society of America.
39. Taylor is cited in Bailey, *Common Sense About Sexual Ethics*, 57.
40. See Phipps' treatment of Milton, 89, 149f.
41. Daniel Day Williams' interpretation is typical, and I have paraphrased it here. See *The Spirit and the Forms of Love* (New York: Harper & Row, 1968), 216f.
42. See Ruether, *New Woman, New Earth*, 3f.
43. Margaret Mead, *Sex and Temperament in Three Primitive Societies* (New York: Morrow, 1955) 190.
44. Judd Marmor (ed.), *Sexual Inversion* (New York: Basic Books, 1965), 10.
45. John Money and Patricia Tucker, *Sexual Signatures* (Boston: Little, Brown, 1975) 230.
46. The Maccoby and Jacklin study is summarized in Joseph H. Pleck, "The Psychology of Sex Roles: Traditional and New Views," in Libby A. Carter and Anne F. Scott (eds.), *Women and Men: Changing Roles, Relationships and Perceptions* (New York: Aspen Institute for Humanistic Studies, 1976) 187f.
47. See, for example, the argument in Savramis, 58ff.
48. Cited in ibid., 60.
49. See Ruether, *New Woman, New Earth*, 72.
50. See Herbert W. Richardson, *Nun, Witch, Playmate: The Americanization of Sex* (New York: Harper & Row, 1971; paperback edition, 1974) Chap. 1.
51. Ibid., 11f.
52. See Ruether, *New Woman, New Earth*, Chap. 1; and in Eugene C. Bianchi and Rosemary R. Ruether, *From Machismo to Mutuality: Essays on Sexism and Woman-Man Liberation* (New York: Paulist, 1976) Chap. 1.
53. Cupitt traces this development, 65ff.
54. Thomas Aquinas, *Summa Theologica*, 1, q. 93, 4. Cf. 1, q. 92, 1 and 1, q. 98, 2. Phipps gives a useful interpretation of Aquinas in *Was Jesus Married?* (New York: Harper & Row, 1970) 176ff.
55. Cited in McLaughlin, 48.
56. Cited in ibid.
57. See ibid., 49ff.
58. Ibid., 50.
59. Ibid., 51.
60. See Mary Daly, *Beyond God the Father: Toward a Philosophy of Women's Liberation* (Boston: Beacon, 1973) 51ff.
61. Ibid., 51.
62. Ruether, in Bianchi and Ruether, 74.
63. See Jack Nichols, *Men's Liberation: A New Definition of Masculinity* (New York: Penguin, 1975) 27ff.
64. See Warren Farrell, *The Liberated Man* (New York: Bantam, 1975) 15f.
65. See Marc Feigen Fasteau, *The Male Machine* (New York: Dell, 1975) 11.

66. See Bianchi, in Bianchi and Ruether, Chap. 4; Farrell, Chap. 5; and Fasteau, Chaps. 11, 12.
67. See Fisher, 51.
68. See Bianchi, in Bianchi and Ruether, 87ff.
69. See Germaine Greer, *The Female Eunuch* (New York: McGraw-Hill, 1971) 35.
70. See Nichols, 200f.
71. Bianchi makes this point especially well, 36f.
72. Richard Zaner is especially helpful on this matter. See "The Alternating Reed: Embodiment as Problematic Unity," in Fenton, 53ff.
73. Ibid., 64.
74. Ruether, *New Woman, New Earth*, 148. I am indebted to Ruether's analysis in her Chap. 6 in this paragraph.

4: Sexual Salvation: Grace and the Resurrection of the Body

1. Paul Tillich, *Systematic Theology, Vol. II* (Chicago: University of Chicago Press, 1957) 57. Cf. 166. See also Harold H. Ditmanson, *Grace in Experience and Theology* (Minneapolis: Augsburg, 1977) esp. Chaps. 4, 6.
2. See Dan Sullivan, "Introduction" to Jeanniere, 15f.
3. See Leslie Paul, *Eros Rediscovered: Restoring Sex to Humanity* (New York: Association, 1970) 142f.
4. See Tom F. Driver, "Sexuality and Jesus," in Martin E. Marty and Dean G. Peerman (eds.), *New Theology No. 3* (New York: Macmillan, 1966); also, "On Taking Sex Seriously," *Christianity and Crisis*, Vol. 23 (Oct. 14, 1963).
5. Sullivan, 17.
6. See H. A. Williams, 50f.
7. Ibid., 51.
8. John A. T. Robinson, *The Human Face of God* (Philadelphia: Westminster, 1973) 64.
9. John Erskine, quoted in Phipps, *Was Jesus Married?*, 9.
10. Driver, "Sexuality and Jesus," 243, 240.
11. Jack Dominian, *The Church and the Sexual Revolution* (London: Darton, Longman & Todd, 1971) 66.
12. See Phipps, *Was Jesus Married?*, esp. Chaps. 2, 3, 4.
13. See Lewis B. Smedes, *Sex for Christians* (Grand Rapids, Mich.: Eerdmans, 1976) 78f.
14. See Robinson, *The Human Face of God*, 57ff. If we interpret the Virgin Birth as a non-literal way of attempting to affirm something about Jesus as the Christ, we are left, according to Robinson, with only three possibilities concerning Jesus' conception. One is that Joseph was his human father who impregnated Mary inside wedlock; another is that Joseph impregnated Mary outside wedlock and subsequently legitimized this action by marriage. But both of these possibilities are not strongly supported by biblical evidence. Hence, a third possibility presents itself: that the conception took place outside wedlock by a man unknown to us, and this was subsequently accepted by Joseph. In pressing this point Robinson may be stretching the available evidence, but his overall contention concerning the radical scandal of the Incarnation is clear and appropriate.

15. See ibid., 197ff.
16. Ibid., 199.
17. Both Driver, "Sexuality and Jesus," 236, and Phipps, *Recovering Biblical Sensuousness*, 158, make this point.
18. In speaking of God's incarnation in Jesus Christ, we do well to remember why Paul Tillich was hesitant about the term. The notion that "God has become man" is nonsensical because God cannot become something else— God cannot cease to be God. There is, then, a danger that the doctrine of the Incarnation will be interpreted as a mythological transmutation. Rather than speaking of the divine nature and human nature wedded in Jesus Christ, Tillich finds it more appropriate to assert that in Jesus the Christ "the eternal unity of God and man has become historical reality" and in Christ we meet the manifestation of God "in a personal life-process as a saving participant in the human predicament." See *Systematic Theology, Vol. II*, 148, 95.
19. Ditmanson, 58.
20. Gregory Baum, as quoted in ibid., 24.
21. Paul Tillich, *The Shaking of the Foundations* (New York: Scribner's, 1948), 162.
22. Niebuhr, *The Nature and Destiny of Man, Vol. I*, 237.
23. Ditmanson, 60.
24. Alexander Lowen, *Pleasure: A Creative Approach to Life* (New York: Penguin, 1975) 188.
25. Theodore Isaac Rubin, *Compassion and Self-Hate: An Alternative to Despair* (New York: Ballantine, 1975) 69.
26. Ibid., 189.
27. Lowen, *Pleasure*, 82.
28. See Rubin, 167; Rollo May, 167ff.
29. See Lowen, *Pleasure*, 136.
30. See ibid., 205.
31. See Rubin, 165.
32. See Vogel, 63.
33. See Rubin, 173.
34. See H. A. Williams, 19f.
35. Ibid. Cf. 1 Cor. 8:6; Eph. 1:10.
36. *Human Sexuality: A Preliminary Study* (New York: United Church Press, 1977) 64. In these three paragraphs I am drawing upon the insightful interpretation in this source.
37. Ibid., 49.
38. I am here quoting Dan Sullivan, p. 22, who describes Fairbairn's position.
39. Ibid.
40. Mary S. Calderone, "Eroticism as a Norm," *The Family Coordinator*, October 1974, 340.
41. See Lowen, *Pleasure*, 54f., 144.
42. Ibid., 68f.
43. Ibid., 32.
44. Ibid., 33f.
45. Ibid., 113.
46. John Giles Milhaven is particularly helpful at this point. See "Conjugal Sexual Love and Contemporary Moral Theology," *Theological Studies*,

Vol. 35, No. 4 (December 1974); and "Christian Evaluations of Sexual Pleasure," unpublished paper delivered to the American Society of Christian Ethics, January 1976.

47. Francois Chirpaz, as described and quoted by Milhaven, "Conjugal Sexual Love . . . , " 708f.
48. See Milhaven, "Christian Evaluations . . . , " p. IV-5.
49. Nichols, 85.
50. Sidney Callahan, *Beyond Birth Control: The Christian Experience of Sex* (New York: Sheed and Ward, 1968) 37f.
51. Ibid., 49.
52. See Marcuse, *Eros and Civilization*, 49.
53. Norman O. Brown, *Life Against Death* (Middletown, Conn.: Wesleyan University Press, 1959) 27.
54. Alan Watts, *Nature, Man, and Woman: A New Approach to Sexual Experience* (New York: Pantheon, 1958) 160ff.
55. Sherrard, 42. Cf. 43-47.
56. Paul Tillich, *Systematic Theology, Vol. I* (Chicago: University of Chicago Press, 1951) 72f.
57. Urban T. Holmes, III, "The Sexuality of God," in Barnhouse and Holmes, 266.
58. Douglas, 164.
59. Daniel Day Williams, 284.
60. Abraham Maslow, "Love in Self-Actualizing People," in Hendrik M. Ruitenbeek (ed.), *Sexuality and Identity* (New York: Dell Publishing Co., Inc., 1970). This quotation and those which follow are found on 224-233.
61. Alexander Lowen, *Depression and the Body: The Biological Basis of Faith and Reality* (Baltimore: Penguin, 1973) 305.
62. James Harrison, in his reviews of several books on masculinity, *Sex Roles,* Vol. I, No. 2 (1975) 205.
63. See Phyllis Trible, "Good Tidings . . . , " 12; and "Eve and Adam . . . , " 251ff.
64. "Good Tidings . . . , " 12.
65. Ibid.
66. See Samuel Terrien, "Toward a Biblical Theology of Womanhood," in Barnhouse and Holmes, 17ff.
67. Berdiaev's thought on androgyny is found mainly in his early work, *The Meaning of Creativeness* (1914). I am quoting Sherrard's summary, 61f.
68. Ibid., 64.
69. Bailey, *The Man-Woman Relation in Christian Thought*, 275.
70. See Richardson, 56ff.
71. Ibid., 57.
72. Robert M. Stein, "Liberating the Feminine," in Barnhouse and Holmes, 80.
73. See ibid., 85.
74. See Gayle Graham Yates, *What Women Want: The Ideas of the Movement* (Cambridge, Mass. and London: Harvard University Press, 1975).
75. Ibid., 176f.
76. See June Singer, *Androgyny: Toward a New Theory of Sexuality* (Garden City, N.Y.: Anchor/Doubleday, 1976) esp. 276ff.
77. Ibid., 333. Cf. 52.

5: Love and Sexual Ethics

1. Several theologians are particularly helpful in articulating this understanding of human nature. See Norman Pittenger, *Making Sexuality Human* (Philadelphia: Pilgrim, 1970), Chaps. 2, 3, 4; *Goodness Distorted* (London: Mowbray, 1970), Chap 3; *Unbounded Love* (New York: Seabury, 1976), Chap. 3; Daniel Day Williams, *The Spirit and the Forms of Love*, esp. 220ff.; and Paul Tillich, *Morality and Beyond* (New York: Harper & Row, 1963).
2. See Daniel Day Williams, 222.
3. See Sidney Callahan, "Human Sexuality in a Time of Change," *The Christian Century*, Vol. LXXXV, No. 35 (Aug. 28, 1968) 1078f.
4. See Herbert W. Richardson, who has insightfully traced this historical development, and upon whose interpretation I depend at this point.
5. See Roland H. Bainton, *What Christianity Says about Sex, Love, and Marriage* (New York: Association, 1957) 58ff.
6. Richardson, 64.
7. See Haughton, 52ff.
8. See Richardson, 43f.
9. While I disagree with the major conclusions of his article, William Muehl makes this particular point eloquently. See "Some Words of Caution," in Barnhouse and Holmes, 172.
10. Paul Tillich, *Love, Power, and Justice* (London: Oxford University Press, 1954) 25f.
11. See Anders Nygren, *Agape and Eros*, trans. Philip S. Watson (London: SPCK, 1957), 75ff.
12. Ibid., 78.
13. See Phipps, *Recovering Biblical Sensuousness*, 99, 105.
14. Beverly Wildung Harrison, "Sexism and the Language of Christian Ethics —Some Basic Theses for Discussion," (mimeographed, n.d.) 3f.
15. Reinhold Niebuhr, "Toward New Intra-Christian Endeavors," *The Christian Century*, Vol. LXXXVI, No. 53 (Dec. 31, 1969) 1666.
16. May, 65.
17. Ibid., 74.
18. C. S. Lewis, *The Four Loves* (London: Bles, 1960) 106. While I have benefited from both May and Lewis on this issue, I would also perceive some elements differently. May identifies power and passion more with eros than with epithymia. I believe that these qualities are more directly associated with the dynamics of sexual drive, and that direction and the quest for communion are marks of eros. Regarding Lewis, his insights are always illuminating and refreshing, but he frequently underplays the unity of love (as is evident in his book title); further, at points he betrays a continuing dualism about the body-self.
19. See Gene Outka, *Agape: An Ethical Analysis* (New Haven: Yale University Press, 1972), Chap. 2.
20. Ibid., 62.
21. David Bailey Harned, *Faith and Virtue* (Philadelphia: United Church Press, 1973) 48.
22. See Tillich, *Love, Power, and Justice*, 30. Cf. Outka, 287f.
23. Lowen, *Pleasure*, 172.

24. Dorothee Sölle, *Beyond Mere Obedience*, trans. Lawrence W. Denef (Minneapolis: Augsburg, 1970) 52f.
25. See Harned, 51.
26. Ibid., 52.
27. See Richardson, 113.
28. Rainer Maria Rilke, quoted in Anne Morrow Lindbergh, *Gift from the Sea* (New York: Vintage, 1955) 98.
29. Anne Philipe, quoted by Jeanniere, 159.
30. See Pittenger's fine treatment of love, to which I am indebted here, *Making Sexuality Human*, 42ff.
31. See *Human Sexuality: New Directions in American Catholic Thought*, 92ff. for a helpful elaboration of these qualities and others.
32. In this section I am drawing heavily upon parts of the chapter which I wrote for *Human Sexuality: A Preliminary Study*, esp. 96-105, by kind permission of the editor.
33. H. Richard Niebuhr clarifies these ethical styles and their implications. See *The Responsible Self* (New York: Harper & Row, 1963), esp. Chap. 1.
34. In his many writings Reinhold Niebuhr articulates this polarity of love and justice. See esp. *The Nature and Destiny of Man, Vol. II*, Chap. 9.
35. See Jack Dominian, *Proposals for a New Sexual Ethic* (London: Darton, Longman & Todd, 1977) 38ff.
36. I am indebted to Dominian for his suggestion of the need for expanding this phrase from the official Roman Catholic statements. Dominian is a Catholic psychiatrist. See 76ff.

6: The Meanings of Marriage and Fidelity

1. See Rosemary Haughton, "The Theology of Marriage," in Barnhouse and Holmes, 218.
2. See Yoshio Fukayama, "Religion and Sexuality: A Sociological Perspective," (unpublished paper, July 1976).
3. See Marvin B. Sussman, "Family Sociology," in Margaret S. Archer (ed.), *Current Research in Sociology* (The Hague: Mouton, 1974).
4. See James Ramey, *Intimate Friendships* (Englewood Cliffs, N.J.: Prentice-Hall, 1976) 125f.
5. See Cupitt, 138f.
6. Philippe Aries' insights are discussed by Ruether in Bianchi and Ruether, 41f.
7. See Helmut Thielicke, *The Ethics of Sex*, trans. John V. Doberstein (New York: Harper & Row, 1964) 79-144.
8. Ibid., 104.
9. Ibid., 81.
10. Ibid., 84.
11. Ibid., 90.
12. Karl Barth, *Church Dogmatics, Vol. III/4* (Edinburgh: T. & T. Clark, 1960) 163.
13. Bailey, *The Man-Woman Relation in Christian Thought*, 271f.
14. Bailey, *Common Sense About Sexual Ethics*, 115.

15. Derrick Sherwin Bailey, *The Mystery of Love and Marriage* (New York: Harper, 1952) 53.
16. Ibid., 53f.
17. Bailey, *Common Sense About Sexual Ethics,* 96f.
18. Pittenger, *Making Sexuality Human,* 51.
19. Ibid., 52.
20. "Social Statements of the Lutheran Church in America," Adopted by the Fifth Biennial Convention, Minneapolis, Minnesota, June 25-July 2, 1970, 1f.
21. Ronald Mazur, *The New Intimacy: Open-Ended Marriage and Alternative Lifestyles* (Boston: Beacon, 1973) 13.
22. Anna K. and Robert T. Francoeur, *Hot and Cool Sex: Cultures in Conflict* (New York: Harcourt Brace Jovanovich, 1974).
23. Ibid., 51. Cf. Robert T. and Anna K. Francoeur (eds.), *The Future of Sexual Relations* (Englewood Cliffs, N.J.: Prentice-Hall, 1974), esp. 30ff.
24. Rustum and Della Roy, "Is Monogamy Outdated?" in Jack R. and Joann S. DeLora (eds.), *Intimate Life Styles: Marriage and Its Alternatives,* 2nd edition (Pacific Palisades, Calif.: Goodyear, 1975) 376. Cf. Rustum and Della Roy, *Honest Sex* (New York: New American Library, 1968) esp. Chap. 7.
25. See Rustum and Della Roy, "Is Monogamy Outdated?", 375ff.
26. See John Snow, "Changing Patterns of Marriage," in Barnhouse and Holmes, 63ff.
27. Ibid., 73.
28. Ibid., 72.
29. Jessie Bernard, *The Future of Marriage* (New York: Bantam, 1973) 301f.
30. Ibid., 314.
31. Ibid., 323.
32. Dwight Hervey Small, *Christian: Celebrate Your Sexuality* (Old Tappan, N.J.: Revell, 1974) 184.
33. Karl Menninger, as quoted in ibid., 175.
34. See Paul Ramsey, "A Christian Approach to the Question of Sexual Relations Outside of Marriage," *The Journal of Religion,* Vol. XLV, No. 2 (April 1965).
35. Ibid., 110.
36. Smedes, 202.
37. Daniel Day Williams, 232.
38. Ruether, in Bianchi and Ruether, 81.
39. Ramey, 138.
40. Ibid., 143.
41. Raymond J. Lawrence, "Toward a More Flexible Monogamy," in Francoeur and Francoeur (eds.), *The Future of Sexual Relations,* 66ff.
42. Jessie Bernard, "Infidelity: Some Moral and Social Issues," in James R. Smith and Lynn G. Smith (eds.), *Beyond Monogamy* (Baltimore: The Johns Hopkins University Press, 1974) 138.
43. Ruether, in Bianchi and Ruether, 79.
44. See Francoeur and Francoeur, *Hot and Cool Sex,* 140ff.; Ramey, 101f.; Ruether, in Bianchi and Ruether, 85.
45. Oscar Wilde as quoted by Dan Sullivan in Foreword to Jeanniere, 18.
46. See Sherrard, 44.

47. See, for example, the editor's comments on the limitations in data, in spite of their obvious enthusiasm for the concept, in Smi Smith, 39ff.
48. See Gagnon and Simon, 94, 96f.

7:   The Morality of Sexual Variations

1. See Ira L. Reiss, "Changing Trends, Attitudes, and Values on Premarit Sexual Behavior in the United States," in Felix F. de la Cruz and Gerald D. LaVeck (eds.), *Human Sexuality and the Mentally Retarded* (Baltimore: Penguin, 1974) 286f.
2. Ibid., 289.
3. Hettlinger, 48. (Here the author is characterizing a a position which is not necessarily his own.)
4. William Hamilton, quoted in Hettlinger, 49.
5. Ibid., 50f.
6. Ramsey, 113.
7. See Hettlinger, 53ff.
8. See Jack Dominian's psychiatric opinion, *The Church and the Sexual Revolution*, 55.
9. See ibid., 29.
10. Such expressions as transexuality, transvestism, bestiality, exhibitionism, and voyeurism will be encountered at some time or another by most ministers and others in the helping professions. A basic familiarity with their meanings and dynamics is warranted. Otherwise, the predicament of a clerical acquaintance of mine might occur. Confronted by a stranger who first requested counseling and then identified himself as a transvestite, the puzzled cleric reached for his copy of *Handbook of Denominations in America*.
11. See Plummer, 68.
12. See Gagnon and Simon, 84.
13. Jerome, *Letters* 80.1, as quoted by Phipps, *Recovering Biblical Sensuousness*, 52.
14. Rubin, 93.
15. See Smedes, 211.
16. See Lowen, *Pleasure*, 22.
17. Eberhardt and Phyllis Kronhausen make this distinction in their study, *Pornography and the Law* (New York: Ballentine, 1964).
18. George Frankl, *The Failure of the Sexual Revolution* (London: New English Library, 1974) 92.
19. Charles May, "Does Pornography Have Social Value?" *Engage/Social Action*, No. 6 (May 1975) 41.
20. See Gagnon and Simon, 263ff.
21. See Michael J. Goldstein and Harold S. Kant, *Pornography and Sexual Deviance* (Berkeley: University of California Press, 1973) 146f.
22. Ibid., 151.
23. Ibid., 152.
24. See *Report of the Commission on Obscenity and Pornography* (New York: Bantam, 1970).

25. Ernest van Den Haag, *Censorship: For and Against*, Harold H. Hart (ed.) New York: Hart, 1971) 91.
26. Herbert Marcuse, *An Essay on Liberation* (Boston: Beacon, 1969) 7f.
27. Morton Hunt, *Sexual Behavior in the 1970s* (New York: Dell, 1974) 67.
28. See ibid., 68ff.
29. See Francoeur and Francoeur, *Hot and Cool Sex*, 29f.
30. See Hunt's survey, Chap. 2. Cf. Shere Hite, *The Hite Report* (New York: Dell, 1976) 61ff.
31. Sacred Congregation for the Doctrine of the Faith, *Declaration on Certain Questions Concerning Sexual Ethics* (Washington: United States Catholic Conference, 1976) 9f.
32. David Cole Gordon, *Self-Love* (Baltimore: Penguin, 1972) 48.
33. Ibid., 51.
34. Singer, 299.
35. Ibid., 305f.
36. See Hunt, 199.
37. See, for example, Gagnon and Simon, 92.
38. Ibid., 89.
39. Hunt, 203.
40. Gagnon and Simon, 92.
41. Hunt, 204.
42. See John W. Dixon Jr., "Paradigms of Sexuality," *Anglican Theological Review*, Vol. LVI, No. 2 (April 1974) 162.
43. Lowen, *Pleasure*, 75.
44. The hymn is "Lo! He Comes with Clouds Descending," written by Wesley in 1758.
45. Smedes, 236. I am indebted to the manner in which Smedes has interpreted Christian liberty.

8: Gayness and Homosexuality: Issues for the Church

1. This chapter is a revised and expanded version of my article, "Homosexuality: An Issue for the Church," *Theological Markings*, Vol. 5, No. 2 (Winter 1975), and reprinted in *Christianity and Crisis*, Vol. 37, No. 5 (April 4, 1977), by permission of both editors.
2. For a description of the gay movement within the church, see Sally Gearhart and William R. Johnson, *Loving Women/Loving Men* (San Francisco: Glide Publications, 1974) esp. Chap. 3.
3. See *Social Action*, Vol. XXXIV, No. 4 (December 1967), a special issue entitled "Civil Liberties and Homosexuality," which in spite of its date is still pertinent.
4. More expanded interpretations of the Bible on this issue may be found in numerous places. I am indebted to a number of authors, but particularly Derrick Sherwin Bailey, *Homosexuality and the Western Christian Tradition* (London: Longmans, Green, 1955; reprinted by Shoe String Press, Inc., Hamden, Conn., 1975); John J. McNeill, S.J., *The Church and the Homosexual* (Kansas City: Sheed Andrews and McMeel, 1976); Joseph C. Weber, "Does the Bible Condemn Homosexual Acts?" *Engage/Social Action*, Vol. 3, No. 5 (May 1975); Helmut Thielicke, *The Ethics of Sex;* and

H. Kimball Jones, *Toward a Christian Understanding of the Homosexual* (New York: Association, 1966). Especially helpful on hermeneutical issues in this context is James T. Clemons, "Toward a Christian Affirmation of Human Sexuality," *Religion in Life*, Vol. XLIII, No. 4 (Winter 1974).

5. See McNeill, 42.
6. Bailey first emphasized this interpretation in 1955, but since then it has been reaffirmed by others. McNeill provides a good summary of the scholarship in the intervening years, 42ff.
7. See Gerhard von Rad, *Genesis: A Commentary* (Philadelphia: Westminster, 1961) 205ff.; and David L. Bartlett, "A Biblical Perspective on Homosexuality," *Foundations*, Vol. XX, No. 2 (April-June 1977) 135.
8. McNeill, 50.
9. Martin Noth observes, "Leviticus deals almost exclusively with cultic and ritual matters." *Leviticus, A Commentary* (London: SCM, 1965) 16. Norman H. Snaith also notes, "Homosexuality here is condemned on account of its association with *idolatry*." *Leviticus and Numbers, The Century Bible* (London: Nelson, 1967) 126.
10. See U.C.C., *Human Sexuality: A Preliminary Study*, 76f.
11. McNeill, 55.
12. See Weber, 34.
13. Bartlett, 141.
14. Several writers have used different labels in the attempt to understand the differing positions. Interpretations of the theological possibilities and illustrative examples, however, will vary.
15. See Louis Crompton, "Gay Genocide: From Leviticus to Hitler," address delivered to the Gay Academic Union, New York University, November 30, 1974 (mimeographed).
16. See, for example, the remarkable article by Louie Crew, "At St. Luke's Parish: The Peace of Christ Is Not for Gays," *Christianity and Crisis*, Vol. 37, Nos. 9 & 10 (May 30 & June 13, 1977).
17. See Karl Barth, *Church Dogmatics*, *III/4* (Edinburgh: T. & T. Clark, 1961) esp. 166.
18. See Muehl, "Some Words of Caution"; also, William Muehl and William Johnson, "Issues Raised by Homosexuality," *Y.D.S. Reflection*, Vol. 72, No. 4 (May 1975).
19. Jim Cotter, "The Gay Challenge to Traditional Notions of Human Sexuality," *Christian*, Vol. 4, No. 2 (1977) 145.
20. Gregory Baum, "Catholic Homosexuals," *Commonweal*, February 14, 1974, 480f.
21. Ruether, in Bianchi and Ruether, 82f.
22. See C. A. Tripp, *The Homosexual Matrix* (New York: The New American Library, 1976) 266.
23. Compare the Kinsey statistics with the more recent estimates of Morton Hunt, *Sexual Behavior in the 1970s*. A useful discussion of the comparison is in the review of Hunt's book by Wardell B. Pomeroy in *SIECUS Report*, Vol. II, No. 6 (July 1974) 5f.
24. See John Money and Anke A. Ehrhardt, *Man and Woman, Boy and Girl* (New York: New American Library, 1972) 238ff.; also, McNeill, 113ff.
25. See Tripp, 236ff.
26. The therapist is Dr. Gerald C. Davison, President of the Association for

Advancement of Behavior Therapy. See Kenneth Goodall, "The End of Playboy Therapy," *Psychology Today,* Vol. 9, No. 5 (October 1975).

27. Hooker's report is published in *Foundations for Christian Family Policy* (New York: New York Council of Churches, 1961. See also her article, "Homosexuality," in *International Encyclopedia of the Social Sciences* (New York: Macmillan, 1968).

28. See McNeill's summary of the evidence, 115ff.

29. Muehl, "Some Words of Caution," 171.

30. See McNeill, 136.

31. Peggy Way, "Homosexual Counseling as a Learning Ministry," *Christianity and Crisis,* Vol. 37, Nos. 9 & 10 (May 30 & June 13, 1977), p. 128.

32. Thielicke, 282.

33. Ibid., 283f.

34. Friends Home Service Committee, *Towards a Quaker View of Sex* (London: Friends House, 1963) 45.

35. McNeill, 148. After a publishing delay of two years, this book was finally granted an ecclesiastical *imprimi potest* (permission to publish), which does not imply official agreement with the contents but is certification that the book has met prudent standards of scholarship in regard to a controversial topic. (See McNeill's Preface, esp. xiif.) Some months after it had been published, however, the *imprimi potest* was withdrawn, and the Vatican ordered McNeill to public silence on the issue of homosexuality.

36. See Norman Pittenger, *Time for Consent: A Christian's Approach to Homosexuality* (revised ed.) (London: SCM, 1976); *Making Sexuality Human; Love and Control in Sexuality* (Philadelphia: United Church Press, 1974); and, "A Theological Approach to Understanding Homosexuality," *Religion in Life,* Vol. XLIII, No. 4 (Winter 1974).

37. See Reinhold Niebuhr, *The Nature and Destiny of Man, Vol. II,* Chap. 8.

38. Pittenger makes this point well, *Time for Consent,* 74f.

39. See the analysis of causation theories in Simon and Gagnon, 132ff.

40. Alan Bell, 142.

41. Simon and Gagnon, 137.

42. See Cotter, 134ff. Precisely because gay people (like heterosexuals) vary widely in their understanding and experience of their own sexuality, there is no unanimity among them about language. While it is clear that an increasing majority wish to be called *gay,* there are some who insist that the term ought to be reserved for those who are "out of the closet," who are open to the public about their affectional orientation. Further, some gay women strongly prefer the term *lesbian,* maintaining that their experience and life-style is significantly different from that of the gay male. The language situation has some parallels to the movement from Negro to Black and (increasingly) to Afro-American. The point is that the majority group must respect and affirm the right and need of an oppressed minority to their own linguistic self-definitions. For economy of language I have generally adopted the practice which appears to be acceptable to the majority of gays—that of using *gay* to refer to both female and male persons and to those who are closeted as well as those who are publicly avowed— though I am painfully aware that some readers may find this personally unsatisfactory.

43. Bell, 136.

44. Psychiatrist George Weinberg calls this "homophobia," defining phobia as "an irrational, excessive, and persistent fear of some particular thing or situation." While I do not believe it fair to attribute sincerely held positions against homosexuality's acceptance to irrational fears only, I also believe it important to examine the probability that fear is part of the experience of most heterosexuals on this issue. See Weinberg's *Society and the Healthy Homosexual* (Garden City, New York: Anchor/Doubleday, 1973), esp. Chap. 1.

45. See G. Rattray Taylor, *Sex in History* (New York: Harper and Row, 1970) 80ff.

46. Rubin, 243.

47. Douglas, 113; cf. 94.

48. See Weinberg, Chap. 1.

49. David Bartlett appropriately argues this basic point about grace versus works of the law in his very useful treatment of Pauline theological perspectives and homosexuality. Applying the argument in Galatians regarding circumcision, he notes, "heterosexual people insist that homosexual people should 'go straight' in order to be Christian, or ordained, or elected to office, just as circumcised Christians insisted that uncircumcised Christians needed to be circumcised in order to be full members of the church. However, if heterosexual people and homosexual people could really hear the word that they are in a right relationship to God because of God's grace, and if they could receive that word in faith, then they would not need to spend so much energy defending themselves or browbeating others" (Bartlett, 145). My only qualification of these words is the reminder that the gay person's felt need for self-defense and self-justification is much more understandable than is the heterosexual's, given the long history and continuing presence of homophobia and homosexual persecution.

50. See Lewis I. Maddocks, "The Law and the Church vs. the Homosexual," in Ralph W. Weltge (ed.), *The Same Sex* (Philadelphia: Pilgrim, 1969). For an example of a denominational statement which strongly endorses civil liberties without making moral judgments about same-sex relationships, see "Pronouncement on Civil Liberties Without Discrimination Related to Affectional or Sexual Preference," *Minutes, Tenth General Synod, United Church of Christ*, 1975, 69f.

51. The first major case of a successful public referendum to rescind gay rights legislation occurred in Dade County (Miami), Florida in June 1977.

52. In 1976 the U.S. Supreme Court affirmed without comment a lower court decision upholding the Virginia sodomy statute as constitutional. The lower court had held that such sodomy legislation was constitutional inasmuch as the state could establish "that the conduct is likely to end in a contribution to moral delinquency." This was a serious setback to the elimination of such restrictive and punitive laws. See *Doe v. Commonwealth's Attorney for City of Richmond*, 403 F. Supp. 1199 (1975).

53. The special issues of two journals, devoted to this matter, are particularly useful: *Christianity and Crisis*, Vol. 37, Nos. 9 & 10 (May 30 & June 13, 1977); and, *Christian*, Vol. 4, No. 2 (Annunciation 1977). *Christian* is a British theological quarterly.

54. See Way, 126.

55. This study was done by Martin S. Weinberg and Colin J. Williams and is cited in McNeill, 173.
56. The action was taken by the United Church of Christ Executive Council at its meeting in Omaha, October 30, 1972.
57. See David Blamires, "Homosexuality and the Church: The Case for Honesty," *Christian*, Vol. 4, No. 2 (Annunciation 1977) 165ff.
58. Way, 130.
59. John Cavanaugh, *Counseling the Invert* (Milwaukee: Bruce, 1960) 263.
60. See McNeill, 165.
61. Money is quoted by Marilyn Riley, "The Lesbian Mother," *San Diego Law Review*, Vol. XII (July 1975) 864.
62. See Thomas Maurer, "Toward a Theology of Homosexuality—Tried and Found Trite and Tragic," in W. Dwight Oberholtzer, *Is Gay Good?* (Philadelphia: Westminster, 1971).
63. Chris Glaser, "A Newly Revealed Christian Experience," *Church & Society* Vol. LXVII, No. 5 (May-June 1977) 11.

9: The Sexually Disenfranchised

1. Throughout this section on physical disability I am particularly indebted to the work of my friends in the disability section of the Program in Human Sexuality, University of Minnesota Medical School, shared both in conversations and in writings cited below.
2. Theodore M. Cole, "Sexuality and Physical Disabilities," *Archives of Sexual Behavior*, Vol. 4, No. 4 (1975) 389; Thomas P. Anderson and Theodore M. Cole, "Sexual Counseling of the Physically Disabled," *Postgraduate Medicine*, Vol. 58, No. 1 (July 1975) 120.
3. Anderson and Cole, *ibid.*
4. See Theodore M. Cole, Richard Childgren, and Pearl Rosenberg, "A New Programme of Sex Education and Counselling for Spinal Cord Injured Adults and Health Care Professionals," *Paraplegia*, Vol. II (1973) 112ff.; Anderson and Cole, 121; Cole, 392f.
5. Anderson and Cole, 121 (italics added).
6. Cole, Chilgren, and Rosenberg, 114.
7. Daniel H. Labby, "Sexual Concomitants of Disease and Illness," *Postgraduate Medicine*, Vol. 58, No. 1 (July 1975) 103.
8. Lois Jaffe, as quoted in the *Minneapolis Tribune,* March 8, 1976. Prof. Jaffe's insights, shared with me in correspondence and in her articles, have particularly informed my perspectives in this section.
9. JoAnn Kelley Smith, *Free Fall* (Valley Forge, Pa.: Judson, 1975) 18, 79.
10. See Labby for a fuller discussion of sexual possibilities and limitations in various types of diseases.
11. See Lois Jaffe, "Sexual Problems of the Terminally Ill," in Harvey Gochros (ed.), *The Sexually Oppressed* (New York: Association, 1977).
12. See Lois and Arthur Jaffe, "Terminal Candor and the Coda Syndrome," in Herman Feifel (ed.), *New Meanings of Death* (New York: McGraw-Hill, 1977).
13. Smith, 106.
14. I first described this in *Rediscovering the Person in Medical Care*, 90.

15. Mary S. Calderone, "The Sexuality of Aging," *SIECUS Newsletter,* Vol. VII, No. 1 (Oct. 1971) 1.
16. Ibid.
17. Theodore M. Cole, "The Physician's Role in Working with the Sexuality of the Elderly," in J. T. Kelly and J. Weir (eds.), *Perspectives on Human Aging* (Minneapolis: Craftsman, 1973) 95.
18. Ivor Felstein, *Sex in Later Life* (Harmondsworth, England: Penguin, 1973) 20f.
19. Cole, "The Physician's Role . . . ," 97.
20. See Felstein, 23ff.
21. See the summaries of the research in Isadore Rossman, "Sexuality and the Aging Process: An Internist's Perspective," in Irene Mortenson Burnside, *Sexuality and Aging* (Los Angeles: University of Southern California Press, 1975) 19ff.
22. See the summary in Alexander Runciman, "Problems Older Clients Present in Counseling About Sexuality," in Burnside, 56.
23. A good summary of the Masters and Johnson research regarding the aging is made by Runciman, 56ff. See also Irene Mortenson Burnside, "Sexuality and the Older Adult: Implications for Nursing," in Burnside, 26ff.
24. See Mona Wasow and Martin B. Loeb, "Sexuality in Nursing Homes," in Burnside, 35ff.
25. See Bonnie Genevay, "Age Is Killing Us Softly . . . When We Deny the Part of Us Which Is Sexual," in Burnside, 70.
26. Calderone, "The Sexuality of Aging," 1.
27. Susan Sontag as quoted by Genevay, 69.
28. See ibid., 74.
29. Burnside, 47.
30. Ibid., 50.
31. Felstein, 123.
32. Calderone, "The Sexuality of the Aging," 1.
33. See the report of these findings by Paul H. Gebhard, "Sexual Behavior of the Mentally Retarded," in de la Cruz and LaVeck, 29-49.
34. Ibid., 45.
35. Ibid., 49. It is important to remember that the higher incidence of "situational homosexual behavior" in sex-segregated institutions does not undercut the argument in the previous chapter concerning the lack of choice which most persons feel in their *basic* psychosexual orientation.
36. See Warren R. Johnson, "Sex Education of the Mentally Retarded," in de la Cruz and LaVeck, esp. 58-60.
37. Ibid., 58 (italics added).
38. Sheldon C. Reed and V. Elving Anderson, "Effects of Changing Sexuality on the Gene Pool," in de la Cruz and LaVeck, 124.
39. Edmond A. Murphy, "Effects of Changing Sexuality on the Gene Pool: A Response to Sheldon Reed," in de la Cruz and LaVeck, 136.
40. See Robert W. Deisher, "Sexual Behavior of Retarded in Institutions," 145ff.; David Gordon Carruth, "Human Sexuality in a Halfway House," 153ff.; and Michael J. Begab, "Institutional and Community Attitudes, Practices and Policies: General Discussion," 163ff. (all in de la Cruz and LaVeck).

41. Sol Gordon, "A Response to Warren Johnson," in de la Cruz and LaVeck, 68.
42. See Gebhard, 42f.
43. Deisher, 149.
44. Janet Mattinson, "Marriage and Mental Handicap," in de la Cruz and LaVeck, 185.
45. Robert B. Edgerton, "Some Socio-Cultural Research Considerations," in de la Cruz and LaVeck, 247. See also Robert B. Edgerton, *The Cloak of Competence* (Berkeley: University of California Press, 1967), and Janet Mattinson, *Marriage and Mental Handicap* (London: Duckworth, 1970).
46. See, for example, Brian G. Scally, "Marriage and Mental Handicap: Some Observations in Northern Ireland," in de la Cruz and LaVeck, 192ff.
47. See the summary by W. Roy Breg, "Physical and Biological Aspects: General Discussion," in de la Cruz and LaVeck, 105f.
48. Edgerton, "Some Socio-Cultural Research Considerations," 246.
49. Ibid., 245f.
50. *Buck v. Bell*, 274 U.S. 200, 207 (1927).
51. Some advance in the Court's sensitivity, however, is evident in a 1942 opinion overturning a state's compulsory sterilization law for "habitual criminals." See *Skinner v. Oklahoma*, 316 U.S. 535 (1942). This more enlightened attitude has yet to be firmly established for the retarded, though some legal scholars believe that the Court may do so when presented with an appropriate case.
52. Robert A. Burt, "Legal Restrictions on Sexual and Familial Relations of Mental Retardates—Old Laws, New Guises," in de la Cruz and LaVeck, 207.

10: The Church as Sexual Community

1. Daly, 4.
2. Edward Sapir, as quoted in Yates, 133.
3. May, *Love and Will*, 236.
4. Yates, 132f.
5. Robert S. Ellwood Jr., "A Return to 'Father Knows Best,'" in Barnhouse and Holmes, 103. Ellwood has helpfully traced these stereotypical modes of perception.
6. See Sam Keen, "Toward an Erotic Theology," in Fenton, pp. 26ff.; Keen, *To a Dancing God* (New York: Harper & Row, 1970) 143; Vogel, 98f.
7. Daly, 19.
8. See U.C.C., *Human Sexuality: A Preliminary Study*, 45ff.
9. See ibid.; cf. Letty M. Russell, *Human Liberation in a Feminist Perspective: A Theology* (Philadelphia: Westminster, 1973) 97ff.
10. See ibid., 43; and Terrien, 21.
11. Ruether, *New Woman, New Earth*, 65.
12. See ibid., 51; and Richardson, 61.
13. McLaughlin, 46.
14. See Gayle Graham Yates, "An Androgynous Image of God," *Theological Markings*, Vol. 6, No. 1 (Spring 1976) 26.
15. See ibid., 28.

16. Holmes, in Barnhouse and Holmes, 257.
17. See ibid., 258ff.
18. Ibid., 265.
19. Ibid., 264.
20. See Richardson, 8. In discussing creation, however, Richardson has a one-sided emphasis upon the volitional element—creation by "command," by "fiat," etc. This becomes an excessively masculine imagery.
21. Paul Hessert, "Toward a Theology of Sexuality," *Explor*, Vol. 1, No. 2 (Fall 1975) 79f.
22. McLaughlin, 50f.
23. Charles Davis makes this point in somewhat different language, 130ff.
24. Russell, 20; cf. Daly, Chap. 1.
25. See Margaret Farley, "Sources of Sexual Inequality in the History of Christian Thought," *The Journal of Religion*, Vol. 56, No. 2 (April 1976) 162ff.
26. Ibid., 166.
27. Ibid., 175.
28. Jeanniere, Vogel, and Davis all make this point.
29. Ernest Becker, *The Denial of Death* (New York: Free Press, 1973) 84.
30. I am depending here upon Becker's interpretation of Rank, 160ff.
31. Ibid., 163.
32. Becker contends that the child's anxious questions about sex may not, at the fundamental level, be about sex *per se*, but "about the meaning of the body, the terror of living with a body." Ibid., 164.
33. Norman Pittenger, *Unbounded Love* (New York: Seabury, 1976) 85. Pittenger's process theology interpretation of resurrection is most helpful at this point.
34. See Fisher, 209.
35. See ibid.
36. See Dixon, "Paradigms of Sexuality," 157f.
37. Douglas, 69.
38. See Haughton, 64f.; and Taylor, Chap. 12.
39. Taylor, 229.
40. Haughton, 77.
41. See ibid., 81.
42. See especially the interpretations of Lawrence in Haughton, 82f.; Krook, 280ff.; and William E. Phipps, "D. H. Lawrence's Appraisal of Jesus," *The Christian Century*, Vol. XCI, No. 45 (April 28, 1971) 521ff.
43. See Phipps, *Recovering Biblical Sensuousness*, 86ff.
44. See Krook, 346.
45. Evgueny Lampert, *The Divine Realm: Towards a Theology of the Sacraments* (London: Faber & Faber, 1943) 97.
46. Sherrard, 3.
47. See Michael Novak, as quoted in Phipps, *Recovering Biblical Sensuousness*, 95f.
48. See Dixon in Barnhouse and Holmes. I am indebted to his interpretation at this point.
49. Ibid., 254f.
50. See my *Moral Nexus: Ethics of Christian Identity and Community* (Philadelphia: Westminster, 1971) Chap. 10. I have drawn upon the insightful work of Frederick W. Dillistone with regard to these metaphors.

51. Ibid., 174f.
52. Norman Pittenger, *Life as Eucharist* (Grand Rapids: Eerdmans, 1973) 14f. Cf. John A. T. Robinson, *The Body*, 9.
53. Lowen, *Pleasure*, 242; cf. 245.
54. See Ruether in Bianchi and Ruether, 114f.
55. Russell, 165.
56. Peter L. Berger, "Cakes for the Queen of Heaven: 2500 Years of Religious Ecstasy," *The Christian Century*, Vol. XCI, No. 45 (December 25, 1974) 1223.
57. For a fuller discussion of these briefly-noted issues, see U.C.C., *Human Sexuality: A Preliminary Study*, Chap. 5.
58. Bianchi gives a helpful overview of the socialization process in Bianchi and Ruether, 54ff.
59. See Fasteau, Chaps. 11, 12, 13; Farrell, Chap. 5; and Nichols, Chaps. 9, 12.
60. Hannah Arendt, *On Violence* (New York: Harcourt, Brace & World, 1970), 6f.
61. See Phipps, *Recovering Biblical Sensuousness*, 53ff.
62. See the summary of this evidence in James W. Prescott, "Body Pleasure and the Origins of Violence," *Bulletin of the Atomic Scientists*, Vol. 31, No. 9 (November 1975) 10-20.
63. Ibid., 11.
64. Ibid., 14.
65. See the summary of such anthropological evidence in Savramis, Chap. 2; cf. Marcuse, *Eros and Civilization*.
66. See Rollo May, *Power and Innocence: A Search for the Sources of Violence* (New York: Norton, 1972) esp. Chap. 8.
67. James Weldon Johnson, as quoted in Grace Halsell, *Black and White Sex* (Greenwich, Conn.: Fawcett, 1972) 15.
68. See Robert Staples, as quoted in U.C.C.: *Human Sexuality: A Preliminary Study*, 24f.
69. See Ruether, *New Woman, New Earth*, Chap. 5, on whose analysis I am depending in this paragraph.
70. Eldridge Cleaver, as quoted by Robert Bellah, *The Broken Covenant: American Civil Religion in Time of Trial* (New York: Seabury, 1975) 105f.
71. See Fisher, Chap. 4.
72. See ibid., 89.
73. See ibid., 93.
74. See ibid., 96.
75. See ibid.
76. See Ruether, *New Woman, New Earth*, Chap. 8; Daly, 174-178; Davis, 82-86; Fenton, 142f.; and Lowen, *Pleasure*, 95-101.
77. Ruether, ibid., 195.
78. Lowen, ibid., 96.
79. Davis, 82f.

Epilog

1. W. H. Auden, "For the Time Being," from *The Collected Poetry of W. H. Auden* (New York: Random House, 1945) 443f., used by permission.

Index of Subjects

Index of Names

Index of Biblical References

Dichotomy - concupiscence - epithymia

Page 9 Jesus views

Page 12 New Life

Page 83 - Settled in Jesus

Page 91 - Giving & receiving

Page 96 -

Page 110 - agape & eros

Page 131 - typical tanaka

Page 200 children addicted